A GUIDE TO
TRAINS

The World's Greatest Trains, Tracks & Travels

A Guide to

TRAINS

The World's Greatest Trains, Tracks & Travels

GRAEME CARTER, COLIN GARRATT,
DAVID JACKSON, HOWARD JOHNSTON,
WILLIAM D. MIDDLETON, KARL ZIMMERMANN

CONSULTANT EDITOR
DAVID JACKSON

FOG CITY PRESS

Published by Fog City Press
814 Montgomery Street
San Francisco, CA 94133 USA

Copyright © 2002 Weldon Owen Pty Ltd
Reprinted 2002

CHIEF EXECUTIVE OFFICER John Owen
PRESIDENT Terry Newell
PUBLISHER Lynn Humphries
MANAGING EDITOR Janine Flew
ART DIRECTOR Kylie Mulquin
EDITORIAL COORDINATORS Tracey Gibson, Kiren Thandi
PRODUCTION MANAGER Caroline Webber
PRODUCTION COORDINATOR James Blackman
BUSINESS MANAGER Emily Jahn
VICE PRESIDENT INTERNATIONAL SALES Stuart Laurence
EUROPEAN SALES DIRECTOR Vanessa Mori

PROJECT EDITOR Kerry Davies
PROJECT ART DIRECTOR Sue Burk
PROJECT DESIGNER Lena Lowe
PICTURE RESEARCHERS Tracey Gibson, Marney Richardson

ISBN 1 877019 46 1

Color reproduction by Colourscan Co Pte Ltd
Printed by Kyodo Printing Co (S'pore) Pte Ltd
Printed in Singapore

A Weldon Owen Production

[Of the parallels between the railways and the Church] both had their heyday in the mid-nineteenth century; both own a great deal of Gothic-style architecture which is expensive to maintain; both are regularly assailed by critics; and both are firmly convinced that they are the best means of getting man to his ultimate destination.

REVEREND W. AWDRY (1911–1997), British author, best known for his children's books about Thomas the Tank Engine

CONTENTS

FOREWORD

This is a guide to the railroads of today, and how
they got to be the way they are, from their
beginnings as the first means of travel that was
faster than a horse could gallop.

There's the story of the first, frantic decades of experiment
and expansion that so dramatically changed the lives of
millions. There's a little nostalgia, too, for the later years
when the railways ruled the world and the incomparable
steam engine ruled the railways. But not too much of this,
for those days are long gone, and now there is an equally
exciting story to tell, as countries around the world
rediscover their railways and invest in them. New lines,
new trains, are setting new land transport standards and,
if they lack the "romance" of steam, they project an aura
of power and drama that is attracting a whole new
generation of railroad buffs.

But you don't have to be a railroad buff to want to
know more about that speeding passenger train you saw
yesterday, or that long, long freight train that held you
up at the grade crossing. Nor do you have to be a railroad
buff to enjoy a ride, in the 21st century, on a meticulously
restored "old-time" railroad, or to thrill at the idea of
taking a great train journey yourself. May this book
both inform you and help you to feel something of
the enduring fascination of railways.

DAVID JACKSON
Train watcher

INTRODUCTION

This book follows the evolution of rail from the first steam engines to the sleek high-speed trains of today. This all-encompassing guide salutes the successes and documents the failures of the great rail networks and empires around the globe. It explores the massive impact that the development of rail has had, and continues to have, on our everyday lives.

The railroads not only gave people the ability to travel great distances in a relatively short space of time, and at reasonable cost, but also brought about the creation of towns and cities, expanded industries, and enhanced communications. No matter how steep or inhospitable the terrain, the skills of visionary engineers such as Isambard Kingdom Brunel made sure the railroad would get through.

In wartime, warring countries built lines as part of their battle strategies. Military control of America's railroads, which could move troops and supplies quickly, proved a decisive weapon in the American Civil War. The Great War in Europe saw rail transporting troops and supplies.

For the holidaymaker, traveling by train offers the perfect opportunity to see a region in close up, and often in great comfort. *A Guide to Trains* includes extensive chapters on preserved lines and great railway journeys around the world, taking the reader across Australia's red center, through 86 tunnels to the Copper Canyon in Mexico, and from New York to Canada on the Adirondack … and much more.

THE EDITORS

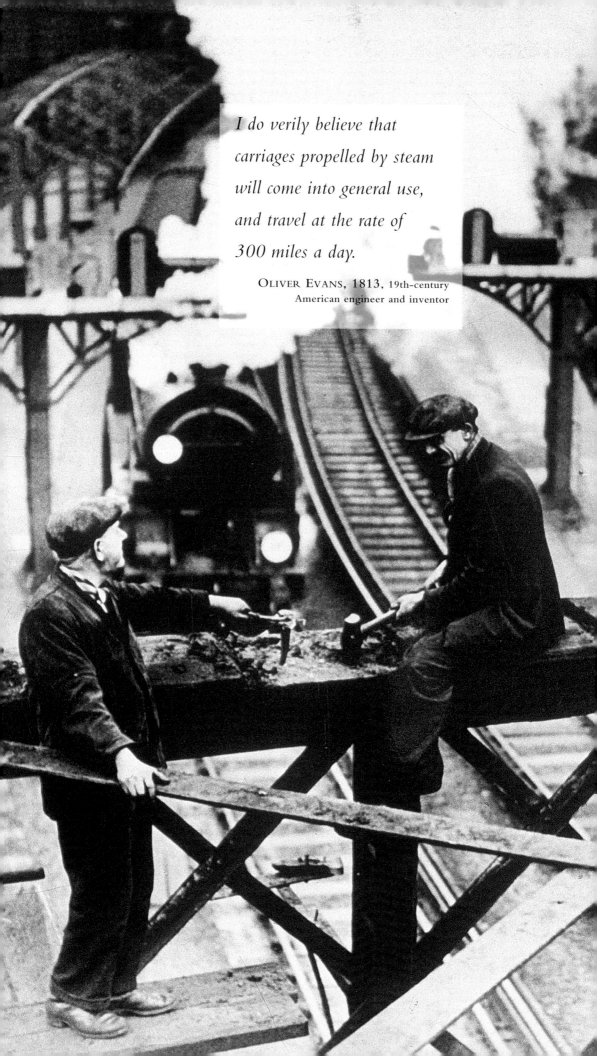

I do verily believe that carriages propelled by steam will come into general use, and travel at the rate of 300 miles a day.

OLIVER EVANS, 1813, 19th-century
American engineer and inventor

CHAPTER ONE

THE HISTORY *of* RAIL

RAIL'S RENAISSANCE

Railroads embrace the 21st century with spectacular new passenger trains and giant freighters.

I t is barely two centuries since a steam locomotive first hauled wagons on rails at a grimy Welsh ironworks in Britain in 1804. Fewer than 30 years later, the first intercity railway opened between Liverpool and Manchester in England, showing dramatically that people as well as goods could travel by rail at what were then phenomenal speeds.

From those beginnings railroads spread throughout the world—and changed that world forever as they made populations mobile and brought economic revolution. Fortunes were made and lost, and legends created, while the great railroads became institutions in our cities and made "the depot" a focal point in small towns. The train itself, racing through the landscape beneath its plume of white steam, made an indelible impression on all who saw it —fearsome at first, ultimately commonplace, but always in some degree exciting.

The years prior to World War I have been called the "Golden Age" of railways. Everyone and everything moved by train. Commuters packed into steam and later (if they were lucky) electric trains for their daily journeys between their homes in the ever-spreading suburbs and their workplaces. Businessmen and "commercial travelers,"

INNER-CITY RAIL *systems, such as Australia's Sydney Monorail (above) and the Paris Métro (right), transport people quickly and efficiently.*

with their suitcases full of samples, rode hundreds of miles by train to seek out customers. For their vacations these same people took other trains to resorts that the railroads had created, but all year round the affluent could ride in considerable luxury to wherever fashion and fancy, and the railroads, led them. And day and night the freight trains kept rolling, delivering the nation's needs.

UNDER THREAT

Two exhausting world wars, with the Great Depression between them, changed all this on both sides of the Atlantic Ocean. Road transport began to take a substantial amount of business from the railroads in the 1930s. While some fought back with glamorous new passenger trains and innovative freight services, many were either too rundown or too set in their ways to do so. After 1945, the competition from road and air transport intensified, and then came the boom in private motoring,

bringing huge increases in public spending on roads. By the 1960s, most railroads in the Western world were in decline. Some said the day of the train was over.

Today, it is clear the pessimists were wrong. Typically, the railway is rationalized and computerized, and once again established as a key component of any effective national transport system as governments

RAIL FREIGHT SERVICES *such as this long "intermodal" freight train, here crossing the desert in Arizona, have worldwide support on environmental grounds.*

are facing up to road traffic congestion and its associated environmental issues. Railroads are still struggling in most countries for more than a minor share of merchandise freight business, but they are handling the indispensable bulk flows of coal, iron ore, and the like more efficiently than ever before. In 2000, more than 290 million tons (296 million t) of coal were transported by train from Wyoming's Powder River Basin to power generators, with equally impressive iron ore hauls in Australia, Brazil, and South Africa.

City after city is meeting commuters' needs with new rail systems, including "light rail," with its sleek electric cars running right into city centers. Sleeping-car trains crisscross Europe and carry vacationers in comfort in North America and Australia, while historic, rejuvenated

trains such as the *Venice Simplon-Orient-Express* have created a whole new luxury travel market. Most spectacular of all are the 21st century's high-speed passenger trains. These services are winning business and leisure travelers back from the jet-plane by linking major cities at up to 200 miles per hour (320 km/h).

A UNIVERSAL PLEASURE
At first sight nothing could be further removed from the "romance" of the steam train than one of these immaculate streamliners as it streaks almost silently through the countryside, or a 17,000-ton (17,340 t) coal train rolling smoothly along behind a pair of giant diesel locomotives, each with

the strength of 6,000 horses. But the train—any train—can still excite people, from those who dedicate themselves to preserving lines and restoring old trains to life, to those who find pleasure in studying the workings of railway systems in all their complexity. Some people are intrigued by the intricacies of modern train operation and control, while the technology of locomotives and railcars absorbs others. Still more transfer their enthusiasm and skills to the challenge of model railways.

On one thing everyone will no doubt agree: The great journeys of the world are those—and there are a great many of them—that can still be traveled by train.

HIGH-SPEED TRAINS *such as Japan's "Bullet Train" led rail's revival. This Series 700 Nozomi was brought out in 1999.*

HIGH-SPEED TRAINS

People are well accustomed to reaching far-flung destinations by air, but contemporary intercity and international high-speed train travel is now commonplace across the globe.

The most dramatic expression of rail's revival in the new millennium is the way that train travel at 125–200 miles per hour (200–322 km/h) is now taken for granted in an ever-increasing number of countries around the world.

Japan's *Shinkansen,* or "Bullet Trains," showed the way when they began on the all new Tokaido Line from Tokyo to Osaka in 1964. Running every 15 minutes at speeds up to 131 miles per hour (210 km/h), they showed how a high-speed and high-frequency rail service could challenge the previously all-conquering airlines for intercity passenger transport. From that truly spectacular beginning *Shinkansen* routes have multiplied, with speeds rising higher year by year.

As with the *Shinkansen,* purpose-built lines have also revolutionized travel in Europe, especially in France,

AMTRAK'S ACELA EXPRESS *is the American railway's most serious effort to draw travelers back to the rails (above). Japan's "Bullet Trains" (above left) were the first to challenge other modes of high-speed transport.*

where the *TGV* (*Train à Grand Vitesse*) began running in 1981. Newly built *TGV* lines are laid out for speed, without sharp curves, and the trains, which are semi-permanently coupled with articulated coaches (sharing bogies), can also run at higher than normal speeds on existing lines. *TGV*s operate all over France, and the railway has

now introduced double-decker train sets to meet the great demand for the services.

The success of the *TGV* technology has led to its worldwide export: Spain's *AVE* (*Alta Velocidad Española,* or Spanish High Speed) trains were built in France using a mixture of both French and Spanish parts. *Thalys,* the international high-speed train connecting France, Belgium, and Germany, also uses *TGV* technology, and even South Korea is now importing units for its new fast routes.

In 1991 Germany launched its *InterCityExpress* (*ICE*). In addition to raising speeds (the first trains ran at 175 miles per hour/282 km/h), the *ICE* set new levels of comfort. It was built to the maximum dimensions allowed, giving more room in the passenger

EUROSTAR VERSATILITY

In 1994 *Eurostars* were introduced between London (Waterloo) and Paris, via the Channel Tunnel, cruising at 186 miles per hour (300 km/h). Later the service was extended to Brussels.

Eurostars are electric trains that can pick up power three ways: 750v DC from the third rail alongside the tracks in the south of England, 25kv AC from the Channel Tunnel overhead wires, and 3kv DC overhead in Belgium.

A new dedicated high-speed line from the Tunnel entrance to the center of London is under construction. *Eurostar* train sets also run on services from London to northern England.

THE SLEEK LINES *of a German ICE 3 offset the ultra-modern railway station at Frankfurt. There is now also a version of the ICE (InterCityExpress) that incorporates tilt train technology, allowing it to travel at even faster speeds around bends.*

compartments. The first *ICE*s had conventional power cars at each end of the train, but the *ICE3*, introduced in 2000, has under-floor motors in half of the carriages. As in France, Germany is building new high-speed lines to exploit the full capability of the new trains, but there is also a version of the *ICE* that incorporates the technology of tilt trains, enabling it to travel faster around bends, thus shortening journey times on conventional lines. Top speed has risen to 205 miles per hour (330 km/h), and *ICE*s now run between most major German cities, and into Switzerland and Austria.

The new breed of express passenger trains also turn their attention to interior design. The opulence of the "Grand Old Trains," still to be seen in the superb restorations of the *Venice Simplon-Orient-Express* and others, in truth was only available to the privileged few. Today's express trains, running every few minutes on many lines, make the most of modern materials and design to offer all of their passengers a style of journey that is very different to anything they may have known in the past.

BRITISH EXPERIMENTS

The relative lack of electrified mainlines in the early 1970s prompted British Railways to opt for 125-mile-per-hour (200 km/h) tilt trains, and there followed an unsuccessful experiment with the APT (Advanced Passenger Train). The same technology was later successfully applied in Sweden (the X-2000) and Italy, whose *Pendolino*s are now imported into Britain.

The fastest British trains are currently the *InterCity 225*s, which ply the electrified East Coast Main Line (London to Edinburgh) at up to 140 miles per hour (225 km/h).

SPEED IN THE U.S.A.

The United States came late to the concept of high-speed trains. Although foreign train sets were tested earlier, it was only in 2000 that an American high-speed train, Amtrak's *Acela Express*, was introduced. Able to run at speeds of up to 150 miles per hour (242 km/h), *Acela Express* is in service on the East Coast Corridor between Washington D.C., New York, and Boston.

A TRIO *of French TGVs (Train à Grande Vitesse) wait to depart from the Gare Montparnasse in Paris.*

NIGHT TRAINS

*From deluxe boudoirs to sleek modern sleepers,
night trains have an atmosphere all their own.*

The sleeping-car train is almost as old as the railroad itself. George Pullman's first sleeping car ran from Bloomington, Illinois, to Chicago in 1859. Little more than a decade later, trains that covered long distances included one or more cars with beds so passengers could sleep through the night. From this evolved the accommodation offered by the great transcontinental trains of North America, Asia, and Russia, where the need to provide for both night and day travel led to the development of the "convertible" car. In Britain and Europe, where distances were shorter, dedicated sleeping cars entirely made up of private compartments were more common. Different grades of accommodation appeared, with extraordinary opulence for those who could afford it. In the United States the name synonymous with such cars was Pullman. In Europe the Belgian-based Compagnie Internationale des Wagons-Lits and the German Mitropa organization had near-monopolies on both sleeping-car and dining-car operations at one time.

THE LURE OF NIGHT

Speed was never especially high on the agenda—it could disturb passengers' sleep and have them arriving at their destinations inconveniently early. To many, riding the night train was a pleasure in itself. And, despite setbacks, the opportunity is still there.

After World War II the car and cheaper air travel almost destroyed the long-distance passenger train in the United States. In Europe, too, the phenomenal growth of the high-speed train network since the 1980s reduced intercity journey times, with the loss of many historic night trains. But on both sides of the Atlantic those that remain have been re-equipped to provide high accommodation standards for leisure riders. And in Europe in particular, new sleeper trains offer an acceptable alternative to air travel for the business traveler.

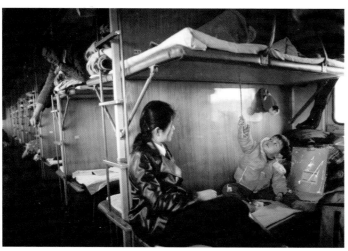

GLAMOR *was a hallmark of sleepers in the 1930s (above), while today in China "soft" class (above left) affords a degree of luxury not evident in the much more basic "hard" sleeper class (left).*

TRAVELERS RECEIVE SILVER SERVICE *in sleepers on India's Palace on Wheels, (above). A 1932 poster promotes the British Night Scotsman (below).*

Amtrak, which took over the national passenger train network in the United States in 1970, entered the 21st century with 16 long-distance trains of bilevel Superliner cars or the latest Viewliners, single-deck cars with upper and lower rows of windows to give a large, roomy feel.

Border-crossing *Euronight* trains traverse Europe from Scandinavia to France and Spain, and from Holland and Belgium through Germany to Switzerland, Italy, Austria, and Hungary. The European overnight trains are well patronized, especially in high summer. In the winter-sports season, also, extra trains run from the major cities to the ski resorts. They offer various types of accommodation, the most common being single or double sleeping compartments in traditional European style, and couchettes (compartments with four or six berths).

In Britain, sleeper trains with purpose-built, air-conditioned cars run between London and Penzance in the west of England, and London and Scotland.

On the other side of the world, Japan, now best known for its flying *Shinkansen,* still has sleeping car trains on its classic 3-foot-6-inch-gauge lines between Tokyo and Miyazaki, near the southern tip of Kyushu, and to Sapporo on the island of Hokkaido.

AUSTRALIAN SLEEPERS
Australia offers a diesel train that runs at 100 miles per hour (160 km/h) and, in a rare combination, includes a sleeping car. There are also two memorable stainless steel streamliners, the Sydney–Perth *Indian Pacific* (*IP*) and the Adelaide–Alice Springs

THE NIGHT SCOTSMAN
Leaves King's Cross nightly at 10.25.

Ghan. Built in the 1960s, the *IP*, with its Roomettes and Twinettes, lounges and dining cars, was modeled on the best United States trains of the type, just as they faded from the American scene. Both trains have been restyled and refurbished, and are among the world's best rail experiences, both day and night.

HOTEL TRAINS

Europe's remarkable "hotel" trains target the business travel market but are attracting tourists as well. *CityNightLine* trains offer three grades of sleeper compartment in double-decker cars painted a striking midnight blue. They run on such routes as Dortmund to Vienna and Zürich to Berlin. *TrenHotel* trains provide sleepers of similar quality in Talgo articulated cars, named for their original Spanish manufacturer. These cars are fitted with adjustable-gauge axles and thus can run on routes from broad-gauged Spain to the rest of Europe.

LUXURY *on* WHEELS

Just as certain trains of the 19th century offered luxury travel for the wealthy, today's prestige trains are again a mark of status.

I n 1842 Britain's Queen Victoria made her first railway journey and so launched the era of luxury travel. The advantages for the monarch of rail travel over travel by coach were clear, and what better publicity could the railways possibly receive? As the British manufacturers vied for royal custom, they built ever more opulent coaches, culminating in the London & North Western Railway's 1895 saloon. Its luxury was unparalleled—it had a grand lounge, with sparkling cut glass, luxurious blue drapes, and polished wood paneling. The Queen used it to visit the counties of her realm.

BRITAIN'S ROYAL TRAINS *were the height of luxury. A silver-plated bed adorned the monarch's sleeping salon aboard this train from the early 20th century.*

THE BID FOR LUXURY
Other rulers followed with increasingly fantastic designs. Bavaria's King Ludwig, whose extravagance bankrupted his kingdom, had a saloon with toilet seats covered in swansdown. Soon the world's nobility, from Indian maharajahs to Russian dukes, all had private saloons. The Pope's train included a throne room.

American luxury trains, by contrast, were the brainchild of one man, George Pullman, who developed them to convey businessmen over long distances in comfort. He built the first true "Pullman car," the Pioneer, in 1864. This "hotel on wheels" offered hitherto unheard of luxury in its sleeping berths. Competition inevitably flowed from

Pullman's success, such as from Webster Wagner's equally luxurious "Palace Cars." Soon trains had club cars, parlor cars, and hairdressing salons. There was even a bridal suite on the *Pennsylvania Limited.*

From this developed the ultimate status symbol— the private car. These were typically self-contained, with a lounge and bedroom, as well as a dining area and rooms for guests. Not content with one car, some tycoons had complete private trains.

"Non-royal" luxury only came to Europe after Belgian Georges Nagelmackers' return from America in 1870. He founded an Ostend–Cologne sleeping-car service but had to

stave off bankruptcy in 1873 by allying himself with the rich American William Mann. Together they established Compagnie Internationale des Wagons-Lits et des Grandes Express Européens (Wagons-Lits) to operate Pullman-style expresses all over Europe and even across Russia. These Wagons-Lits trains set new standards—the *Orient-Express* and the trains of the Trans-Siberian Railway quickly became the stuff of legend.

Luxury trains now entered a "golden age" on both sides of the Atlantic, but things were never quite the same after the destruction wrought by World War I. Then, after World War II, air travel threatened their existence.

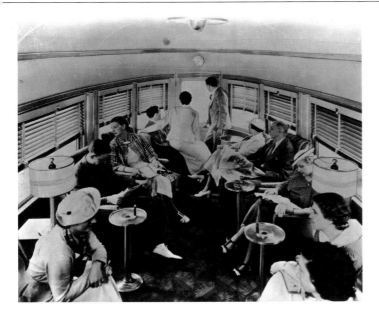

THIS STREAMLINED OBSERVATION CAR *was appointed with easy chairs, lamps, and standing ashtrays.*

A NEW GOLDEN AGE

The last 20 years of the 20th century saw a remarkable rebirth of deluxe trains, as a holiday experience rather than merely transport. The *Venice Simplon-Orient-Express* (*VSOE*) brought back to life the romantic spirit of the original *Orient-Express*, whisking passengers from London to Venice in restored 1920s Pullman and Wagons-Lits cars. With cabins a riot of polished marquetry and brass fittings, "dressing for dinner," music in the piano bar, and spectacular scenery passing the windows, the *VSOE* is perhaps the ultimate nostalgic survivor.

Others have followed, including Scotland's *Royal Scotsman,* which is perhaps the most luxurious. Although modern, the carriages evoke yesteryear luxury and tradi-tional Scottish style. State cabins are decorated in tartan fabrics and polished wood, and even single cabins are spacious enough to fit a wardrobe, dressing table, and en suite bathroom. With its lounge and open-veranda observation cars, the train makes leisurely progress through the Scottish Highlands, offering far more comfort and style than any previous Scottish train.

India's *Palace on Wheels* luxury cruise train is similarly both modern and nostalgic. Started 20 years ago with vintage saloons, it now has custom-built carriages, each decorated in the unique style of individual princely states, some with paintings, others with carved wood or gold ornamentation. Each saloon has just four double en suite cabins, with three stewards per coach. There are

THE ROYAL SCOTSMAN *employs a number of top-class chefs (right) for its journey through the Scottish Highlands. Lounge cars on the Blue Train are furnished for comfort and style (below).*

lounge, bar, and restaurant cars, and a library. The *Palace on Wheels* runs through the deserts of Rajasthan at night, bringing its passengers to sights such as the Taj Mahal and fort at Jaipur by morning.

South Africa's *Blue Train* is, by contrast, cutting edge. The newest, launched in 1997, includes facilities such as video players and cell phones. Des-cended from the 1920s *Union Limited* luxury service, today's *Blue Train* is an impeccable way to travel.

Remarkably, a century and a half after Queen Victoria's first rail journey, not only do luxury trains still exist, but, with this recent renaissance, they are now enjoying a new golden age.

COMMUTER TRAINS

The establishment of the railways enabled a new approach to life and work. Commuting allowed workers to live outside crowded cities.

Commuting was created by the railroads. The dream of living in an area well away from work was only made possible by the rapid, cheap transport that railroads could offer. As early as the 1850s British railway companies realized that they could encourage people to build houses alongside their networks (and attract regular travelers) by providing cheap travel to the industrial centers.

Some companies became property developers themselves. One example is the Metropolitan Railway of London, which promoted an idyllic "Metroland" in the green fields beside its lines in the 1920s. New, cheaper, and more spacious houses, in rural or "village-style" locations, had great appeal compared with polluted, cramped cities.

Regular customers on suburban lines who bought weekly, monthly, or yearly season tickets at reduced rates were first given the title of

DIGNITARIES *attend the opening in 1863 of London's Metropolitan Line, the first to venture into the heart of a city.*

"commuters" in the United States. In the 21st century, the benefits of commuting by rail are still obvious—a single line of urban railway can carry up to 50,000 people every hour in each direction, more than four times the capacity of a fast eight-lane highway.

Today, almost universally, day-to-day commuters are the most numerous type of train passenger, but also the least profitable. They travel at reduced fares, yet all need to ride on the trains at roughly the same times—morning and evening peak periods. This requires the expensive infrastructure of platforms, stations, tracks, and trains, which then spend most of the rest of each weekday and every weekend standing virtually idle.

Generally commuters travel short distances (usually taking up to an hour) on mainline company tracks but, even so, some railways have been built to attract commuter traffic in particular. In many countries the first railways built were what would now be called commuter lines, such as the

FAST TRACK TO THE SKY

Airport links are a vital part of today's commuter rail networks. Holiday travelers and business people pay premium fares for fast and convenient trains that run directly from city stations to airport. London's 85-mile-per-hour (137 km/h) *Heathrow Express* and Stockholm's *Arlanda Express* were among the first, with many more to follow in cities around the world.

Nürnberg–Fürth line in Germany, Paris–St. Germain in France, and St. Petersburg–Tsarskoye Selo in Russia.

Special rolling stock and locomotives were built, not always with much attention to commuter comfort. The object was to carry as many people as possible without making the train too long. Trains could be loaded and unloaded very quickly, with a door to each compartment, so more trains could be run during the rush hour. In continental Europe and the United States the larger loading gauge allowed the use of double-decker trains.

Later there came "open" stock, with a central aisle and seats on either side. This accommodated more standing passengers, although loading and unloading could be slow. High-performance steam engines, built to accelerate the trains quickly, allowed the maximum number of trains per hour. And then came electrification, with the vast networks of London, Berlin, Paris, and New York being established before 1914.

Over the last three decades increasing road congestion has seen traditional commuter networks reinvigorated with new lines, trains, and stations. On some routes train speeds

KUALA LUMPUR'S *rail system uses a metro line and the Star Light Rail Transit, enabling workers easy access to the busy Malaysian city.*

WORKERS *cling to a train prior to departure in Jakarta. Train transport might be cheap in Indonesia, but it is hazardous for all concerned.*

and frequencies increased, with supporting innovations including the establishment of "park and ride" areas at major stations or the termini at the "country" end of the line. The interchange between buses, metros, and rail networks is also being improved. Today light-rail systems are frequently integrated with the "heavy rail" of traditional railways using the same tracks.

URBAN AND RURAL LINKS
The German city of Karlsruhe was the first in Europe to link urban and rural areas this way, enabling passengers to travel into and out of the city center without having to change vehicles. The Karlsruhe city tramway operator began to share tracks with German Railways (DB) in 1992, on the 17½-mile (28 km) Stadtbahn line with a through service to the city center

using light-rail vehicles. Eight new stations were built and new dual-voltage light-rail vehicles (DC-AC, with on-board transformer and rectifier) were introduced. The services persuaded many commuters to leave their cars at home and were soon expanded.

Karlsruhe also became an international model, to be emulated in the United States and other European cities. Britain's Tyne & Wear Metro, serving Newcastle-on-Tyne, has extended its network, with the light-rail vehicles sharing heavy-rail tracks.

Since the downturn in rail's popularity that began in the 1960s, with the increased use of automobiles, the trend is now reversing. Road congestion is again convincing people of the value of the railways in efficiently moving large numbers of commuters, with governments willing to subsidize lines where this is found to be necessary.

BIG, FAST FREIGHT TRAINS

The needs of industry brought about the first railways;

today, freight transport still inspires innovation.

Demand for the easy movement of coal gave us the first railways. The trains were slow and lumbering but were more efficient than canal barges—and cheaper to operate. The use of small wagons loosely coupled to an engine changed little over the first 100 years of rail. Vehicles spent days being loaded or unloaded in massive marshaling or storage yards. But by World War II railroads such as the Norfolk & Western in the United States were hauling huge tonnages in high-capacity wagons. Today bulk commodities such as coal are handled as efficiently as any traffic on rail.

A FREIGHT TRAIN *heads south through Central Italy (above). A Canadian National freight train (above left) carries goods across inhospitable terrain.*

INTERMODAL *freight trains cross Louisiana's Lake Ponchartrain on the Norfolk Southern Railroad.*

One of the keys to this is the concept of the block train that carries only one type of product and usually serves a single customer. Spectacular examples are the mile-long (1.6 km) Burlington Northern Santa Fe and Union Pacific coal trains from Wyoming's Powder River Valley. Their roller-bearing wagons each carry 100 tons (102 t) or more at up to 60 miles per hour (almost 100 km/h) to power stations in the south and east. They have counterparts in Canada and South Africa, and in the giant iron-ore trains in the Pilbara region of Western Australia. Trains such as these have spurred manufacturers to build diesel-electric engines with 6,000 horsepower.

The challenge in countries with frequent passenger trains is to handle vital freight flows without obstructing passenger services. In Britain even coal trains now travel at 60 miles per hour (97 km/h) in order to free up the lines.

AUTOMATIC SYSTEMS

The movement of coal in Britain went through a total revolution in the 1960s. The small, 16-ton (16.3 t) wagons that carried coal from the colliery to its final destination, often power stations, were replaced by much bigger air-braked hopper wagons. These wagons are coupled in rakes of up to 50 vehicles, the maximum length that sidings and loops can handle. They are loaded from an overhead bin at the colliery as the train is hauled underneath by the locomotive, using automatic slow-speed controls, at a rigid 0.5 miles per hour (0.8 km/h). At the power station, the coal is emptied from the wagons'

CONTAINERS *are often double-stacked (above). Two coal trains meet on the Burlington Northern Railroad (left).*

truck or ship, it makes possible the hotshot merchandise trains that criss-cross North America, often with containers double-stacked. These trains, up to 100 wagons long, run colossal distances, rivaling road for speed, and air for cost.

Another American solution to the need to load and unload trains fast is to "piggyback" standard road-truck trailers onto trains. In many European countries, however, low bridges and narrow tunnels make this difficult, so complete road trucks travel on special low-height wagons on RoLa (Rollende Landstrasse or "Rolling Motorway") services.

And in response to the increasing pressure on road networks, Britain now runs 75-mile-per-hour (121 km/h) express mixed-freight trains between London and Scotland up to three times a day. Only express mail trains are able to beat them.

underside doors, which are automatically opened and closed by the discharge plant as the train passes. Both the colliery and power station have "balloon" loops of track so the locomotive never has to uncouple. The train simply goes around a continuous circuit from colliery to power station back to colliery, hence its name, "merry-go-round."

This system is still used today, but 100-ton (102 t) bogie wagons have replaced the 16-ton wagons, and each train is controlled by a single driver. An even more radical development is that coal imported into Britain from overseas is now containerized for the journey from seaport to power station.

Containerization and the intermodal concept—moving goods smoothly from shipper to destination using at least two kinds of transport—have revolutionized rail freight. For general freight, the 20- or 40-foot-long (6 or 12 m) container, or "box," is almost universal on both sides of the Atlantic. Transferred mechanically between train and road

LINKING EUROPE AT SPEED

The opening of the Channel Tunnel in 1994 offered enormous potential advantages for fast freight. Here was the opportunity to move goods across Europe and Britain at speed by rail. In an initiative backed by the European Union, member railways have agreed in principle to a "Trans-European Rail Freight" (TERF) network of 75-mile-per-hour (121 km/h) "freight freeways," to connect Spain, Italy, Hungary, and Britain with countries in between.

PRIVATIZATION

*In a world where environmental protection is constantly balanced
against cost efficiency, the railways have not been excluded.*

It is a paradox that many of the world's railroads were largely built privately, but ultimately became owned by the state, either through political policy or economic necessity. The first railroad companies from the pioneering days quickly amalgamated as they connected with other systems and, as the networks consolidated, they invariably formed an integral part of a nation's identity, therefore becoming desirable property for government control.

AMTRAK'S NATIONAL FLEET *is the
exception to the historic private ownership of United States railroads (above).
European rail freight operators lease this
Blue Tiger diesel-electric locomotive—
the manufacturer retains
ownership.*

Railroads should, perhaps, stay privately owned, rather than be a direct burden on the taxpayer. However, competition from road transport and the cost of meeting environmental responsibilities and other regulatory demands can threaten railways' viability. There are many systems that simply do not cover costs and have to be underwritten by government—or closed.

A BALANCING ACT

The cost of maintaining the track and the infrastructure on which trains run is vast, and ever more so as train speeds rise. Given the global proliferation of road transport, government strategic control is essential if railways are to develop their full potential.

To balance burgeoning road transport against a modern, fast, punctual, safe, and profitable railway is an extremely complex equation.

A properly defined "integrated transport system" that utilizes all modes of transport effectively and under a frame-work of government legislation, would be a universally desirable objective.

However, no government has had the courage or sense of environmental wellbeing to deal with these core issues, with the sole exception of Switzerland, whose system of integrated transport is a model for the world. In fact, the trend has been to shy away from state responsibility and revert to partial privatization on the premise that market forces, controlled by the profit motive, will put matters right.

COST AND EFFICIENCY

In North America, where railroads have always been privately owned—apart from the United States national network, Amtrak—major companies have sold much track mileage to smaller "short line" operators deemed better able to run it profitably. This practice has saved many lines from closure. Among state-owned systems, "open access" agreements have become fashionable, in which the state keeps ownership of track and infrastructure, and private companies run the trains. Some of Germany's passenger services are now privately operated on this basis.

In Australia, super-freighters cross the continent behind locomotives hired on "hook and pull" contracts in which the

BRIGHT COLORS AND MODERN DESIGN *give identity to Britain's 25 privatized railways, such as national freight operator English, Welsh & Scottish Railway (left), cross-London commuter line Thames Trains (above), and South West Trains (below), which serves large areas of southern England.*

owners provide only locomotives and crews. New Zealand has gone a stage further with the entire rail system sold to a private consortium. In Japan, too, the railway network is state backed but also has private interests involved. Of the biggest rail economies, only in Russia, China, and India are the railroads still completely state owned and operated.

BRITAIN'S EXPERIENCE
Nowhere has privatization gone so far than in Great Britain. In 1994 the government attracted international attention by privatizing the entire rail network, splitting what was, in effect, one state-owned company into some 125 separately owned organizations. There was massive opposition, with the government accused of "selling the family silver."

However, British Railways had for many years been vilified (often unfairly) by the popular media as inefficient, bureaucratic, and a rampant consumer of taxpayers' money.

Those who supported privatization claimed that it would improve the system by introducing a customer-led culture.

In fact, it brought severe culture shock, with 25 different franchised operators leasing trains from separate rolling-stock operators, and running them on tracks and into stations owned by yet another company.

For the first time, overseas operators took an active part in running Britain's railways. The major rail freight franchise went to a single United States corporation, which introduced American rail technology, including United States-built diesel locomotives.

Other new operators came from non-rail backgrounds, including the road transport industry. Inevitably many long-serving railway workers departed, to be replaced by managers and staff with no rail experience. The long traditions of the railways' corporate identity became fragmented, and the process of assimilation proved to be a long and painful one, with many issues still unresolved.

Passenger complaints skyrocketed and rail's share of Britain's freight business fell by the turn of the century to less than 10 percent. Only the rail buffs rejoiced, as the new independent operators sought to establish their identities by bringing in an amazing variety of new liveries. Britain's trains had never been so colorful.

HOW IT ALL BEGAN

For centuries wheeled vehicles ran on rails, some even powered by sail, before the Industrial Revolution pushed inventors to develop new methods for locomotion.

There is nothing new about using tracks for wheeled vehicles. Made of stone, wood, and iron, rails have been used since Babylonian times.

Wooden railways were common in 16th-century Europe, mainly at mines. The vehicles that ran on them were often small hand-pushed trucks guided by a pin that ran in a slot between plank-like rails. Austrian copper miners working in Cumberland, England, brought these vehicles with them in the 1560s, but they had little influence on future development.

The real impetus was the beginning of the Industrial Revolution, stimulated by

JAMES WATT *(1736–1819) developed the beam engine. This led to the basic design for the world's first steam locomotives.*

coal, which needed an all-weather means of transport from pit-head to navigable water. The earliest recorded wagonway was built at Wollaton, a mining town near Nottingham, between 1603 and 1604. By 1660, wagonways appeared on Tyneside, an area that became the nursery of railways.

Wagonways, on which wagons were moved by horses or by gravity, were up to 12 miles (19 km) long, with cuttings, embankments, and bridges. The 1726 stone Causey Arch had the largest span in Britain at 105 feet (32 m). Without an advance on animal power, however, traffic was still slow moving.

But earlier that century French engineer Denis Papin and two English inventors, Thomas Savery and Thomas Newcomen, had developed steam engines to pump water from mine shafts. In the 1760s Scottish engineer James Watt improved on Newcomen's basic design.

NICHOLAS CUGNOT

Nicholas Cugnot, a French artillery officer, was the world's first motorist. Yet within minutes of his first trip he had the world's first motoring accident and soon also became the world's first convicted dangerous driver.

His three-wheeled road wagon (below) appeared in 1769. The steam-powered machine had two cylinders driving a single front wheel of solid iron, and Cugnot said his invention would carry four people at 2 miles per hour (3 km/h). But the weight of the huge copper boiler on the front of the carriage made it almost impossible to steer. On its maiden run the machine ran into a stone wall, demolishing it. Undaunted, Cugnot spent the next year building a larger version for the French War Ministry, designed to pull field guns. He demonstrated his new machine on a Paris street in 1770.

Cugnot promised that it could carry 5 tons (5.1 t), but the steering once again let him down and, as he tried to turn a corner, the carriage turned over. Magistrates sent him to jail as a public nuisance and impounded his machine.

CATCH-ME-WHO-CAN, *Trevithick's locomotive, ran on a circular demonstration track near what is now Euston Square, London, from July to September 1808.*

The beam engine was a supported beam with a large cylinder at one end, and a tube with a piston at the other to pump the water. This was the genesis of railway power. Until George and Robert Stephenson's *Rocket* in 1829, locomotives were basically a scaled-down beam engine going for a walk.

In the northern mining town of Leeds, engineer Matthew Murray (born in Newcastle in 1765) produced the first steam locomotives to be commercially successful. He developed the ideas of Watt and Cornish inventor Richard Trevithick by adding a slide valve, which was a major step forward, followed by improved cylinder-boring and precision machining.

In 1801 Trevithick began experimenting with steam engines for the iron foundry at Coalbrookdale. With the soaring cost of horse fodder, in 1810 John Blenkinsop asked for Murray's assistance to provide steam power on

the wagonway at nearby Middleton Colliery. His engines used two vertical double-acting cylinders with a single-flue boiler, which gave smoother action. The patent toothed drive on both the engines and track allowed the locomotives to pull heavy loads yet still be light enough to not break the rails.

Wrought-iron rails enabled the locomotive to approach maturity. Eventually the various ingredients were drawn together to create the "modern" railway, which began with the opening of the Stockton & Darlington line in 1825, and the Liverpool & Manchester in 1829.

Let the country make the railroads, and the railroads will make the country.

Edward Pease (1767–1858), Promoter of the 1825 Stockton & Darlington Railway

RICHARD TREVITHICK (1771–1833)

Born at Camborne in the tin-mining region of Cornwall, the son of a mine manager, Richard Trevithick eagerly participated in local efforts to evade James Watt's monopoly on the stationary steam engine, and to harness high-pressure steam in order to increase engine output while saving on coal.

In 1800 he built and had patented three high-pressure steam road carriages for trials in Camborne, London, and Coalbrookdale, but the poor roads caused problems.

As the result of a bet, he built a steam locomotive in 1804 for the Penydarren Iron Works, near Merthyr Tydfil in South Wales. It successfully hauled 10 tons (10.2 t) over the 9½-mile (15 km) tram-way, but it broke the iron plate rails. Despite this mishap it was the first time a steam locomotive had been used to haul both freight and fare-paying passengers.

Trevithick's 1808 *Catch-Me-Who-Can* gave rides on a circle of track in London and was an advance on the Penydarren locomotive, with a vertical cylinder driving directly onto the wheels on one side, without the clumsy flywheel or the trombone-like slide arrangement.

Despite important innovations such as the return-flue boiler, blast-pipe, and coupled wheels, and his demonstration that smooth wheels and smooth rails would work well together, Trevithick frittered away his considerable talents on ill-conceived mining ventures in South America, and he died, penniless, aged 62.

THE FIRST LOCOMOTIVES

The opening of new lines in England's industrial north

created a mood ripe for engineering innovation.

The first steam locomotives of 200 hundred years ago occupied a formative age of railways lasting a quarter of a century, until the opening of the Liverpool & Manchester Railway (L&MR) in 1830.

LOCOMOTION NO. 1 *ran on the world's first public steam railway in 1825. This model was presented to the British Science Museum by T. A. Common in 1936.*

After the early work of Richard Trevithick, among others, three key figures in the development of the steam locomotive were George Stephenson, William Hedley, and Timothy Hackworth.

George Stephenson was possibly the most famous railway engineer ever, and he is rightly acclaimed as the "Father of Railways." The best known of his numerous achievements is the 1829 locomotive *Rocket,* which he used on the L&MR.

PIONEER *engine builder Timothy Hackworth was the first locomotive superintendent for a railway company.*

Importantly, it combined the blast-pipe (which he had earlier developed) with the tubular boiler, and it had pistons directly driving the wheels. The last steam locomotive to be built in Great Britain, in 1960, used the very same engineering principles.

Born in 1781 at Wylam, Northumberland, Stephenson trained as a colliery engine-wright and, independently of Sir Humphrey Davey, invented a miner's safety lamp. He also discovered that iron wheels could efficiently run on iron rails, doing away with the need for cog-drives.

NEW TECHNOLOGY

From 1814 Stephenson experimented with steam locomotives at Killingworth Colliery. He became the engineer of the Stockton & Darlington Railway in 1825 and, following his success in building the L&MR, was in demand for other projects.

Stephenson's first engine, *Blucher,* ran, though not very well. However, the dark, dank, and harsh coalfields

of Durham were a hotbed of new technology. In the same year, William Hedley was to join Timothy Hackworth in building locomotives.

Hackworth was one of a group of enterprising colliery owners and engineers and, like Stephenson, was born in Wylam, in 1786. When Hackworth was a foreman blacksmith at the Wylam Colliery he met Hedley, who was born in nearby Newburn in 1779 and trained as a colliery manager.

He linked the work of Trevithick and Stephenson and showed that a smooth-wheeled locomotive could pull an economic load on smooth rails. In 1805 Hedley was appointed manager at Wylam Colliery, which had just ordered Trevithick's second Penydarren loco-motive. The state of the track, however, meant that the engine could not be used. Trevithick refused to build another engine, and Hedley stepped into the breach.

With Hackworth's help, from 1813 to 1815 Hedley built three successful loco-

**A STEPHENSON FAMILY
PORTRAIT** with George seated
and Robert standing to his left.

motives using flue-return
boilers and wheels coupled
through gears. They were
modified by 1817 as eight-
wheelers to spread their
weight on the brittle iron
rails, and they pulled 50-ton
(51 t) loads until 1829, when
they were replaced by two
four-wheelers of the same
design. These new engines,
Puffing Billy and *Wylam Dilly*,
still survive.

TRACKS AND TRIALS

The 20-mile (32 km)
Stockton & Darlington Railway opened in 1825, the first
public steam railway to be
empowered by an Act of
Parliament. It was to be a
good testing ground for locomotives and new ideas in
track construction. The line's
builder, George Stephenson,
used his new engine, *Locomotion No. 1*, gaining valuable
experience that he put to
good use four years later
building the L&MR.

Although nowadays held
up as an icon of engineering
achievement, *Locomotion
No. 1* as a working
locomotive was in
truth something of
a flop. It was
frequently too
short of steam

for the long hauls demanded
and, faced with proposals by
the directors to abandon steam
entirely and convert to horse
power, Hackworth was
determined to produce a
better engine.

His blast-pipe improved
the fire and, using a flue-
return boiler, he considerably
increased the heating surface
on *Royal George* in 1827,
successfully providing power
and reliability along with its
economical operation.

Other engineers were
developing similar ideas at
the same time, including John
Rastrick, born in 1780. He
was apprenticed to his father
in Northumberland and, after
studying iron making in
Shropshire, was soon placed
in charge of a foundry. In
1823 he became the engineer

of the horse-worked
Stratford & Moreton
Railway in Warwickshire
and worked for George
Stephenson and the
L&MR's promoters to
develop new railway lines
for northern England.

In 1829 Rastrick built the
Shutt End Colliery Railway
in Staffordshire and joined
engineer Jonathon Forster.
They built both the *Agenoria*
(now preserved) and the first
locomotive to run in the
United States, the *Stourbridge
Lion*. Rastrick was also one
of the judges at the Rainhill
locomotive trials on the
L&MR in 1829, which were
won by George and Robert
Stephenson's *Rocket*.

Hackworth began to use
multi-tube boilers (as used in
Rocket) from 1830, and later
inclined cylinders driving
directly onto coupled wheels,
as on his *Derwent* in 1845.
As a builder of slow, heavy
freight locomotives, he was
soon left behind by more
progressive designers.

BUILDING ON A VISION

George Stephenson was a
visionary. When asked his
opinion on the best gauge for
a new railway, he said that all
should be the same, as one
day they would all be linked
to each other. George and his
son Robert, who had his own
successful career as a railway
engineer, ran two companies
that had become world famous
by the time George
died in 1848.

PUFFING BILLY
*proved itself a reliable
workhorse at the
Wylam Colliery.*

THE FIRST INTERCITY RAILWAY

While engineers improved the design of steam locomotives,

the challenge of building lines to link cities and ports was still to be met.

In 1820 in Great Britain, Liverpool's merchants (importing cotton and exporting finished goods), together with Manchester's cotton mill owners, had long been looking for an alternative to the costly, inadequate services of the canals and roads linking the two cities, just 30 miles (48 km) apart.

Monopolistic practices were raising transport costs to exorbitant levels, and the cotton industry was growing at such a speed that existing capacity was hopelessly inadequate. Wealthy Quaker Joseph Sanders met surveyor and engineer William James in 1821, a time when trade was booming. James had foreseen the coming of the railways, and from 1800 to 1820 he surveyed and tried to promote many railway lines at his own expense. His survey company was the largest and wealthiest in Britain, but none of his ideas was adopted.

BUILDING THE LINES

Sanders was delighted when James proposed a railway between the seaport of Liverpool and the industrial city of Manchester, which James undertook to build in 18 months. His offer was accepted and he began the first survey of the line, with Robert Stephenson (George Stephenson's son) as his assistant. James overstretched himself, however, and was declared bankrupt in 1823. George Stephenson succeeded him as the new line's engineer.

In 1825 the Stockton & Darlington Railway opened, and a parliamentary bill was introduced for the Liverpool & Manchester Railway—but it was thrown out because Stephenson could not answer stiff questioning about his survey. Stephenson was sacked, to be replaced by civil engineers John and George Rennie. The bill was finally passed in May 1826, and

TICKETS *from the Liverpool & Manchester Railway, 1832 (above), on which the Stephensons' Rocket (below) ran after winning the Rainhill Trials of 1829. John Rastrick, one of the trial judges, sketched Rocket's boiler into his notebook (right).*

Stephenson was reappointed as the railway's engineer.

The line required several heavy engineering works, including the digging of a 70-foot-deep (21 m) cutting through solid rock at Olive Mount near Liverpool, a 1¾-mile (3 km) tunnel under Liverpool to the docks, and a 4-mile (7 km) embankment over a marshy area known as Chat Moss. Initially it looked as if the marsh would defeat

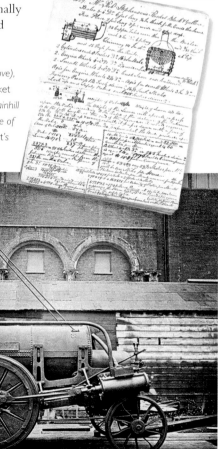

NINE VIEWS *of the Liverpool & Manchester Railway, one of Stephenson's earliest engineering triumphs, are captured in these colored aquatints by T. T. Bury, c. 1833.*

Stephenson. As the embankment was built up, it just disappeared into the bog.

The work took almost two years (1826–1827), and was hugely expensive. Parallel trenches were dug across the moss to drain a 48-foot-wide (15 m) causeway, and vast quantities of peat and fascines (bundles of brushwood and heather) were laid across it. When it finally stabilized, it was covered with earth and gravel, with ash spread for the sleepers and track.

THE RAINHILL TRIALS

The directors initially considered horse-traction or using stationary steam engines, but decided to hold a contest to see whether suitable steam locomotives existed.

There were three "serious" entries, George and Robert Stephenson's *Rocket,* Timothy Hackworth's *Sans Pareil,* and John Braithwaite and Swede John Ericsson's *Novelty.* The trials were held in 1829 on a section of the line at Rainhill.

For Hackworth it all went wrong. First there were minor mechanical problems, then came regulation infringements. Cylinder failure finally ended *Sans Pareil*'s chances. Both *Rocket* and *Novelty* reached the grand speed of 30 miles per hour (48 km/h), but *Rocket* was consistently more reliable than its rival, and won the prize. The contest was closely followed around the world, with news of it published daily as far away as Boston, Massachusetts.

Rocket's mechanical innovations remained at the heart of steam locomotive technology to its very end: a multi-tube boiler, using induced draught to regulate the rate of combustion and steam production, with direct drive from the cylinders to the rail wheels. The cylinders were inclined at approximately 45 degrees and the 7½-ton (7.6 t) machine could develop 25 horsepower.

The fundamental feature of the locomotive was the link between steam usage in the cylinders and production of steam in the boiler. By using the energy in the exhaust steam discharged through the blast-pipe nozzle on the smokebox, Stephenson was able to create the induced draught on the fire through the boiler tubes—the harder the engine worked, the greater was the pull on the fire, increasing the amount of steam that was produced.

TRAGEDY AND TRIUMPH

The directors of the Liverpool & Manchester Railway ordered seven more Stephenson locomotives for its opening on September 15, 1830, by the Duke of Wellington.

Tragically, the great day was marred by the death of Liverpool Member of Parliament William Huskisson, who stepped in front of *Rocket.*

But the railway, which Huskisson had actively supported, was an outstanding success. The company's shares doubled, and the line paved the way for locomotives and railways over the next quarter of a century.

33

BRITAIN'S RAILWAY MANIA

Buoyed by the success of early railways, British investors went on a spending spree that opened up lines across the country.

The late 1990s saw frenzied investment in "dot.com" business, where fortunes could be won, and lost. Yet the phenomenon is not new. Nearly 160 years earlier the railways were the new technology and investors rushed to put their money into them. The ease with which investors could become involved fueled the boom. But more often than not they lost their money as expensive surveys and the legislative process used up their investment capital, for railways that would never be built.

In Great Britain this madness for railways soon became known as "railway mania." The period of financial excitement for railways from 1844 to 1846 was the most startling, though it wasn't the first such boom. The first "mania" was from 1824 to 1825, when changes in British company legislation and the easy availability of money saw prospectuses published for 70 railway lines, of which 50 made it to Parlia-

ment. Although the Liverpool & Manchester was the only substantial line to emerge from this, there were several proposals for trunk routes linking Britain's major cities, giving a foretaste of what was to come. The poor harvest of 1825 and a series of banking failures ended this euphoria.

BOOM AND BUST

The opening of the Liverpool & Manchester in 1830 fueled a second boom, from 1835 to 1837. In all, 50 Acts for new railways were passed for lines totaling around 1,600 miles (2,576 km), and financial backing was forthcoming for the most unrealistic schemes. Potential shareholders were only required to provide a deposit of five percent, so even small investors could gain a railway interest. But,

as building costs surged ahead of estimates and Parliament tightened legislative requirements, the boom was again followed by a slump.

It was the intensity of the mania of 1844 to 1846 that was remarkable. In 1846 alone 4,540 miles (7,310 km) of line were sanctioned, which almost doubled the existing system, and capital authorizations broke all records. The boom was the result of several good harvests, favorable loan terms from the Bank of England, and a relaxation of some parliamentary restrictions. Yet some landowners resented the intrusion of the railway developers and came into conflict with them. This even led to pitched battles between

RAILWAY SHARES
(above) won and lost fortunes, while the rail-ways grew. The Liverpool & Manchester (right) opened in 1830.

the laborers and impromptu "armies" of men employed by the landowners. Other land-owners actively encouraged railways by investing in them.

The decade from 1840 saw Britain's railway map transformed. In 1840 there were 1,500 miles (2,415 km) of railway. By 1850, however, the total mileage had shot up to 6,000 (9,660 km). Had all the railways authorized during railway mania been built, the figure would have been close to 12,000 miles (19,320 km). The result was that by 1850 Britain's railway system was largely complete, with trunk and secondary routes criss-crossing the landscape. Only southwest England, Wales, and northern Scotland, with their more difficult terrain and limited traffic prospects, were not immediately affected, although these regions were also covered with lines over the following 15 years.

However, once the shaky foundations of the new capital market were exposed, a slump, hastened by worsening economic conditions, followed. Railway share prices halved between 1846 and 1849, with just 17 miles (27 km) of new railway authorized in 1849. Yet the lessons were not entirely learned, and there were subsequent booms in both 1852 to 1853 and the early 1860s, although none ever repeated the excesses of the great 1840s railway mania.

THE ENGINEERS

All this expansion would have come to nothing without parallel advances in technology, and the locomotive engineers obliged. In just five years following

STEPHENSON'S ROCKET
was developed during the first "mania," from 1824 to 1825.

the 1829 success of the *Rocket,* George Stephenson moved on to his 2-2-0 Planet design, which was larger and more powerful and formed the basis of all subsequent steam locomotives. In 1841 George's son Robert invented the link-motion valve gear, used on thousands of locomotives for the next 100 years. Belgian engineer Egide Walschaert invented his own valve gear in 1844, its application becoming almost universal. By this time leading engineers had set up their own locomotive building works to supply engines to the newly formed railway companies, and the railway age was almost fully developed.

GEORGE HUDSON, "RAILWAY KING" (1800–1871)

Widely credited as Britain's "Railway King," George Hudson was a colorful character who financed construction of many railways and advocated a unified system. But he was later undone when his underhanded financial dealings were exposed. He came from relatively humble roots, a farmer's son from an East Yorkshire village. He entered the railway scene in 1827, when, under questionable circumstances, he inherited a fortune from a distant relative, enabling him to invest in early railway schemes.

Meanwhile, he became active in local politics and by 1836 was leader of the Tories on York City Council. This paved the way for his election as chairman of the York & North Midland Railway, which proved highly profitable. Although Hudson used dubious accounting practices, he was seen as a supreme strategist and financial genius. In 1844 he created the Midland Railway by merging other lines. By this time Hudson controlled more than 1,000 miles (1,610 km) of line, including the main route north from London to Rugby, York, and Newcastle. His power and influence grew and he was a favored guest of the wealthy and influential.

In 1845, by then an elected Member of Parliament, he made a desperate bid to prevent the building of a direct London-to-York railway, which threatened the prosperity of his railway interests. He was unsuccessful, and a subsequent committee of inquiry into his operations discovered serious financial manipulations, including the payment of vast sums in dividends from capital funds. These maneuvers brought about his downfall in 1849.

Nevertheless, in the 22 years he was directly involved with railways, Hudson helped build a powerful network. After the scandal, he moved abroad and spent much of his later life fighting claims against him for misappropriated funds.

EXPANSION *in the* UNITED STATES *and* CANADA

North America readily took to the railroad as a means of transportation, building thousands of miles of track across its vast distances.

Though England was its birthplace, railroading quickly took hold in North America. The vastness of the United States and Canada provided an ideal environment for this new transportation mode. The railroads were an effective tool in enhancing the reputation and influence of the cities that hosted them. Later they also helped to bond countries.

THE FIRST SYSTEMS

The first railroads in the United States were built at the same time as canals, which they soon made obsolete. In 1828 the Baltimore & Ohio (B&O) began laying rails from Baltimore to Ellicott's Mills, 13 miles (21 km) away. The same year work also began on the Chesapeake & Ohio Canal in nearby Georgetown. Both eventually reached Cumberland, the railroad doing so in 1842. Generally acknowledged as America's first railroad, the B&O (which operated with horses for power until 1831) staked Baltimore's claim as a major trading center with the developing West—as the Erie Canal had done in 1825 for New York City, which was fast becoming the country's preeminent port.

Other major port cities were in the competition as well, and they bettered their

THE CROSSING OF CANADA *by the Canadian Pacific Railway was a mammoth task, blasting through hundreds of miles of solid rock. This lithograph (above) depicts a canyon on the route. U.S. rail bonds (above) became sought-after commodities.*

chances by becoming railroad termini. When the *Best Friend of Charleston* chugged out of its namesake city on Christmas Day 1830, the South Carolina Canal & Rail Road Company became the nation's first railroad to offer a schedule of service using steam locomotives. Philadelphia's Main Line of Public Works, a complex system combining canals and railroads that stretched across Pennsylvania to Pittsburgh, was completed in 1834. New York's Mohawk & Hudson railroad opened that same year to complement the Erie Canal. Boston soon joined, with the Boston & Worcester in 1835 and the Western Railroad, later called the Boston & Albany, in 1841.

DEVELOPING THE WEST

As the "Western frontier" continued to move west, the railroads stretched to serve it. Established railroads grew (sometimes through subsidiary companies), and in other cases independent lines were built, often to ultimately be joined through end-to-end mergers. Before long every town wanted its own line, and the boom was on, leading to an overbuilding that would in years ahead substantially burden the industry.

Numbers tell the story eloquently. In 1830 the total length of track throughout the United States was 23 miles (37 km). It had grown to 2,808 miles (4,521 km) by 1840—more than in all of Europe. It had reached 9,021 miles (14,524 km) by 1850—more than half of the world's rail mileage. By 1860 it had grown to 30,626 miles (49,308 km), by 1880 to 93,267 miles (150,160 km), and by 1900 to 193,346 miles (311,287 km).

For roughly 20 years from 1850, the massive growth in the Midwest and West was fueled by land grants—gifts of public land to the states and later directly to the railroads from the federal government. The railroads used this land to build their rights of way and facilities, and also sold parts of it to new settlers.

THE LAND GRANTS

The most famous of these land-grant-aided rail routes across the West was the Central Pacific (CP)–Union Pacific (UP) line from Sacramento to Omaha. This was the first transcontinental railroad. When the last spike was driven in May 1869, it marked the completion of an American epic that had begun in 1862 with the signing of the Pacific Railroad Act. From the west had come the CP, building through the rugged Sierras with Chinese laborers, many of whom died in the hazardous business of blasting tunnels and cuts through the mountains and building bridges.

From the east came the UP, whose largely Irish workforce had a far easier time of it in terms of topography, but they had to deal with Indians retaliating against this unprecedented incursion across their lands. Using skills learned in the Civil War, General Grenville M. Dodge was in full charge of the building as chief engineer. Dr. Thomas C. Durant, UP vice-president, handled the often corrupt financial dealings.

When news of the line's completion was telegraphed to a proud populace, it wasn't the end of the story. Still to come were revelations of corruption and bought politicians. Also ahead were years of right-of-way realignment and upgrading. Both land grants and government loans were based on mileage completed, so CP and UP had raced to their meeting point, building cheaply in the process.

CREATING CANADA

The story was much the same when the Canadian Pacific completed its transcontinental railway in 1885, an accomplishment no less heroic than that of the CP and UP.

In fact, it literally created Canada as it exists today by bonding the Western provinces with the East and assuring that they did not become part of the United States. For both nations, their binding by rail was a major milestone, and forever afterward a cultural icon.

THE GOLDEN SPIKE *of the Union Pacific Railroad was driven at Promontory, Utah, on May 10, 1869, completing the first transcontinental crossing of the United States.*

NORTH AMERICAN ENGINEERING

As America extended its railroad tracks, American engineers began to develop a distinctive locomotive style.

The persistent theme of railroad engineering's development in the United States, and the characteristic that sets it apart from similar processes around the world, is "bigness"—big engines and railway cars to serve a big country with a big loading gauge and big clearances. It's no coincidence that one of America's most famous steam locomotives was called the "Big Boy." This massive articulated locomotive, with a 4-8-8-4 wheel arrangement and the capability of generating 7,000 horsepower, trundled long freight trains over Union Pacific's Sherman Hill in Wyoming. The Big Boy was the quintessence of American steam power— a technology taken as far as it could go.

HUMBLE BEGINNINGS

The roots of the American steam locomotive reach back more than a century from 1941, when the first Big Boy rolled off the erecting floor. The earliest steam locomotives built in the United States couldn't have been more different from the behemoths into which they evolved. Peter Cooper's cabless *Tom Thumb* of 1829, which was basically a vertical boiler on a flatcar, ran on the Baltimore & Ohio more as a harbinger of what might be than a workaday locomotive.

THE DE WITT CLINTON *of 1831 (at right) was exhibited alongside the new locomotive No. 999 for the New York Central & Hudson River Railroad (which had earlier absorbed the Mohawk & Hudson) at the Columbian Exposition in Chicago, 1893.*

In South Carolina, the similarly vertical-boilered *Best Friend of Charleston* (1830) was more successful. With its horizontal boiler, steam dome, and forward smokestack, the Mohawk & Hudson's *De Witt Clinton* (1831) pointed much more clearly to what was to come. All three of these locomotives were built in the United States, showing that the former colony was ready to forge its own style of railroading—one appropriate to its wide-open spaces.

By the end of the 1830s, the 4-4-0, aptly named the "American type," had become the country's standard locomotive, a position it held for roughly half a century. This was a locomotive type to which all its successors in the

decades ahead held a clear design kinship. A key development was the swiveling lead bogie, or truck.

The 1830s saw the introduction of many additional design features that later became standard for American steam power: a cab to shelter the crew, for instance, and the cowcatcher (or pilot), which prevented derailment when a locomotive tangled with livestock. The sand box (later sand dome), said to be used first in Pennsylvania when a grasshopper infestation slicked the rails, was another product of the decade.

George W. Whistler developed America's first steam locomotive whistle in 1836. Reflecting the size and stature of the locomotives themselves,

THE MILITARY *made great use of the railroads during the Civil War. This Union locomotive was built by William Mason.*

American whistles were deep, robust, and powerful, in contrast to the shrill cries typical in Britain and on the Continent. The headlight became common in the 1840s.

The next great locomotive wheel arrangement in the United States was the 2-8-0 Consolidation, introduced in 1865. With lower driving wheels, these were classic freight locomotives designed for strength over speed. The 2-8-0 in time superseded the 4-4-0 as the country's most widespread locomotive. Natural evolutions were the Decapod (2-10-0, a gritty freight hauler), the Mogul (2-6-0), and the Ten-Wheeler (4-6-0). In the 1890s the trailing truck was developed, which allowed fireboxes to grow substantially, and led to the preeminence of the Pacific (4-6-2) and Mikado (2-8-2).

IMPROVEMENTS

Although locomotives grew in both size and sophistication, two innovations that had the potential to make railroading much safer languished. In 1868 Eli H. Janney patented the knuckle coupler, which could replace the link-and-pin system that maimed many a brakeman. Then George Westinghouse patented his air-brake system. It was another 25 years, however, with the passage in 1893 of the Safety Appliance Act, that these essential improvements went into general use.

Meanwhile, steam locomotives just got bigger and better. The introduction of oil-fired locomotives in the 1910s and automatic stokers in the 1920s was critical as locomotives became more powerful, beyond the capacity of firemen to supply coal.

But by the end of the 1930s the diesel locomotive was ready. When Electro-Motive Division's bulldog-nosed set of FT diesel-electric demonstrators toured the country in 1940, the cat was out of the bag. Though fine steam locomotives continued to be built well into the 1950s, there was no turning back. The future belonged to the much more efficient—if less charismatic—diesel locomotive.

HEADLIGHTS FOR TRAINS *were developed in the United States in the 1840s. They were not adopted in Great Britain, where lines did not have unprotected crossings.*

EUROPE'S FIRST RAILWAYS

Europe began to develop railways in the 1830s, at first relying on British engineering—but Germany soon caught up.

European engineers and entrepreneurs watched the emergence of the railway in England with interest, but it was some years before they made much progress on their side of the Channel. Even then it was often under the supervision of English engineers such as George and Robert Stephenson, who surveyed the first mainlines in Spain and Norway. Another Englishman, Joseph Locke, laid out the French mainline from Paris to Le Havre. Many lines were also built by British contractors and laborers, the latter gaining a reputation for hard work and hard drinking.

BRITISH EXPORTS

These pioneers took British-built locomotives with them, in addition to many of their engineering standards. Not least of these was the 4-foot-8½-inch track gauge that now

A BRITISH children's alphabet book featured an artist's depiction of Der Adler (The Eagle), for the letter "E."

allows through running from one side of Europe to the other (with the exception of Spain and Portugal). The beginnings of the railway in France also closely paralleled those in England. The first French line was built in the mining district of St. Etienne, near Lyon. As with the British Stockton & Darlington Railway, it was conceived as an industrial railway to move coal. Passengers came later. At its opening in 1830 the line was horse-worked, as it was for another 14 years.

The first steam-worked railway was the Paris & St. Germain, in what is now the Parisian suburbs. It opened in 1837 using locomotives built at the Stephenson works at Newcastle-on-Tyne in England. Four years later trains ran on France's first international route from Paris to Basel in Switzerland. The government laid the foundations for today's French rail network in 1842, with legislation to determine main trunk routes which the state would build for private companies to lease and operate. This remained the structure of French railways for almost 100 years, until nationalization came in 1938.

Germany built the biggest railway system in Europe, but its first step was a small one, a 4½-mile (7 km) line from Nürnberg to Fürth. It was known as the Ludwigsbahn because of its enthusiastic sponsorship by King Ludwig of Bavaria. The opening featured a British-built locomotive, *Der Adler* (The Eagle). Its British driver, William Wilson, then worked the line for 27 years. Of greater significance, however, were the completion in 1837 of the Saxon State Railway's arterial line from Dresden to

MARC SÉGUIN (1786–1875)

An inventive engineer whose interests extended to theoretical physics and suspension bridges, Marc Séguin built the first effective French steam locomotive in 1829, after visiting George Stephenson in England. Séguin pioneered the multiple-firetube boiler (which Stephenson later adapted for his *Rocket* locomotive) and, less successfully, used an axle-driven fan to strengthen the draft. He demonstrated his engine on the St. Etienne–Lyon line, though the line continued to be horse-worked until 1844.

Leipzig, a distance of 72 miles (116 km), and the first Prussian railway, Berlin to Potsdam, which acquired some of the first American-built locomotives imported into Europe. From this point the growth of the German rail network was assured.

Progress toward a cohesive national system was slowed, however, by the determined independence of the sovereign German states. Militant Prussia planned its lines and gave them financial support. Eccentric Baden was for some time the odd one out when it opted for 1,600-millimeter-gauge (5 foot 3 inch) track.

It was the formation of the Imperial German Empire in 1871 that finally provided a unifying influence and almost tripled Germany's railway mileage in the lead-up to World War I. By 1910 Germany's network totaled over 36,000 miles (58,000 km), while Britain's totaled 23,000 miles (37,000 km).

ELSEWHERE IN EUROPE

West and south of Germany, Belgium and Austria both began building railways in the 1830s. Belgium, independent after 1831, also sought out George Stephenson as its technical advisor and had north–south

DURING THE CONSTRUCTION
of Austria's Semmering line (above), 700 workers died. The steam engine Kopernicus (below) was a fine example of early German engineering.

and east–west rail routes in operation by 1844. Austria ran trains on a line from Vienna to Brno in Bohemia (now the Czech Republic) from 1837 and also began the task of building the railway south from Vienna through the Semmering Mountains. Completed in 1853, the line had 15 tunnels and 16 soaring viaducts in 36 miles (58 km); 700 men died during the line's construction.

Holland and Italy both made inauspicious starts to railway building, beginning in 1839, and there was little substantial development until the 1860s. Switzerland's first internal line, from Zürich to Baden, began in 1847. Spain's first was in 1848, though it took another 10 years for the Spanish to build their first mainline, from Madrid to Alicante. By then Europe's railway map was well on its way toward its final shape.

To *the* Alps *and* Beyond

The late 1800s saw rapid growth in European rail travel, with great engineering feats and locomotive development.

The benefits of fast and direct rail travel came to Europe only after the railways conquered its great mountain ranges.

The line from Vienna over the Semmering Pass opened in 1854, breaching the mountain barrier between northern and southern Europe, and in 1867 trains began running over the 4,496-foot (1,373 m) Brenner Pass, which linked Innsbrück in Austria with Bolzano in Italy.

UNDER NOT OVER

Then on September 17, 1871, France and Italy jointly opened the first rail tunnel through the Alps, the 7½-mile (12 km) Mont Cenis or Fréjus Tunnel. It had taken 14 years to build (it would have been longer without dynamite and the pneumatic drill, which were invented in the 1860s) but it transformed communications between north and south.

The tunnel made possible the inauguration of such trains as the *Paris–Rome Express* and

EUROPEAN *rail travel was promoted widely in the late 1800s (above). This illustration of a planned Channel Tunnel (right) was drawn in 1858.*

the *Indian Mail* trains. The latter ran from Calais on the French Channel coast to the Adriatic seaport of Brindisi, carrying English mail for India and the Far East, and cut days off the transit time by steamer.

RESORT TRAVEL

Germany and Switzerland were linked directly with Italy in 1882 via the St. Gotthard Tunnel and again in 1906 when the Simplon Tunnel opened. These were huge engineering tasks at the time; today the tunnels are conduits for volumes of traffic that were unimaginable when they were conceived. These were

the years when the railway companies did all they could to encourage Europe's pace-setting aristocracy to take the train to their favorite resorts, paving the way for future mass travel.

The railway had reached Venice, via a 222-arch viaduct across the lagoon, in 1846 and now brought that decaying city a new lease on life. Nice, Monte Carlo, and the rest of the French Riviera became accessible to the English leisured classes by train in the 1860s. By 1898 even St. Petersburg in Russia was linked to Cannes by an *Express,* which ran via Nice

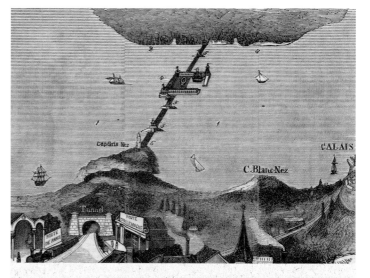

SUBMARINE RAILWAY

In 1881 trial borings were made near Calais in France and Dover in England for what would have been the greatest Victorian enterprise of them all, a tunnel under the English Channel. The project was abandoned for political reasons (not least because the generals feared an underwater invasion) and it was to be a century and more before the dream became reality.

and Vienna and took 68 hours to complete the journey.

In the next decade, royalty discovered Biarritz and San Sebastian on the Atlantic coast straddling the border between France and Spain, and was able to reach them from Paris by the first-class-only *Sud Express*. This French train connected at the frontier with its broad-gauge Spanish equivalent for Madrid, with advertised connections from there all the way to exotic Casablanca in North Africa. But exotic destinations were already somewhat familiar. In 1889 the Wagon-Lits Company's luxurious *Orient-Express* had begun running from Paris to Constantinople (Istanbul), through Vienna, Budapest, Belgrade, and Sofia.

For most of the 19th century European train speeds were generally low, despite the introduction of more and more powerful locomotives to haul increasingly heavy trains.

A train that averaged only 29 miles per hour (47 km/h) could be called an *Express*. Indeed, in 1889 an observer noted that one British company had a goods train with a schedule faster than that of the French *Riviera Express*.

By 1900, however, France was leading Europe, with three trains timetabled at an average of more than 60 miles per hour (100 km/h) and no fewer than 27 at more than 55 miles per hour (88 km/h). To make this velocity more acceptable to passengers, the French relaid some mainlines with heavy steel rails that

The world is a book,

and those who do not

travel read only a page.

Attributed to SAINT AUGUSTINE OF HIPPO (354–430), Numidian Christian theologian

weighed up to 132 pounds per yard (60 kg/m). The almost universal adoption on the Continent of the automatic compressed air brake, invented by the American, George Westinghouse, also made a substantial contribution to the comfort and safety of the passengers.

Among the many steam engine innovations in the period, the introduction of superheating made the greatest impact. This is a process of reheating and drying steam before it enters the cylinders. Perfected in Germany at the turn of the century, it led to a substantial step forward in haulage power and the widespread use of the process.

COMPOUND STEAM
Compounding, or double expansion of steam, had its first practical application in France in the 1880s, and was successfully adopted for both passenger and freight locomotives there and in other European countries, notably Germany, over the next several decades.

Compound locomotives were costly to build and called for skill on the part of their drivers. However, they could be strikingly efficient and economical in operation. Some of the best of the breed became synonymous with the Nord Railway of France, where compound Atlantic-type locomotives (4-4-2s), introduced in 1899, performed prodigious feats of speed and haulage in a career that was to last almost 40 years, in the Golden Age of Steam.

EUROPEAN ENGINEERING

Initially European countries relied on British and American engineering, but soon introduced their own innovations.

European mechanical and civil engineering had a tremendous effect on railways' development around the world.

At first it was Great Britain, where railways were invented, which exported its technology, particularly locomotives, to the rest of the world. For a few short years both America and Europe relied heavily on imports, until their own engineers acquired sufficient skills to start a domestic locomotive-building industry.

In 1841, just 10 years after *John Bull,* a state-of-the-art Planet design developed by Robert Stephenson & Co, had arrived in the United States, the last British locomotive was imported. Very soon the trend was reversed and America, particularly the Baldwin Locomotive Works of Philadelphia, started to supply locomotives to Europe, especially as "railway mania" outstripped the capacity for a home-grown product.

This practice continued in an ad hoc form until the early 1900s and was revived during World War II. However, by the 1850s Germany, France, and Belgium in particular began to develop strong locomotive-building industries of their own, and fundamental

differences in engineering meant that the "foreign" locomotives, designed for a rough and short life in the United States, often fared poorly in Europe.

Early locomotives like *Rocket* and those of Edward Bury in the 1830s had frames made of iron bars. Increasingly sophisticated bar frames became the American standard, but British and most European builders later moved to precision-cut steel plate.

EUROPEAN EXPORTS

A number of European engineers introduced significant innovations. French designer Anatole Mallet built the first successful compound locomotive in 1885, which had a massive influence on the design of large American steam locomotives. From the late 1880s German engineer August von Borries introduced Mallet-type compounds on the Prussian State Railways, with 3,500 examples built

EDWARD BURY'S Comet *locomotive featured an inside bar frame to which the wheels and cylinders were attached.*

over the next three decades. At the same time, Europe adopted the American practice of using a wide firebox over a trailing truck. This allowed the burning of poorer quality coal, common in countries such as Belgium.

It was another Frenchman, Henri Giffard, who invented the injector in 1858, replacing the motion-driven pumps that were previously used to inject water into the boilers. Though the steam drying of saturated steam—superheating—was conceived in 1842 by the English locomotive builders, Hawthorn, it was another five decades before improvements in metallurgy and lubricants made superheating a practical option. The first superheating patents were taken out in 1850 by Quillac and Montcheuil, in France, but it was not until 1898, when Wilhelm Schmidt

ANATOLE MALLET *built the first compound engine, influencing the design of American trains, such as this 2-6-6-2.*

AN INJECTOR uses live or exhaust steam to feed water into a locomotive's boiler. This photograph is of a sectioned model.

applied his superheater to two Prussian 4-4-0s, that engineering turned the corner. Belgian engineer Jean-Baptiste Flamme successfully modified the design in 1903, after which it was used worldwide.

IMPROVING EFFICIENCY

The supply of cheap coal and labor stifled efforts to improve efficiency, but during the 1930s Depression efficiency took on a new importance, and the extra cost of modified designs could be justified.

In 1929 French engineer André Chapelon proved that the power and efficiency of existing locomotives could be improved by a minimum 40 percent by "streamlining" internal steam passages. He reduced steam pressure losses caused by over-elaborate steam pipes. The result, his Kylchap exhaust, undoubtedly aided the British LNER

Pacific No. 4468 *Mallard* in 1938 in achieving its world speed record of 126 miles per hour (203 km/h).

Unencumbered by the tight restrictions on loading gauge, the United States was, by 1910, building powerful 2-8-0s, while Europe often still considered tiny 0-6-0s as its "top-link" freight engines.

American developments such as all-welded boilers and the air brake— pioneered by George Westinghouse in 1869 and standard by the

A SUPERHEATER dries and heats steam to boost locomotive performance.

turn of the century—took nearly 50 years to gain all-round approval in Britain. The British were wedded to the vacuum brake and the conversion to air brakes is not complete even today.

But it was two types of valve gear for locomotives, Stephenson's from England, and Walschaerts', invented by Belgian engineer Egide Walschaerts, that were universally adopted throughout the world.

GEORGE WASHINGTON WHISTLER (1800–1849)

The journey of two young North Americans, George Washington Whistler and William Gibbs McNeill, to Great Britain in 1828 sowed important seeds in the railway world. Upon his return to the United States, Whistler directed the building of the Lowell (Boston) workshop's first locomotive in 1835. He imported an engine from Stephenson's at Newcastle, England, dismantled it to learn how it was constructed, and copied the components to build his own. Along with McNeill he then engineered the Baltimore & Ohio Railroad, from 1838 to 1841.

In another career highlight, Whistler, faced with finding a route over the spine of the Berkshires in West Massachusetts, built a series of seven stone-arch bridges, the first of their type in America. By now an eminent civil engineer, he was chosen by the Czar of Russia to build a railway from Moscow to St. Petersburg—Russia's first mainline, opened in 1852 (above). When the first Russian lines were

built there was no effort made to adopt the European standard gauge of 4 feet 8½ inches (1,435 mm). The 5-foot (1,524 mm) gauge that Whistler proposed for Russia was the same as the regional "Southern" gauge adopted by John Jervis for the South Carolina Railroad in 1833.

However, Whistler died from cholera before the railway was completed. Today, it is his son, James McNeill Whistler, the celebrated artist, who is better remembered.

BATTLE *of the* GAUGES

Different gauges served different rail purposes, but the lack

of a standard gauge for mainline rail worldwide has created problems.

Today's standard gauge of 4 feet 8½ inches is derived from the width of early horse-worked railways, approximate to the space needed for two horses working side by side. Wheel ruts left by Roman chariots were of similar proportion.

When George Stephenson pioneered the first railways in northern England, he chose the distance between the two inner rails as 4 feet 8½ inches, prophetically stating that all railways should be the same width. But his words were not heeded, to the great detriment of railways world-wide. Though standard gauge predominates throughout Europe, North America, and China, there are many areas of the world in which it doesn't. These include Russia (5 feet), the Indian subcontinent (5 feet 6 inches, meter, and 2 feet 6 inches), Africa (mainly 3 feet 6 inches or meter), and Latin America (3 feet, meter, standard, 5 feet 6 inches, and even the narrow 75 centimeters).

In Britain, Stephenson's gauge was challenged when Isambard Kingdom Brunel, engineer to the Great Western Railway, decided that precisely 7 feet 0¼ inches was preferable and referred contemptuously to Stephenson's gauge as that of the wagonways. Brunel's determination was for fast, comfortable, spacious, smooth-running, quiet trains. It was a magnificent vision and, though Britain's other mainline railways continued building to Stephenson's standard gauge, the fabulous Great Western spread its 7-foot tentacles from London westward to Bristol, Exeter, Plymouth, and Penzance, and Neyland in West Wales, and north to Wolverhampton in the Midlands—a total of 544 miles (876 km) of trunk mainlines.

Inevitably, matters came to a head when broad and standard gauges met, as they did at Gloucester in 1844. Chaos resulted; through running was

CHAOS ERUPTED *when passengers switched trains at Gloucester, as depicted in the* Illustrated London News *in 1846 (left). The magic of England's broad gauge is captured in this painting (above) from the 1870s.*

ISAMBARD KINGDOM BRUNEL
*(1806–1859), a visionary engineer, left
a legacy of bridges, tunnels, and viaducts.*

impossible and passengers and luggage had to be transferred between trains. A unified gauge was deemed essential, and a Royal Commission was established the next year to settle the issue, logic seeming to favor standard gauge. However, in June 1845 a train on the Great Western Railway ran the 77¼ miles (124 km) between London and Swindon at an average speed of 60 miles per hour (97 km/h). Brunel's vision was turning into reality. The commission, however, ruled in favor of Stephenson's gauge, and the Great Western began running a mixed gauge, with a third line added to allow standard-gauge trains to run on the broad-gauge track beds. But it was close to 50 years before the Great Western, in one memorable weekend in 1892, converted its last sections of broad-gauge track to standard gauge.

AROUND THE WORLD

Different gauges evolved in different countries for many reasons. Building railways in virgin territories, as in Africa, for instance, was costly. The ventures were speculative since the railway had to create the industries. Narrow gauges were favored because they were infinitely cheaper to construct, particularly when heavy earthworks were involved, such as embankments, tunnels, cuttings, and viaducts. Once the industries expanded, the restrictions of a narrow gauge became evident in slower and less comfortable trains. Africa would have benefited from a unified gauge, but its railways were built piecemeal by

different colonial powers, with local interests in mind.

The disparate nature of Africa's railways are mirrored in many other parts of the world. Narrow gauges were ideal where traffic was limited and remained localized in concept. Even India's three gauges were not necessarily an inherent problem. The broad gauge operated many trunk routes, leaving the meter gauge to serve remoter and less populated areas, and the

*Depend on it, they will be
joined together one day.*

GEORGE STEPHENSON (1781–1848),
the "Father of Railways"

2-foot-6-inch gauge was ideal for the rural lines, where economic development was limited. But India's recent rise to become a major industrialized nation has highlighted the limitations of the meter gauge, and a massive and costly conversion to 5 feet 6 inches is being undertaken.

Australia did not achieve uniform standard gauge between its major state capitals until 1995, and goods bound for Queensland destinations north of the state capital of Brisbane still have to be transshipped to trains on 3-foot-6-inch gauge. Spain, Portugal, and Ireland also have good reason to regret their choice of 5-foot-6-inch and 5-foot-3-inch (1,600 mm) gauges.

47

COLONIAL DEVELOPMENT

Whether it is now seen as exploitation or visionary genius,

colonialism delivered the benefits of railways to many countries.

By the end of the 1830s railways were seen as exciting new technology in Britain, mainland Europe, and North America, and as a catalyst for opening up both commerce and industry. However, railways would not have spread so rapidly beyond the industrializing countries had it not been for the global force of colonialism. This force was embraced by France, Germany, Belgium, and, most powerfully, the British Empire. The benefit the railway had given to the mother country was to be conferred across the varied terrain of the far-flung lands of the Great Britannic Rule.

Soon the great British iron towns, along with the locomotive and rolling stock builders, throbbed feverishly to the new rhythm of building for the Empire. Civil engineers mapped out wild, untamed, and little explored territories; it was a Herculean task carried out by supermen, many of whom were cut down by disease in the prime of their endeavors.

RAIL TO THE WORLD

Colonial countries exported locomotives in pieces, landing them on virgin beaches. They were then assembled with the help of native labor and driven through the fever-laden jungles to the steaming interiors. How else were the goldfields of the Ashanti exploited or the Cadbury chocolate empire founded?

Britain's rule in India led to the construction of one of the world's greatest railway networks. The motives may have been mixed—to facilitate political control, to provide relief from the subcontinent's endemic famines, or just to capitalize on the unleashed urge to travel of a previously static population—but the

CECIL RHODES (1853–1902), *whose visionary railway from Cape Town to Cairo was never completed.*

railways played a huge role in the emergence of India as a major industrial nation.

In Canada, British capital created the Grand Trunk Railway (GTR), the first major component of what became Canadian National Railways (GTR's directors continued to meet in London until 1914). The great feat of building the Canadian Pacific

THIS INDIAN MINIATURE PAINTING *of the early 20th century depicts the ubiquitous steam engine, which played a major role in India's development.*

THE CUBAN SUGAR NETWORK

Spanish colonists in Cuba built a railroad to transport sugar even before Spain's first trains ran in 1848—a line from Havana to Bejucal opened in 1837. By 1922 there were 3,000 miles (4,800 km) of public railway on the island; until nationalization in 1950 roughly half of these lines were controlled by American interests and half by British. Several thousand more miles of mainly narrow-gauge track served Cuba's sugar mills. Many of these survived at the start of the 21st century and were still worked by steam locomotives, such as this American fireless engine, a magnet for rail enthusiasts around the world.

transcontinental railroad was spurred by the need to connect the remote colony of British Columbia on the Pacific Coast with Montreal in the east.

By 1900 almost all of Africa had been colonized, with huge areas under British control, not least in the fertile and mineral-rich south. The British were the continent's most prolific railway builders, and Cecil Rhodes, the driving force behind the British South Africa Company, intended to use his vast fortune from gold and diamonds to make Britain the master of Africa. The basis of the domain was to be the Cape to Cairo Railway.

This great vision was not to be, and Africa, to its loss, inherited a vast range of unconnected, localized railway systems. They were also of different gauges: standard, 3 foot 6 inches, meter, and 950 millimeter, along with numerous smaller lines. This was inevitable given the array of colonial powers involved. Britain shared the continent with Germany in East and Southwest Africa, Italy in Ethiopia, France in Algeria and Morocco, Belgium in the Congo, and Portugal in what are today Mozambique and Angola.

I will send the locomotive as the great Missionary over the World.

GEORGE STEPHENSON
(1781–1841), British engineer and the "Father of Railways"

OTHER COLONIES

Other important railways built under colonization were the British railways of Malaya and Burma, while the Dutch bequeathed to Indonesia a remarkably dense network of lines in what was then their East Indies, especially on Java.

The vast railway inheritance of South America also came into being through foreign powers, although this was primarily the result of their developing commercial interests rather than colonization as such. Again the British were by far the most prevalent. The vast railway network of Argentina was almost entirely British owned and enabled Argentina to become one of the world's leading economies, known as the food basket to the world, with prodigious quantities of beef, wheat, and fruit conveyed by rail to the exporting ports of the Atlantic Ocean. Argentina's railways were the largest commercial undertaking to operate outside of Britain.

The British colonies in Australia, moving toward prosperity through their export industries, also needed railways to link their far-flung communities, enable new settlement, and reduce the cost of bringing huge wool and grain export crops to the coast. Vast distances meant that many lines were built to minimum standards, and the individual states, which were not united as a nation until 1901, followed their own inclinations in track gauge, engine design, and operating systems. Even so, it was still the railways that underpinned their economies and shaped their futures.

BLOWING SAND *buries a rail car used in the 1950s by the De Beers diamond mine in Namibia, Southwest Africa.*

49

RAILS *around the* WORLD

*The development of railways worldwide has always been
determined by each country's political and economic circumstances.*

I n 1999 the World Bank estimated that there were almost 750,000 miles (1,201,337 km) of railway in the world. The 21st century will no doubt record changes. Some countries continue to extend and modernize their railroad systems with panache and success. A few, such as Great Britain, aim for the best of both worlds, with a dense network of highly developed railways on which 90 percent of its railway traffic is vested, paralleled by demands for a fast, safe, efficient, and even profitable rail network. There are also many countries that have allowed their railroads to decline to a point at which only massive capital invest-ment, unlikely to be available, would allow them to ever again be the efficient transport systems that they once were.

JAPANESE EFFICIENCY

The automated efficiency of the "Bullet Train" is a world-wide symbol of Japan, but there is more to the Japanese railroads than the *Shinkansen.* Throughout the islands there is a tracery of more than 12,000 miles (20,600 km) of 3-foot-6-inch-gauge lines. In 1987 Japanese National Railways was split into six regional companies (which run the *Shinkansen,* among other trains). There are also 15 private companies and more than 150 small operators.

Freight trains are fewer now than in former years but

TOKYO'S COMPLEX RAILWAY NETWORK *is complemented by subways and light rail to serve one of the world's busiest and most crowded urban areas.*

passenger services are often intense, and use the latest in rolling stock. This includes 80-mile-per-hour (130 km/h) tilting diesel trains that run on the Soya line on Japan's most northerly island, Hokkaido, and the equally fast *Kamome* (Seagull) electric sets that serve Nagasaki on Kyushu. Sleeping-car expresses run on several routes, and the line running to Hokkaido includes the 33½-mile (54 km) Seikan undersea tunnel. Further south the narrow-gauge tracks cross to the island of Shikoku via the seven Seto-Ohashi bridges, opened in 1990. Japan also has an impressive number of subway (metro) and light-rail systems, including Tokyo's ever-expanding network.

LATIN AMERICA

Latin America has embraced concessioning (privatization) in order to restore the fortunes

of its once-proud railroads. Years of official neglect have taken their toll. In Argentina, Brazil, Chile, Mexico, Peru, and elsewhere railroads are now being run by consortiums with aggressive investment plans (and in many cases the expertise of North American railroad partners).

Mexico concessioned its 124-year-old, government-owned railway, Ferrocarriles Nacionales, in 1997–1998. The expectation is that the three new operating com-panies will attract long-lost freight back to the railroads. Two concessionaires have similarly taken over Peru's mountain-climbing trains, which include those to fabled Machu Picchu. In large, busy cities such as Rio de Janeiro and Buenos Aires even the metro systems are privately operated (and are growing). And Brazil has new, dedicated

mineral haulers whose 2-mile-long (3 km) trains rival those of their more well-known competitors, South Africa and Western Australia.

PRIVATE COMPANIES *have taken over the operation of Peru's railways, including those over the precipitous Andes. This train is on its way to Machu Picchu.*

TURKEY'S EXPANSION

In the Middle East, the railroads of Turkey stand out. The network of 5,400 miles (8,600 km) of main routes, many of them through spectacularly difficult terrain, was largely complete by 1950, at which time it was carrying three-quarters of the country's surface freight traffic. From there, successive governments gave priority to road building with inevitable consequences: rail lost custom and the system

decayed. But at the turn of this century the state-owned railroad (TCDD) embarked on an ambitious plan of line construction and modernization, with a crossing of the Bosphorus to link Europe to Asia as the ultimate target.

RUSSIAN REJUVENATION

Russia is one of the world's great railroad nations, with its 55,000 miles (87,000 km) of general-traffic routes and 37,000 miles (60,000 km) of industrial lines. Russia also has the world's greatest distance of electrified rail—more than

24,000 miles (39,000 km)—almost all 5-foot (1,520 mm) track gauge. In Soviet times its traffic volume was enormous; travelers wrote of passing processions of huge, closely spaced freight trains. In the 1990s this traffic declined, and by the end of the century the system as a whole was rundown and in great need of modernization.

The railways remained a state-owned monolith but, with government pledging rail would still be the backbone of Russia's transport system, the mammoth task of upgrading track and communications was set in motion. The key projects were the introduction of high-speed trains for the Moscow–St. Petersburg line, and the building of a completely new freight line, the Baikal–Amur–Magistral, which diverges from the Trans-Siberian Railway near Irkutsk to provide an alternative, largely parallel, route East.

WORKERS LOAD IRON ORE *onto the freight cars of a train at the Carajas Grande mine in Para, Brazil.*

THE COMING *of the* DIESEL

The diesel engine was invented in 1893, but it was another 40 years before it began to make an impact on railways.

The first application of diesel to rail traction was in a Sulzer-Diesel locomotive completed at Winterthur, Switzerland, in 1913 for the Prusso-Hessian State Railway, Berlin.

The 1,000-horsepower experimental unit had a direct drive to the axles. How to transfer the power to the wheels presented a problem, especially with regard to enabling the locomotive to start heavy loads. Many early engines used a series of gears (direct drive) with coupling rods connecting the driving wheels. The challenge was how to make the equipment strong enough for daily use.

The invention of diesel-electric drive offered a solution.

The engine is coupled to an electric generator, which is in turn connected by cables to electric motors on the axles. The amount of power to the motors is easily controlled, and the equipment is more robust and lighter in weight. This continues to be the chosen method for most diesel locomotives today.

DIESEL SPEED

Various experimental loco-motives, some successful, were built and, despite the work being carried out in Europe, it was America that started to lead the way.

The first commercially successful U.S. diesel-electric locomotives were produced in 1925 by a consortium of General Electric, Ingersoll-Rand, and the American Locomotive Company (Alco). They were built for the Central Railroad of New Jersey. The 300-horsepower six-cylinder locomotives, with a B-B wheel arrangement, weighed 60 tons (61 t). The box-like design wasn't pretty, but it worked, changing the railroads' perceptions of diesel power. It quickly became clear that, where speed was important, diesel-electric traction was going to perform.

In 1932 the world's first high-speed diesel train, the *Flying Hamburger,* was intro-duced in Germany and scheduled to run at a top speed of 93 miles per hour (150 km/h) from Berlin to Hamburg. The two-coach

A DIESEL MOTOR *of the 1890s (left). In the United States diesels offered rail a cost-reducing response to the popular Model T Ford (above).*

RUDOLF DIESEL (1858–1913)

German engineer Rudolf Diesel is famous for his design of the compression-ignition oil engine named after him. Although an oil-powered engine was first invented in 1890 by Englishman Herbert Stuart Akroyd, (1864–1927), Diesel's was the first in which the heat from the compression alone was sufficient to ignite the fuel. Diesel invented his engine in 1893, and it was then developed by Maschinenfabrik Augsburg, Nürnberg (still in business today and known simply as MAN), which put it into production in 1897. It was first used commercially, in ships, in 1903.

THE BURLINGTON ZEPHYR

Just two years after the *Flying Hamburger*, the first diesel-electric streamliner came into service in America in 1934.

The *Burlington Zephyr* was a revolution in design and appearance. The light-weight, three-car stainless-steel train only required 600 horse-power. Its manufacturer was E. G. Budd, who set out to demonstrate just how light the train was by using a tug-of-war team to pull it.

The sharp streamlined styling and corrugated stainless-steel bodysides caused quite a stir. But then that's hardly surprising. With revenues collapsing as buses and the motorcar gained a hold, the railroads needed to arrest falling passenger numbers. Patronage of the Burlington Railroad had fallen from 18 million in 1923 to 7 million in 1933.

The *Zephyr* ripped to shreds the existing, transcontinental speed record. The 1,015 miles (1,634 km) from Denver to Chicago had once taken 26 hours 45 minutes. The record of 18 hours 53 minutes, set in 1897 by a lightweight steam train, was decimated by *Zephyr*'s 13 hours 5 minutes at an average of 78 miles per hour (126 km/h).

The Union Pacific quickly introduced its streamliner for the Chicago–Portland route in 1934, followed by other railroads. The three-coach *Zephyr* only seated 72 people, and soon railroads running streamliners were ordering more cars, with 11-car and then 17-car rakes becoming standard on the Union Pacific.

articulated units were powered by two engines of 410-horsepower each. Ironically the train was intended, not as a prestige operation (which it quickly became), but as a secondary train on the main route.

In Britain diesel railcars were introduced on branch and secondary lines, which by then were under serious threat. In the middle of the Depression, to try to cut costs and stop passengers turning to newly introduced buses, railcars were seen as a possible solution.

DIESEL TAKES HOLD

In 1933 the first railcars were introduced onto the Great Western Railway, and were soon followed by the London & North Eastern. The coming of war meant that work, still experimental, was halted. The major turning point came in the United States in 1939. The General Motors Electro-Motive Corporation brought out the FT diesel-electric demonstrator, which out-performed all steam engines. No. 103, a four-unit freight locomotive, delivered a mighty 5,400 horsepower.

Within a year it operated on 21 railroads across 37 states, and covered 83,000 miles (133,630 km). It performed in temperatures from minus 40°F to plus 110°F (minus 40°C to plus 43°C), at altitudes ranging

BRITAIN'S FIRST *mainline diesel took a test run from St. Pancras Station in late 1947.*

from sea level to 10,200 feet (3,111 m).

This marked a watershed in diesel locomotive technology—and the eventual demise of steam. No. 103's performance on steep gradients with heavy trains established the future of diesel-electric locomotives and secured General Motors the front-runner position in building diesels for America and, significantly, for export. It had the technology, and this kept it in business when many steam-locomotive builders worldwide were unsuccessful in making the switch to diesel engine production, ultimately resulting in their closure.

ELECTRIFICATION

Electrified railways were first used in answer to steam's shortcomings but it was soon a preferred method of traction.

E lectricity, with current supplied from a central source, is the ultimate in railway power. We think of electric trains as quiet, fast, efficient, and above all clean.

German engineer Ernst von Siemens showed them to be feasible in 1879 and they found their first practical applications where the smoky steam engine had become intolerable. Perhaps the most dramatic conversion was in the tunnels of London's Metropolitan Railway, which had used steam underground for almost 30 years before electrification brought relief in 1890. The transformation for long-suffering passengers can only be imagined.

Five years later, the first major railway electrification in the United States came about after Baltimore's city fathers demanded that the Baltimore & Ohio Railroad solve the smoke problem on its line through the town. Similar pressures led to the conversion of New York's spectacular elevated line, the

ELECTRIC ENGINES, *first used on London's underground lines (left), were made possible by Germany's Ernst von Siemens (above).*

"El," and to the electrification of the railway tracks into the Grand Central Terminal and Penn Station.

But it was the danger of working steam engines in steeply graded tunnels that gave the reason for the Great Northern Railroad's 6-mile (10 km) electrification of its line over Stevens Pass in the Cascade Mountains in 1909. The first great Swiss Alpine tunnel, the St. Gotthard, was worked with steam engines at its opening in 1881 but the Simplon Tunnel, opened in 1906, was electrified from the start and the St. Gotthard was converted a few years later.

MAINLINE ELECTRICITY

As early as 1903 fearless German engineers pushed a pair of experimental electric railcars up to 130.5 miles per hour (210 km/h) on a track

that was certainly not built to cater for such a speed. They survived, and the exercise proved electricity's potential for mainline rail traction.

The capital cost of electric installation was high, however, and, where coal for steam engines was cheap, electrification came first to urban railways rather than mainlines. By 1914 Britain had electric lines in provincial cities, notably Newcastle-on-Tyne and Liverpool, as well as in London. The latter's lines led to the development before World War II of the famous Southern Electric system, which at one time claimed to be the world's most successful commuter network. It was also one of the few that ever made a profit.

Electric trains soon began running in the great European cities. Across the Atlantic, too,

ERNST VON SIEMENS' FIRST DEMONSTRATION *of the practical application of electric traction took place at the Berlin Trades Exhibition of 1879. Using a third conductor rail to supply current, the engine had a modest output of three horsepower.*

suburban and outer-suburban lines were converted at a rate that, by 1930, gave the United States the world's greatest mileage of electrified surface railways.

By that time the favorable economics of electric operation were at last leading to its use on densely trafficked trunk routes. The Pennsylvania Railroad electrified its New York-Philadelphia-Washington "eastern corridor" in 1935, using Raymond Loewy-styled GG1 electric locomotives.

But it was where coal, the standard fuel of steam engines, was not plentiful that the great mainline electrification projects first took shape. In 1914 in the United States the Milwaukee Road began stringing conductor wire over 650 miles (almost 1,050 km) of its line west from Butte, Montana, and by 1921 its trains were rolling through the canyons of the Bitter Root and Cascade Mountains behind electric locomotives.

Switzerland, with no coal but an abundance of hydro-electric power, became an electrification pioneer and leader in the technology. The entire Swiss Federal Railways' system, and most of the many private Swiss railways, have

long been electrically operated. The soaring cost of coal after World War I was a direct influence in the conversion of main routes in France and, especially, Italy, which by 1939 had Europe's greatest electrified mileage.

Only Britain held back. Except for the commuter network in the south of England and a short-lived coal hauler in the northeast, no significant electrification scheme was inaugurated until 1954, when steam was replaced on the heavily graded line between Sheffield and Manchester.

CONTINUED EXPANSION

Since the mid-1960s, when Japan's *Shinkansen* showed the way, railways have met competition for passenger business with clean, attractive, and super-fast electric trains from

city to city as well as within them. The almost universal use of high-voltage, industrial-frequency alternating current has effectively reduced the cost of electrification. While the "mobile power station" diesel locomotive is still first choice for heavy hauling over the vast distances of North America and Australia, where the volume of traffic justifies them, the overhead wires are reaching ever further.

At the start of the 21st century, electrification of the entire 5,777 miles (9,297 km) of Russia's Trans-Siberian Railway is almost complete. China and India are extending their electrified mileage every year. And, the European electrified network—despite the historic problems of voltage-change at national borders—continues to grow.

PRE-WAR RECORD BREAKERS

With ongoing improvements in engineering and locomotive design also came an obsession with speed and competition worldwide.

Although there were speed record claims around the turn of the 20th century (all disputed), it was not until the 1930s that accurate records were set, and then broken. By then detailed recording equipment had been developed—as opposed to the train-timers' stop-watches on which previous claims were based—and the railways were maintained and signaled to standards allowing ever-higher speeds. One of the records set in this period, the world speed record for steam, still stands today.

The first authenticated speed of 100 miles per hour (161 km/h) by steam traction was achieved in 1934, by the London & North Eastern Railway's Pacific locomotive

No. 4472, *Flying Scotsman*. This sparked four years of rivalry between Great Britain, Germany, and the United States, and which was only

SPECTATORS lined the King's Cross Station platform in 1934 to farewell the Flying Scotsman *and "Junior Scotsman."*

THE "RACES TO THE NORTH"

Rivalry in Britain between the companies running the East and West Coast Main Lines (London–Scotland routes) led to the "Races to the North" in 1895.

There had been a brief early skirmish in 1888 from London to Edinburgh, but the rival companies agreed on a truce and minimum timings. However, with the planned opening of the Forth Railway Bridge north of Edinburgh, affording the East Coast a shorter route to Dundee, the racing returned in 1895—and over the longer distance to Aberdeen. The races stirred huge public interest, with crowds flocking to the stations to see the flyers change engines in the middle of the night. The competition ended when the East Coast train completed the 520-mile (837 km) journey in 8 hours 40 minutes, averaging an unprecedented 63 miles per hour (101 km/h), and the West Coast then bettered this by 8 minutes, a figure not improved upon until electrification came in 1978.

halted by the declaration of World War II. In Germany a streamlined three-cylinder 4-6-4 engine No. 05.002 created a world speed record in May 1935 of 124.5 miles per hour (200 km/h) on level track near Berlin. It was a well-prepared and publicized demonstration with a four-coach load of Third Reich functionaries, in the lead-up to the 1936 Berlin Olympics.

In the same year in Britain the West and East Coast rivals, the London Midland & Scottish (LMS) and London & North Eastern Railways (LNER), were battling for supremacy. The LNER set a record of 113 miles per hour

CONTESTED CLAIMS

In the years before speedometers and sophisticated recording equipment were available, there were a number of record claims that were contested, either at the time or later. The New York Central & Hudson River Railroad claimed to have achieved the first "ton" (100 miles per hour, or 161 km/h). On May 10, 1893, the Alco 4-4-0 No. 999 was said to have hauled a lightweight *Empire State Express* at 112.5 miles per hour (181 km/h) over a mile at Batavia, New York. The claim was disputed, but its 6-foot-8-inch driving wheels and 24-inch piston travel gave it the potential for very high speeds.

Meanwhile in Britain 4-4-0 No. 3440 *City of Truro* of the Great Western Railway (above) was timed at 102.3 miles per hour (165 km/h) down Wellington Bank in Somerset in 1904. The train was a Plymouth–London mail train, run in hot competition with the London & South Western Railway. The timing was unofficial and by stopwatch, and so *City of Truro's* record has also been disputed, but detailed analysis appears to confirm it.

Most contentious of all is the American claim that the Pennsylvania Railroad's 4-4-2 No. 7002 in 1905 hauled the *Broadway Limited* at a top speed of 127 miles per hour (204 km/h).

A BICYCLE TEAM *raced against the* Empire State Express *in 1896 (left). The* British Mallard *(below) 40 years later set a steam record that has never been bettered.*

(182 km/h) in August 1936. The following year an LMS train bettered it at 114 miles per hour (184 km/h), but the train almost derailed as it approached Crewe Station.

In summer 1938 Gresley's streamlined LNER A4 class 4-6-2 No. 4468, *Mallard,* reached 126 miles per hour (203 km/h) going down Stoke Bank near Grantham, on July 3, 1938. This world record has never been beaten.

Although at the time it had no impact on passenger services, a series of trials on a 14-mile (23 km) military railway between Marienfelde and Zossen, near Berlin, Germany, was a marker for what could be achieved.

In October 1903 a pair of electrically powered standard-gauge coaches broke their own world record for electric traction of 101 miles per hour (163 km/h) set in 1901. They reached 128.5 miles per hour (207 km/h), then 130.5 miles per hour (210 km/h).

Thirty years later Germany was at the forefront again, this time with the diesel-electric traction record. In 1933 trials the *Flying Hamburger* set an unofficial record of 124 miles per hour (200 km/h). It was also the first train in the world to regularly run at 100 miles per hour (161 km/h). The following year the Burlington Railroad's *Zephyr,* on a trial run from Denver to Chicago, attained an average speed of 77.6 miles per hour (125 km/h), and a maximum speed of 112.5 miles per hour (181 km/h). Undeterred, the Germans came back in 1939 with the *Flying Silver Fish,* which hit 134 miles per hour (216 km/h). In this year the Reichsbahn monopolized the first 32 places in the European daily speed table of fastest start-to-stop schedules.

Meanwhile Burlington and its competitor railroads began to knock down previous U.S. records, reducing the Chicago-to-Minneapolis running time to a record six and a half hours.

THE HIGH-SPEED ERA

To compete with air travel and super-highways, the railways

have continued to develop train technology to produce ever-higher speeds.

Post-war regeneration in Europe established the foundation for high-speed trains—though progress was initially slow. Ravaged by war, the railways took 15 years to appreciate that a new form of high-speed travel was the way forward.

There were some exceptions, however. In France the Paris–Lyon electrification began in 1946, and within seven years French Railways offered start-to-stop timings in the range of 70–75 miles per hour (113–121 km/h). By 1959 the *Mistral,* a first-class-only service from Paris to the Riviera, averaged more than 80 miles per hour (129 km/h) and covered the 195 miles (314 km) to Dijon in 2½ hours. For many years the *Mistral* was the world's fastest train.

ACHIEVING HIGH SPEED

The *Trans-Europ-Express* (*TEE*), launched in 1957, was the brainchild of the Dutch. Aiming to woo the business traveler away from airlines, it linked six countries with a unified network. But, with slow journey times, the peak of 100 services dwindled to nothing by 1987.

The Japanese showed the world what should be done, with a brand new straight-line railway, and trains and signaling designed for high speed. The Tokyo–Osaka Tokaido Line, opened in 1964, was standard gauge rather than the Japanese 3-foot-6-inch gauge.

SAFETY AT SPEED

High-speed trains running on dedicated tracks have a remarkable safety record. In Japan the *Shinkansen* (above) entered the 21st century having run since 1964 without a single passenger fatality, except those caused by passengers' own behavior.

"Bullet Trains" were the only trains on the line, eliminating congestion. The trains averaged 101 miles per hour (163 km/h) and could reach 131 miles per hour (210 km/h). New lines are still being opened and the latest trains have a normal top speed of 186 miles per hour (300 km/h).

The first dedicated high-speed line in France opened between Paris and Lyon in

TILT TRAINS *tilt as they go around curves. This compensates for the angle of the track and allows the trains to go faster.*

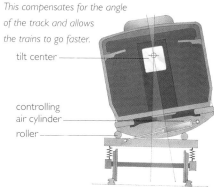

tilt center

controlling air cylinder

roller

1981. It was followed by a route to the Atlantic in 1989, and by the Channel Tunnel line in 1993. Speed records were soon being broken and in 1990 a French *TGV* (*Train à Grande Vitesse*) set a new record of 319 miles per hour (514 km/h). Regular *TGV* and *Thalys* trains (the inter-European *TGVs*) run at up to 186 miles per hour (300 km/h) in normal service. *Eurostar* trains between London, Paris, and Brussels using the Channel Tunnel are based on the *TGV.* Services started in 1993, also with a top speed of 186 miles per hour.

In Britain, the 1974 diesel-electric-powered *High Speed Train* (*HST*) had a top scheduled speed

BUILT FOR SPEED,
the TGV revolutionized long-distance travel.

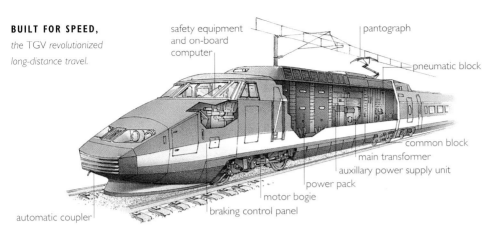

safety equipment and on-board computer

pantograph

pneumatic block

common block

main transformer

auxillary power supply unit

power pack

motor bogie

braking control panel

automatic coupler

as high as 125 miles per hour (201 km/h), and services were gradually extended to all non-electrified intercity routes. An *HST* achieved the world speed record for diesel traction in 1987, reaching 148 miles per hour (238 km/h).

NEW TECHNOLOGY
A British experiment, the Advanced Passenger Train (APT), differed from the *TGV* in being a tilt train, which allowed it to go round curves at higher speeds than conventional trains. The gas-turbine prototype (APT-E) achieved 152 miles per hour (245 km/h) on August 10, 1975. Preproduction APT-P 25kV electric trains for the West Coast Main Line from London to Scotland were dogged by technical problems, and the project was abandoned in 1983.

The *Pendolino,* developed by Fiat in Italy, is similar to the APT. After trials on the Rome–Ancona route, Italian Railways ordered 15 ETR-450 (*Elettrotreno Rapido*) trains, delivered from 1987 to 1991. These typically run on *Cisalpino* services from Italy into Switzerland and Germany. The ETR-460, which can be diesel or electric, will run in Britain from 2002.

Germany has rebuilt existing lines, with new routes only

being added where extra capacity is needed. The first *InterCityExpress* (*ICE*) route opened in 1991 between Hamburg, Frankfurt, and Munich. ICE-1 trains are scheduled to run at 155 miles per hour (250 km/h), and are allowed to reach 174 miles per hour (280 km/h) to make up lost time. During tests in 1988 an *ICE* set a then world speed record of 252 miles per hour (406 km/h). The third-generation ICE-3 trains are scheduled at up to 205 miles per hour (330 km/h).

In the United States, long-distance passenger services were making heavy losses by the end of the 1960s, so high-speed electric multiple units (*Metroliners*) for the North–East corridor (Boston–New York–Washington) seemed like a ray of hope. But the trains reached little more than half their potential 150 miles per hour (242 km/h) due to mechanical problems and track conditions. In recent

years state-owned national passenger company Amtrak has invested in high-speed services. Six-coach 150-mile-per-hour (242 km/h) *Acela* trains, based on the *TGV* but using tilt technology, are now in service, cutting 40 minutes off the usual 4 hours from New York to Boston.

The key to very high speed travel could lie with new technology. Linear induction motors that allow a train to "float" above a track have been in use on airport shuttles since the early 1980s. Transrapid, a German consortium, carried thousands of passengers on a magnetic levitation (maglev) test line and in 2000 secured a contract to build a 22-mile (35 km) maglev line in China, serving Shanghai's new international airport. In Japan, trains on the Yamanashi maglev test line achieved 345 miles per hour (555 km/h).

GERMANY'S TRANSRAPID *maglev train proved its worth in the 1990s.*

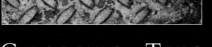

CHAPTER TWO

SERVING *the* CITIES

When a train pulls into a great city, I am reminded
of the closing moments of an overture.

Travels With My Aunt,
GRAHAM GREENE (1904–1991), British novelist

THE LONDON TUBE

The first city to build railways under the ground, London solved many of its traffic problems and also set a precedent for the world.

London's Underground railway, also known as the "tube," is one of the world's largest, with a total of 94 miles (151 km) of deep tunnel and 167 miles (269 km) of subsurface and open-air railway. From 1811 to 1871 London's population trebled from 1.3 million to 3.8 million, making the city the world's largest. Traffic congestion was serious and was not helped by a ban on mainline rail in the city center.

The answer was to build underground, and the first part of the Metropolitan Railway (Paddington–Farringdon) opened in 1863. This was built by the "cut-and-cover" method, in which a large trench was dug—effectively a brick-sided cutting—and then roofed over, a process that caused massive disruption.

The railway used full-size rolling stock and steam locomotives, resulting in problems with ventilation and smoke emission. Even so, within

THE CUT-AND-COVER METHOD *was used to construct the section of line to the Thames Embankment, as depicted in the* Illustrated London News *in 1869.*

a year 12 million passengers journeyed over the 3½ miles (6 km). The line was extended to link the Great Western Railway Paddington terminus with the city center, and also served Euston and King's Cross. What is now the Circle Line was completed in 1884.

The Thames was crossed in 1890 using a deep-level tube. Three inventions made this possible: the Greathead shield to bore through the soft London clay soil; electric trains; and lifts (elevators) to reach platforms 75 feet (23 m) below ground. Escalators were later built. The world's first deep tube, in 1890, was the 3¼-mile 5 km) City & South London Railway

from King William Street (in the city center) to Stockwell. It carried 15,000 passengers per day and was followed by the Waterloo & City in 1898.

Meanwhile, the Metropolitan District Railway and Metropolitan Railway were gradually expanding their subsurface networks to rural locations. They chose these sites for house-building. With easy, cheap access to the center of London from the early 1900s, suburbs quickly grew around the lines. Londoners keen to escape the crowded city snapped up the affordable new dwellings in what was known as "Metroland."

In the 40 years up to World War I, London's population had almost doubled. Underground development was rapid and most of the network in central London was open by the start of the war.

WATERLOO STATION *on the Waterloo & City Line, the second deep-level tube, was completed in 1898.*

THE COMPLEXITY *of Piccadilly Circus station, one of the tube's deepest, is seen in this 1986 cross-section.*

The world's longest rail tunnel, at 17 miles (27.4 km), was created when the Northern Line from East Finchley to Morden via Bank opened in 1939. This record stood until the 1988 opening of the 33-mile (53 km) Seikan Tunnel in Japan.

Following a long period of stagnation, the Victoria Line opened (1968–72), the Piccadilly Line was extended to Heathrow Airport (1977), and the Jubilee Line opened (1979). The Jubilee's eventual extension in 1999 to East London was the first "tube" line to reach the area.

WHAT'S IN A NAME?

The name "tube" came into common usage after the 1900 opening of the Central London Railway (now part of the Central Line). The flat fare of twopence per journey gave rise to the nickname of the "Twopenny Tube." The network began to be called the Underground in 1903, when the Metropolitan District Electric Traction Company was absorbed by the financier C. T. Yerkes' Underground Electric Railways. In 1908 four tube and surface railways agreed to adopt the word Underground for exterior station signs and maps. The London Passenger Transport Board took over the entire system following a 1933 Act of Parliament. In 1948 it came under the control of the London Transport Executive.

Since then, the London Underground has become synonymous with the city it serves, an essential lifeline for commuters as well as a tourist attraction. It is in the morning and evening peak hours that the system comes into its own, with trains every one to two minutes on the busiest lines and each train moving up to 1,650 people. Banks of station escalators carry people at speeds of 162 feet (50 m) per minute, with a vertical rise of 87 feet (27 m) on some. Every day more than 600,000 commuters use the Underground. During peak times each of the network's 273 stations runs at capacity. The busiest are closed for a few minutes at a time, if necessary, to prevent more passengers surging onto the already over-crowded platforms.

Yet it is this frenetic, at times hot atmosphere, with the silence of the hoards of office workers punctuated by the sound of an occasional lone busker, that gives the Underground its unique, almost likeable, atmosphere.

DEAD-END TO DISASTER

The London Underground's impressive safety record was seriously tarnished on February 28, 1975, when a tube train failed to slow down as it approached the Moorgate terminus and smashed into a dead-end tunnel wall. The first two coaches were compressed to half their normal length. With 43 people killed, including the driver, and a further 74 injured, it was Britain's worst rail accident since 1952. The Moorgate inquiry was unable to discover why the driver hadn't stopped. When his body was finally recovered five days after the crash, he was found to have been sitting normally at the controls.

To prevent similar accidents, train stop arms, which operate a lever on the bogie to apply emergency brakes, were fitted on approaches to dead-end tunnels. These are known as "Moorgate controls."

ELEVATED RAIL

Railways built above city streets offered a solution to traffic congestion and polluted steam-operated subways.

Problems with traffic congestion in America's largest city are not a recent issue. As early as 1830 New York had begun to develop a vast network of horse-drawn bus and street railway lines to solve the problem, but the city's unrelenting growth soon overwhelmed the capacity of this surface transit system.

The long, narrow shape of Manhattan Island aggravated the problem, and the city's limited north–south streets were jammed with drays, cabs, buses, and horse-drawn streetcars. By 1860, when New York's population had passed 800,000, annual traffic on the bus and street railway lines exceeded 36 million passengers, doubling over the next five years.

There was no room on congested Manhattan to build more streets, and visionaries began looking for ways to free the city's enormous volume of traffic from the confines of the clogged streets.

Underground railways powered by steam or air pressure were proposed, but subways were not a practical solution until the development of electric power a few decades later. Others looked up and proposed railways that would operate on iron and steel structures built above the city streets.

EARLY EXPERIMENTS

As early as 1868 inventor Charles T. Harvey made a trial run on an experimental cable-powered elevated railway. The trial was only a half mile (0.8 km) long, but Harvey soon began extending the line toward its intended terminal at Yonkers. Cable operation proved impractical, however, and the line began to power its trains with steam locomotives. A rival system was proposed in 1872 when Dr. Rufus H. Gilbert obtained a charter for a patent elevated system made up of tubular iron roadways suspended above the street from Gothic arches. Cars would be propelled through the tubes by air pressure. Nothing ever came of this imaginative scheme, but the company later built the steam-powered Sixth Avenue "El," as the line became known. Other lines quickly sprang up, and by 1880 more than 60 million passengers a year were riding the New York elevated railway, which extended all the way from South Ferry, at the tip of Manhattan, to Harlem.

Brooklyn soon followed Manhattan's lead, and the borough's first elevated line began running in 1885. Kansas City completed a short elevated system in 1886, which was later incorporated into the city's streetcar system. Chicago got its first elevated line in 1891, soon developing an extensive system of lines linked to the central elevated "Loop" that became the distinguishing characteristic and symbol of downtown Chicago. Boston joined the ranks in 1901 and Philadelphia in 1907.

Most of these early lines operated with diminutive steam locomotives, which proved far from ideal. The trains were noisy and rained a steady stream of smoke and

CHICAGO'S *"Loop" is the central link in an extensive elevated rail system, which is currently being upgraded.*

MONORAIL THEN AND NOW

Long a favored topic in such journals as *Popular Science* and *Popular Mechanics*, the idea of elevated monorail rapid transit systems has been around for well over a century. A variety of imaginative monorail schemes was put forward in the late 19th century, such as the Meigs system (opposite), most involving vehicles suspended from a single rail on an elevated structure.

Not as practical as it first seemed, largely because of the difficulties in switching cars between tracks, the monorail never achieved wide acceptance. The only commercially successful example was opened in 1901 at Wuppertal, Germany, operating above a canal (above right).

In more recent years short monorail installations have appeared at a few airports and fairgrounds. In 1998 a monorail system began carrying passengers in downtown Jacksonville, Florida. Other lines soon followed, including the link between the Newark, New Jersey, airport termini and planned extensions to railroad stations, and the system linking the resorts of Las Vegas, Nevada. In Sydney, Australia, a monorail circuit (right) now links the city's central shopping area with parking lots and the Darling Harbor entertainment complex.

cinders on businesses and residents. Hot coals and sparks often dropped onto the streets below. By the mid-1890s electric power had become a feasible alternative, and within a few years all of the lines had been electrified.

The elevated railway was a largely American institution. Europe almost always favored subway or surface rapid-transit lines. Britain's only elevated railway began running at Liverpool in 1892, and Germany developed its elevated systems early in the 20th century, in both Berlin and Hamburg. But then, even in America, elevated systems began to be dismantled in favor of subways. Manhattan's elevated system of close to 300 track miles (483 km), the largest anywhere, was eventually replaced by the New York subway. In Boston the elevated line has also been replaced by subway and surface rapid-transit line. The world's largest surviving elevated system, in Chicago, is, however, being extensively refurbished. Similar work should assure the future of Philadelphia's elevated system. Opened in 1922, it was the last of America's typical steel structures to be built.

Elevated trains have now re-emerged in a new form, as fast-growing cities around the world build rapid-transit metro systems, often on aboveground, prestressed concrete structures that enable quieter operation than their iron and steel predecessors.

NEW YORK'S *elevated line freed up the roads below, but the steam engines that originally plied it, such as this one pictured in 1893, caused noise and pollution problems.*

THE WORLD
TUNNELS
UNDERGROUND

*Cities around the world utilized new technology
and improved safety methods to build
extensive underground railway systems.*

The arrival of reliable electric traction meant that the years from 1890 until the outbreak of World War I in 1914 saw a boom in the construction of underground railways.

City engineers realized that the limitations of cable and steam traction could now be overcome. At the same time, there was a huge growth in the demand for city transport as commerce developed and populations grew.

The last cable-operated city underground rail opened in Glasgow in 1896. In the same year the World Exhibition in Budapest was the catalyst for the first underground electric railway in Europe, a 2-mile (3 km) line built in a shallow subway, with single cars that collected current at 350v DC from an overhead contact wire. This line is still in use today, but the original trains were replaced by new 600v DC articulated cars in 1973.

Also in 1896 the decision was made to build the first underground railway in Paris.

CONSTRUCTION *of the central caisson of the Paris Métro station at Place Saint-Michel was under way in 1907 (right). Manual switching systems were used at the East River Tunnel entrance on the New York subway in 1909 (above).*

The line opened to traffic in 1900, using third-rail current collection. Called the Chemin de Fer Métropolitain, it was soon colloquially known as the Métro, a term that has become generic for an urban heavy rapid-transit system, though "underground" and "subway" are still used in various places.

BUILDING THE LINES

The Budapest and Paris lines were built by the cut-and-cover tunneling method. This entailed digging a trench in the street and roofing it over once the side walls were in place, a technique that caused considerable disruption. It also

required the system to follow the surface street pattern for most of its length. Boring tunnels was an alternative, with the development of the hydraulic shield, but this could only be used where soil conditions were suitable.

Other great European cities adopted underground rapid transit at this time, including Vienna (1898), Berlin (1902), Athens (1904), and Hamburg (1912). In fact these systems all used a combination of underground and elevated or surface construction. The Athens line was actually more like an interurban railway, which linked the city with its port of Piraeus.

UNDERGROUND *tunnels doubled as bomb shelters in London during the Blitz of World War II.*

metro in its capital city of Moscow. Josef Stalin opened it in 1935. Stations on the first line, and later extensions, featured elaborate internal decoration, including heroic statuary and massive chandeliers. The stations are still included in most tourist itineraries. Metro construction continued in Moscow during World War II, if only because the deep-bored rail tunnels provided shelter from air raids, as London's tunnels did during the Blitz.

Meanwhile in the United States the first trolley car subway had been opened in Boston in 1898, but it was converted for use by subway trains from 1901 to 1908. A separate rapid-transit subway was then built, and the original line reverted to use by trolleys.

Underground rail came to Asia with the opening of the first lines in Tokyo in 1927 and Osaka in 1933.

By the 1930s the Soviet Union had also developed the engineering expertise and economic strength to start the construction of a showpiece

INNOVATIONS

In New York the proliferation of elevated lines was tempered by the opening of the first subway in 1904. Four-track sections were built to allow the simultaneous use of local and express trains, a feature still found today.

The Hudson–Manhattan tube line was built in 1908–1909, providing an alternative to a ferry across the Hudson River for passengers from New Jersey (including the many arriving on commuter trains at Hoboken terminal). The first system to be built outside Europe or North America was at Buenos Aires, Argentina, in 1913, using British capital and Belgian-built rolling stock.

After World War I metro construction resumed and the first part of a new system for Madrid (very much modeled on Paris) opened in 1919. Barcelona followed in 1924.

CONTROL SYSTEMS: THE KEY TO ELECTRIC TRAIN OPERATION

The original metro trains were usually single, heavy, slow-moving motor cars, or sometimes two coupled, and various permutations of trailers.

Increasing passenger numbers strained the rather primitive motors and brought the danger of fire, as occurred in a 1903 Paris disaster in which 84 people were killed (right).

This showed the need for multiple-unit control equipment, which would enable the motorman's controller to supply the power in an even and coordinated way throughout the train, which allowed longer trains.

American and European manufacturers, such as Sprague, Siemens-Schuckert, Thomson-Houston, and Westinghouse, developed wire control systems that permitted this, and included features such as automatic acceleration.

In parallel came the development of automatic signaling and train identification systems. These innovations allowed metro trains to run at higher speeds and at very close headways, only a minute or two apart on some lines, even where stops were frequent.

Le Petit Journal

TERRIBLE CATASTROPHE DU MÉTROPOLITAIN
Découverte des premiers cadavres

METRO SYSTEMS
for the FUTURE

Metro systems have constantly improved their technology for efficiency and safety, but the ultimate aim is the driverless train.

The building of city metros skyrocketed over the last quarter of a century. More than 100 systems are now in operation, with new ones or extensions opening each year. Cities throughout the world are desperate to find alternatives to congested street traffic, and to find novel methods of paying for them. Every major population center, even in developing countries, seems to hanker for the prestige and practicality of a metro system.

North America and Europe were once at the forefront of metro development. Plans formulated before or during World War II were brought to fruition and new systems opened in the 1950s in such

NEWEST METROS *have platform-edge screens that open when the train stops.*

diverse locations as St. Petersburg (then Leningrad), Toronto, Nagoya, and Lisbon. They all adopted the conventional approach of steel wheel on steel rail and third-rail current collection.

SPEEDING UP
In the early 1950s trials with rubber-tired trains began in Paris. The aim was to transport more people without resorting to longer trains, and the expensive construction of longer platforms. Trains with rubber tires were found to accelerate faster than those with steel wheels, allowing

more trains on the lines. Track was re-equipped with horizontal running strips, flanked by vertical guide bars. The bogies included vertical rubber-tired wheels for traction, while horizontal wheels provided guidance, and steel wheels were kept for emergency use and switching.

Public service on a shuttle line started in 1952 and the system proved successful. Conversion of four complete Métro lines to this "pneu" operation took place from 1956 to 1974, and the French railway industry persuaded other countries to buy their systems. Montreal converted to the rubber-tired system in 1966, as did the other French metro cities of Lyon and Marseille. In 1969 Mexico

THE CONTROL ROOM *at the rail station of the vast Frankfurt International Airport complex.*

City converted, as did Santiago de Chile in 1971. The cost of converting existing lines to pneu was high, however, and technological advances in train control and motor equipment have since enabled the same performance with steel-wheel trains, which have reappeared on new Paris Métro lines.

THE DRIVERLESS TRAIN

The first trials with rubber-tired trains also experimented with automatic train control (ATC). The ultimate goal was a driverless metro, operating at higher frequencies than conventional block signaling allowed. Trials were successful on the shuttle, but technology and lack of finance blocked conversion of a major line until 1967. Paris uses the "wiggly wire" system, with acceleration and braking codes picked up from a cable laid between the tracks. The London Underground started experiments with a different sort of ATC in the late 1960s, equipping the new Victoria Line with this system as it opened in 1968–1971. Safety codes are transmitted through the running rails. In 1962 New York introduced ATC in the Times Square–Grand Central shuttle, also using a track code system.

Some metro operators have met with a degree of public disquiet at the concept of the driverless train and have retained a human operator on the train (whose main tasks are to operate the doors, and press the start button).

Despite this resistance, reliable ATC is now in everyday use on many systems, some taking the plunge to eliminate the driving cab but retaining staff on the trains to provide information, security, and ticket control. These systems include some airport shuttles, the French VAL system in Lille and Lyon), Osaka's Intermediate Capacity Transport System, the Vancouver Skytrain, and the Docklands Light Railway in London.

Other visible innovations include platform-edge screens, with automatic doors that match those on the train. An obvious safety feature, the screens also serve to balance air pressure and have been adopted by the latest metro lines in London, Paris, and Singapore.

CUTTING COSTS

New technology, such as automation and small-profile and lightweight equipment, can make it cheaper to build and operate a metro system, without the high volume of traffic required to cover costs on conventional systems.

The best known are the French VAL system and the Bombardier Skytrain system (introduced in Vancouver). VAL is rubber-tired and automated, with no auxiliary steel wheels, and a central slot for guidance at switches. Skytrain has steel wheels and rails but is automated and uses linear induction motors to provide drive without pick-up shoes or moving rotors. Both are proprietary systems that have been sold to other metros in Asia and North America.

In general, however, most new metro systems are built using relatively conventional semi-automated technology and steel wheels.

Examples of the latest systems include Bangkok, Hong Kong, and Singapore in Asia; Atlanta, Los Angeles, and Miami in the United States; and Bilbao, Brussels, and Prague in Europe.

THE BILBAO *metro in northern Spain (left) and Vancouver's Skytrain (below) use the latest technology in metro systems.*

TROLLEYS *and* TRAMS

Pioneering horse-drawn streetcars led to electrified systems that have served the world's cities for more than a century.

Streetcar lines ("tramways" outside North America) have their origins in the plateways used in mines and quarries for horse-drawn wagons. The first passenger line in city streets, which also used horse-drawn cars, was the New York & Harlem of 1832. Remarkably, the world's second horsecar line, in New Orleans (1835), is still used for electric cars.

American promoters took the idea to Europe. Horse tramways opened in Paris in 1853 and Birkenhead, Britain, in 1860, followed by London in 1861 and Copenhagen in 1863. The citizens of Sydney, Australia, also welcomed their first horse tramway in 1861. "The motion of the car is extremely easy and comfortable," wrote a local newspaper.

The 1870s were a boom time for the construction of horsecar lines, but the limitations of animal power were obvious, and promoters soon investigated mechanical traction. Steam trams were developed, but they were not very suitable for urban use, although they ran on many suburban and rural light railways and survived in many locations to the 1930s. Compressed air, gas, and petrol engines were tried, and cable lines enjoyed some success.

THE FIRST ELECTRICS

Most of these technically suspect or expensive options faded quickly once electric traction became a possibility. Siemens & Halske opened the first electric railway to provide public service in Berlin in 1881, using current at 180 volts fed through the running rails. Electrified running rails were unsafe in the street, however, so overhead wire was substituted. Underground cables were sometimes used for aesthetic reasons, surviving until tramways ended operation in London in 1952, and until 1962 in Washington, D.C.

The first city streetcar network to use overhead wires with trolley pole collection was installed by American Frank Sprague in Richmond, Virginia, in 1887. By 1900, most American horsecar lines were converted to electric traction, with European cities close behind. Electric tramways also appeared in Japan, Thailand, and various cities in Australia and New Zealand.

Tramways in Britain, or with a British heritage, usually used double-decker trams to

PASSENGERS ON THE UPPER DECK *of North London's steam tram in the 1880s endured the weather (below), but horse tramways also had their problems (above).*

VOLKS MARINE ELECTRIC RAILWAY

A tramway of great historical importance still runs today along the seafront of Brighton, the famous resort on the south coast of England. Pictured above in 1978, this was the first public tramway to be built specifically for electric traction, using a low-voltage current collected from an energized third rail. Early British electrical engineer Magnus Volk built the line in 1883.

DOUBLE-DECKER *electric trams are an ideal way for Hong Kong to deal with its heavily congested streets.*

maximize capacity; the classic double-deckers in Hong Kong are among the last survivors. In continental Europe a single-deck tram towing one or more trailers was more common, while America had larger cars mounted on two bogies.

TRAMS FOR THE MASSES
The 25 years after 1900 were a golden age, and almost every city of consequence around the world operated trolley lines, most under municipal control. The cars provided cheap, reliable transport for the masses, boosting economies and suburban growth.

However, by the 1920s, many streetcar company managers were worried men. The original investment was wearing out: Profits from the good years had gone else-where, with insufficient money put aside for renewals. Automobile manufacturers had begun mass production and reliable motorbuses became available, so it was cheaper to introduce buses that led into the city centers than extend the tracks.

The depression that started in America in 1929 soon affected European economies, and small town streetcar

systems and most interurbans collapsed. The electric "trolleybus" was a stopgap measure to avoid dispensing with the street poles and wires, but tramway managers did not give in without a fight. In North America the President's Conference Com-mittee (PCC) of streetcar operators commissioned research and production of a new bogie car design that would offer the same levels of comfort and performance as the automobile. The outcome, the handsome PCC car, staved off many system closures. Some still operate today, notably in San Francisco, icons for those who admire heritage streetcars.

CLOSURES WORLDWIDE
World War II hastened the decline of tram-ways in Britain and France but did provide an opportunity for reinvestment in Eastern Europe, the Benelux countries,

RESTORED VINTAGE *streetcars, such as this one from Portugal, add color to modern cities.*

and Germany. In Britain, a few city tramways bought new vehicles and built reserved-track extensions, but it was too late. The country's last major system, Glasgow, closed in 1962, leaving just Blackpool's tourist-oriented seafront line.

The 1960s were bad years for public transport in many countries, with the belief that the automobile would suffice for most people (and buses for those who could not afford them), and that cities could be adapted to cope with extra road traffic. Many cities dis-mantled their streetcar systems. Today, as cities face the reality of downtown traffic tangles, there is an exciting streetcar revival in the form of light rail.

LIGHT RAIL

After the decline of trolley lines and tramways during the 1960s,

new approaches and technology saw the rebirth of the lines as light rail.

By the end of the 1960s the more far-sighted planners had begun to realize the disadvantages of the massive swing toward road transport and the subsequent marginalization of public transport. Traffic congestion in major cities was reaching chaotic proportions, peak times were spreading, and the creation of new super highways was destroying the landscape.

Many North American cities saw a rapid decline in their city centers as new suburban malls sprang up to serve populations that had migrated from high- to low-density housing areas that were dependent on the car.

LIGHT RAIL BEGINS

As concerns about environmental pollution surfaced, politicians and planners began to look at flourishing cities in Europe for a solution to their problems. It was there they realized the importance of reserved-track tramways. West Germany was by now the world center of tramway development, particularly in the progress to larger articulated trams operated by one person. At the same time, modernized fleets encouraged more people to use the tramway. Both factors improved the staff-to-passenger ratio, demonstrating the tramways' superior economics to the bus.

LIGHT RAIL *at the Los Angeles Getty Center transports visitors from the ticketing gate into the museum itself.*

What we now call light rail typically carries passengers in stylish, articulated electric cars running between city centers and suburbs—or between cities—on mainly segregated alignments, with "stations" rather than street-corner stops. The structures are simpler than stations on "heavy" railways, so the lines cost less to build. Services can be fast and frequent, and they are easily adapted for peak hours and special events.

The concept recalls the long-gone "interurban" electric railways of the United States. In its present form light rail owes much to innovators in Europe and especially in Gothenburg, Sweden, where, over a 15-year period, an ordinary city streetcar system was extended through new and established suburbs on high-speed reserved track. High-performance cars replaced the old rolling stock, and automobiles were restricted in the central city area.

A new public transport standard was achieved without the expense of digging subways—the attractive new cars stayed on the surface, visible and accessible. Dozens of cities worldwide are now following this lead. The distinction between light and "heavy" rail is becoming blurred as conventional railways and street lines are linked so that "trolleys" can run on existing railway lines.

The Canadian city of Edmonton adapted European

SYDNEY LIGHT RAIL *provides easy inner-city travel in Australia's busiest city.*

KUALA LUMPUR'S *central station is to become Malaysia's transportation hub, linking light rail with other rail services.*

London. Then Manchester converted local rail lines to light rail and joined them with street tramways through the city center to create an integrated system. Trams also run through the city center streets of Sheffield. Other British tramways include Birmingham's West Midlands system and Nottingham.

technology with a new light-rail line in 1978, with trams from Siemens-Duewag in Germany. This proved an immediate success, and San Diego followed suit three years later. Rather than dig expensive subways, city centers utilized pedestrian and transit precincts.

Systems in Cleveland, Pittsburgh, Philadelphia, and Toronto, which survived from the earlier streetcar era, all acquired new rolling stock and are extending again. Los Angeles was a city that threw away its trams and interurbans in the 1960s, determined that it could live with the auto-

mobile. The pall of pollution proves otherwise, and two new light-rail lines and an underground metro line have opened, with a third light-rail line under construction.

San Francisco opened its $80 million line to Fisherman's Wharf in 2000 (and includes 1930s-style cars in its fleet), and equally ambitious extensions are being built in Salt Lake City, Utah. South of the border, there is new light rail in Guadalajara, Monterrey, and Mexico City.

Light rail spread to England in 1980, at first as segregated systems at Newcastle-on-Tyne and in the docklands in

AUSTRALIAN SYSTEMS

The Australian tram went into rapid decline in the 1950s and 1960s, with Adelaide, then Brisbane, and Sydney giving up trams for largely industrio-political reasons.

However, Melbourne's 137-mile (220 km) system, the largest in the southern hemisphere, survived intact, thanks to good management and political support. The first new trams in 20 years arrived in 1975. Several new extensions have since been built, and two suburban railway lines have been converted to light rail.

In 1997 trams also returned to Sydney, with light rail extending from the city center to the inner-city suburbs.

A SPECTACULAR BOWSTRING BRIDGE *carries Sheffield Supertrams over city center streets before the tram conveys passengers to the English countryside.*

CHAPTER THREE

TRAIN TECHNOLOGY

We do not ride on the railroad; it rides upon us.

Where I Lived and What I Lived For,
HENRY DAVID THOREAU (1817–1862), American author and philosopher

How Steam Works

The steam engine radically changed the way people lived, and engineers constantly improved its design.

When water boils it generates steam. When confined in a space and put under pressure, its power can be harnessed. It is the power of steam that lifts a saucepan lid when water is boiling and the principle is the same in steam locomotives —the difference is that it is used in a more complex way.

It was not until the 17th century that serious consideration was given to steam power's potential for practical work. Frenchman Denis Papin designed the first boiler with a safety valve in 1679. Boilers were being made and used in England by the turn of the 18th century.

Once steam began to be used to power locomotives, engineers George and Robert Stephenson introduced several new ideas: a firetube boiler mounted horizontally; cylinders exhausting through the chimney, thus creating a draft on the fire; and inclined cylinders driving directly onto the wheels. These basic principles never changed.

The boiler is at the heart of a steam locomotive. At one end is the firebox, containing the fire and surrounded by water. Steel or copper tubes run through the boiler and, as hot gases from the fire pass through the tubes, they heat the surrounding water. The steam collects above the water level in a dome, with a safety valve releasing it when the pressure becomes too great.

To start the locomotive, the engineer (driver) opens the throttle (regulator) handle in the cab, which is connected to a valve in the boiler. Steam passes into the cylinders, where it is directed by valves into one end. The steam, which is still under pressure, expands and forces a piston inside the cylinder backward and forward as the steam is admitted to first one end and then the other. The pistons inside the cylinders (of which there are at least two, and sometimes three or four) are connected to the driving wheels by rods.

NEWCOMEN'S *1752 pumping engine (above) was one of the first to use steam power. Simplicity was the keynote of Victorian locomotive controls (above left).*

Having served its purpose, the steam is ejected into the smokebox—a visible puff escapes through the blast-pipe and chimney with a "chuff." As it does so, it draws smoke and gases from the firebox, creating a draught to help the fire keep burning fiercely.

Engineers realized that the exhausted steam could do

MALLARD *achieved the world speed record for steam, at 126 miles per hour (203 km/h) in 1938.*

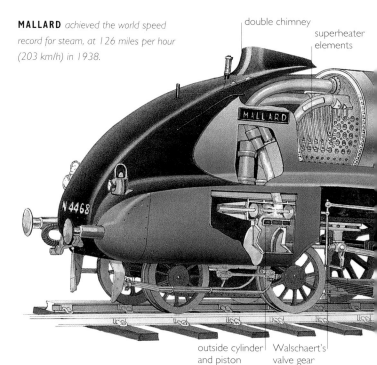

double chimney

superheater elements

outside cylinder and piston

Walschaert's valve gear

THE UNION PACIFIC BIG BOY

The Big Boy was the ultimate articulated steam locomotive. It was easily capable of 60 miles per hour (97 km/h), yet weighed a colossal 552 tons (558 t). One Big Boy is even credited with a speed of 88 miles per hour (142 km/h), hauling a troop train in World War II. The American Locomotive Company (Alco) built 25 of these monsters in three years. Intended for heavy freight trains, the first entered service in 1941.

With a 4-8-8-4 wheel arrangement plus a 14-wheel tender carrying 28 tons (29 t) of coal and 24,000 U.S. gallons (90,840 l) of water, Big Boys were the last triumphant gasp of American steam locomotive design before diesels took over. These 132-foot-long (40 m) leviathans developed 7,000 horsepower and hauled 100-wagon, 8,000-ton (8,080 t) trains over the formidable Sherman Summit in Wyoming. At times the trains were so heavy that two Big Boys were needed to maintain speed up the hill.

more work and developed locomotives with a second set of cylinders through which the exhausted steam was sent. This process, which is known as "compound" working, was introduced in the late 1800s.

Frenchman Anatole Mallet patented a compound articulated locomotive in 1884, in which the boiler and frame sat on two bogies. A fixed rear engine unit with high-pressure cylinders was attached to a swivelling front unit, which carried low-pressure cylinders. Both compound and "simple" locomotives constructed to this principle were extremely powerful.

Another approach to the articulated engine, which allowed the weight to be spread over more wheels than a conventional fixed-frame design, was developed in England by Herbert Garratt. The Manchester firm Beyer Peacock built hundreds of Beyer-Garratt locomotives until 1967, notably for southern Africa and Australia. Garratt's design featured an engine unit at either end, which was fed by a boiler sitting on a frame connecting the two units. Water tanks sat at the chimney end and a coal bunker at the other end.

boiler

water space

firebox

coal

water

4468

driving wheels

water pick-up gear

HOW DIESEL TRAINS WORK

The diesel locomotive is essentially a simple machine, but its development revolutionized the railways.

Diesel locomotives are everything steam locomotives are not. They are clean, rely less on the skill of the crew, and need servicing less often than steam. The crew also has a better working environment, with a better view of the route ahead. Despite higher initial costs, due to their complex manufacture, it is generally accepted that diesel engines are more efficient than steam.

Diesel locomotives are in essence simple machines, consisting of a diesel engine and a transmission system that connects the engine to the wheels. Transmission falls into three types: electric,

mechanical, and hydraulic. However, this simple explanation hides the complex control systems. Initially mechanical, these systems are increasingly electronic.

THE ENGINE

The diesel train engine itself is very similar to those found in road trucks—although they are much larger. Inside the engine, pistons move up and down in cylinders. They are connected to a crankshaft, which converts the reciprocating motion of the pistons into circular motion. Diesel, also called fuel oil, is burned in the cylinders. When the

piston is at the bottom of the cylinder, air is drawn in and diesel fuel is injected into the cylinder. As the piston moves up the cylinder, it compresses and heats the fuel and air mixture until the diesel burns.

This then forces the piston back down the cylinder and turns the crankshaft. A valve opens to release the burned gases from the cylinder, which rises to push the gases out. The cylinder then falls again to repeat the process. This is known as the four-stroke cycle.

A TWO-CAR *Class 156 super sprinter diesel multiple unit departs Manchester Piccadilly Station (below). The 156 typically has a 285-horse-power engine beneath each car, with hydraulic transmission. The Egyptian DE 2550 (right) and the Greek DE 2000 (above) are both diesel-electrics.*

BRITAIN'S CLASS 47 *diesel-electrics were introduced in 1962. This one at Liverpool Lime Street still sports the old InterCity colors but is now operated by Virgin Trains.*

Improvements to the basic diesel engine over its 100-year life include the fitting of turbochargers and intercoolers. A turbocharger uses the hot gases to drive a turbine that, in turn, compresses the air to be used in the cylinder. The compressed air takes more oxygen into the cylinder, which allows more fuel to be burned, thus producing more power. The intercooler works with the turbocharger to reduce the heat that builds up as the air is compressed. Cooler air is more dense and so, again, it will contain more oxygen.

TRANSMISSION TYPES

With the crankshaft now turning, the next stage is the transmission.

Most common is electric transmission, where the engine is connected to a generator or, in modern designs, an alternator. This generates electricity, which is fed to motors connected to the axles, thus driving the train. Complex control systems regulate the current the generator produces and match this to the fuel injected into the cylinders so both produce what the driver expects.

Mechanical transmission is limited to low-power engines. It was very common in early British diesel multiple unit (DMU) railcars and was also used in small shunting locomotives. Some of these even had clutches, like a car, with clutch pedals in the cab for the driver. Most mechanical transmissions, however, use clutchless gearboxes with different ratios of gears giving different road speeds for the fixed range of engine speeds.

Hydraulic transmission has found favor in modern DMUs. It was also popular in Germany where it was used in the celebrated mainline V200 Class locomotives. Hydraulic transmission works by using oil to transmit power from the input (the engine side) to the output (the rail-wheel side) of the transmission. Both input and

DIESEL LOCOMOTIVES *are generally the choice for hauling freight, as for this train working in Mexico.*

output shafts are fitted with turbines. They are housed within a torque converter that contains oil. As the input shaft is turned, it pumps the oil past the output turbine, causing it to move. In this way the motion is transmitted through the converter. When the oil is drained from the converter, no motion can be transmitted. A hydraulic transmission can have several converters set to give different output speeds. Filling or draining one or other of these converters provides a range of speeds, just as with a mechanical gearbox.

The future of the diesel locomotive seems assured given that electrification is uneconomical for many railways. Designs are now being shared between the United States and European countries, further improving this engine's cost-effectiveness.

HOW ELECTRIC TRAINS WORK

Electric trains and locomotives drawing current from overhead wires or third rails are the most powerful form of rail traction.

If diesel locomotives are "cleaner" than steam, then electric traction locomotives, with no emissions, are cleaner still. Electric trains and locomotives receive electricity as either direct or alternating current. In direct current (DC) systems, power is fed through a control system to DC motors driving the wheels. The speed of a DC motor can be adjusted by varying the voltage of its supply. This is done with resistances that are switched into and out of the circuit as needed.

Trains collect current either from a third-rail conductor placed just outside the running rails or from overhead wires. Third-rail systems are common among underground and metro systems, where comparatively low voltages (even as low as 660 volts) are used. Overhead collection is standard for higher voltage (up to 3,000 volts),

THE PANTOGRAPH on this German Railway 5,600-horsepower locomotive takes current from overhead wires energized at 15,000 volts AC, 16⅔ Hz.

mainline DC installations. An engine takes current through a "pantograph" on the roof. This pantograph has a carbon strip to minimize friction as it runs along the wire, and the wires themselves are staggered so they do not wear grooves in the collector.

The relative simplicity of DC electrification led to some

major installations worldwide from the 1890s on. However, construction and maintenance costs were high because DC transmission requires substantial infrastructure, given that closely spaced line feeds are needed to prevent power loss as the distance from the generating station increases. The costs involved in alternating current (AC) systems were lower, although locomotive design was more complex until the advent of modern, solid state switching devices. Some countries, notably Switzerland, Italy, and Germany, used AC electrification before World War I, and today most new mainline installations are high-voltage AC (13,000 to 25,000 volts) at the standard industrial frequency of 50 Hz (60 Hz in America). AC electric locomotives have

ELECTRIC CONVERSION

While the words "electric locomotive" are in common usage, the unit that powers the train is in fact no more than a conversion device,

transforming the energy generated at the power station to the traction motors that power the wheels, as seen in this German AC locomotive. The heat energy from the power station, which comes from burning coal, gas, or nuclear fuel, is converted to electricity and diverted through transformers to lineside feeder stations. In turn, they energize the overhead wires that are suspended from well-insulated steel frames (masts) spaced at regular intervals.

THE MOST POWERFUL *locomotives in the world, rated at almost 14,950 horsepower, were built by Adtranz in 2000 to haul iron ore from Sweden to Norway.*

SHARING THE POWER

The engineer of an electric locomotive leading a heavy train down a steep grade can actually help another train climbing the hill toward him. He does this by using regenerative braking, in which his locomotive's motors, instead of powering the train, are generating current that is returned to the supply line and thus is available to the other train.

traditionally used DC traction motors, converting the current from AC to DC with an on-board transformer or semi-conductor rectifiers. But AC motors are increasingly being used because they are lighter and equally powerful.

However, with AC motors the current from the overhead wires must still be converted from AC to DC, because of the characteristics of the motor control system. Then, to control the train's speed, the on-board electronics change the DC back into AC at a variable frequency, because the motors run at a speed in proportion to the frequency of the current supplied. To accelerate the train the electronics will progressively feed higher and higher frequency current to the motors, forcing them to turn faster.

MULTI-VOLTAGE TRAINS
One unwanted side effect of using variable frequency supplies to the traction motors is signaling interference. Many signaling systems use AC track circuits to detect trains. Stray current from trains can interfere with this, even causing the color of signals to change. Because of this danger, trains using AC traction motors must be extensively tested to prove that they will not interfere with the signals.

The continued need for DC in a train equipped with an AC motor makes designing a multi-voltage train (that is one that uses AC or DC at differing voltages), much easier. Provided the designer ensures the DC link in the train is at the same voltage as the DC supply from the over-head wire, then the current can be used by the train as if it came from the on-board transformer. This is the secret of the *Eurostars* and electric locomotive-hauled trans-European expresses, which cross from one country's electrification scheme to another's without so much as a pause.

Today, electric traction is used on all types of railways from the smallest suburban rapid-transit systems to long-distance, high-speed lines, such as Japan's *Shinkansen* and France's *TGV* lines.

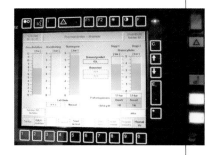

THE INSTRUMENT PANEL *of the driver's cab in modern electric loco-motives (left) includes computer screens (above) to provide up-to-the-minute information to the crew.*

SWITCHERS *and* BANKERS

Unsung workhorses of mainline and industry,

these were the locomotives that worked the yards and steep grades.

I n the railways' early days, when engines became obsolete very quickly, downgraded mainliners often gravitated to humble switching duties (shunting in British parlance). But these engines were invariably cumbersome and ill-suited to the task of moving wagons and carriages around the yards, and the need for specialized locomotives became apparent.

The small tank engine, especially the 0-6-0T, was a favored option all over the world. It was easily maneuvered and the weight of the fuel and water bore directly onto the driving wheels to provide maximum adhesion. For lighter work the 0-4-0T proved an economical alternative, ideal for negotiating restricted areas. Hundreds of thousands of such little engines—and some not so little—were built around the world in the steam age. Steelworks, collieries, shipyards, breweries, and countless other industrial users depended on these workhorses, of which even enthusiasts took little note until "big" steam disappeared from the mainlines.

BRUTE FORCE

As the railways developed, there were more trains, they were heavier, and the destinations of individual wagons more diverse. This caused many larger yards to adopt the hump system, in which long rakes of wagons were pushed

THE MASSIVE MARSHALING YARD in Harbin, northeast China, is the workplace of this classic American-style Mikado 2-8-2, here engaged in heavy shunting work.

uncoupled up an incline and allowed to roll by gravity down the other side into their appropriate sidings.

Humping required more powerful engines, and some gargantuan forms emerged that were capable of brute force over short distances. In Britain and India the 0-8-4T was used, and in Europe the 0-10-0T, while America opted for 0-8-0s, 0-10-2s, and even Mallet tender engines.

From the 1930s the steam switcher went into rapid decline as the diesel became the desired alternative. Diesels did not have to return to the

locomotive shed for coal and fire-cleaning at least once a day; they could be switched on and off for work that often involved periods of idleness; and their even torque provided sure-footed starts with heavy loads. The diesel take-over sped up with North America's development of the road-switcher, a locomotive powerful enough to handle short journeys with freight (and even passenger) trains on the mainlines, and economical enough to be allocated to switching duties.

At the same time, the railways were making great

BRITISH-BUILT *industrial engines: a geared shunting engine in Brazil (above); and a crane tank engine at an Indian sawmill (right).*

numbers of the old mainline steam engines redundant, many of which eked out their final years on switching work. Among the most dramatic manifestations of this were in India and Africa. The last of the magnificent British-built XC express passenger Pacifics ended their days on heavy shunting work at Burdwan, north of Calcutta. And in Zimbabwe the graceful Beyer-Garratt articulated locomotives shunted the yards at Bulawayo, long after steam had officially disappeared from mainlines.

There is less switching now as more and more passenger trains become fixed (multiple) units and as freight travels in block loads, but big sorting yards in America, Europe, Russia, and China are still hives of activity 24 hours per day. And the train-watcher can still stand at stations such as Basel in Switzerland and marvel at the speed at which 60-year-old 0-6-0 electric locomotives switch carriages, luggage, and sleeping cars from one trans-European express train to another.

THE BANKER'S ROLE

Closely related to the switcher is the banker. This is the engine assigned to assist heavy trains over steep gradients, usually by pushing

at the rear. Some special examples have been built. Britain boasted two: the solitary Lickey Banker four-cylinder 0-10-0, which spent its entire life on a 1-in-37 grade near Birmingham; and the London & North Eastern Railway's only Beyer-Garratt locomotive, a 2-8-2+2-8-2 that was built to push coal trains up a 1-in-40 bank in Yorkshire. This latter engine also ended its days on the Lickey grade after the demise of the renowned 0-10-0.

America's most celebrated banker was the Baltimore & Ohio's 0-6-6-0 compound Mallet No. 2400, "Old Maud." The country's first Mallet, it was built in 1904 and became the resident banker on

Pennsylvania's Sand Patch incline, which was notorious for its 1.94 percent grade.

Today, with electric and diesel power almost universal, bankers still push heavy trains up gradients, but they are increasingly rare. Instead, extra locomotives are added to the front of trains, where they can be controlled directly by the single train crew, or they are inserted mid-train and controlled by radio from the front end. It is "distributed power" such as this that makes possible the massive freight trains that are now seen on our railroads.

A CLASSIC BRITISH *0-4-0 industrial shunting engine.*

BUILT *for the* TASK

Difficult track conditions drove engineers to come up with solutions,

producing some engines that looked odd but did the job.

In 1851 Austrian railway promoters held a contest to find the most suitable locomotive type for working the long, twisting grades of the line over the Semmering Mountains, south of Vienna. Four new steam engines were entered and, although none gave a long-term solution for the Semmering, each was a radical example of a purpose-built locomotive.

Many different kinds of locomotive evolved over the years in an effort to pack more power within the engineering limits of track gauge and load capacity, and available width and height. One solution was developed by Robert Fairlie in 1864. The Fairlie locomotive was in essence two engines, with separate boilers sharing a common firebox, back-to-back on one frame

mounted on two bogies, and thus a flexible wheelbase. The most famous Fairlies hauled slate on the 2-foot-gauge Ffestiniog Railway in Wales. They still work there today in tourist service.

AMERICAN INNOVATION
At the other end of the scale were the monstrous American articulateds, including the Southern Pacific "cab forward" locomotives, essentially back-to-front engines designed to alleviate difficult conditions for crews in the tunnels over Donner Pass in the Sierras. They used oil fuel so that the tender could still be in the rear; a previous attempt in

A ROTARY SNOW PLOW *churns the snow on the Cumbres & Toltec line in Colorado (left). Geared Shay locomotives such as this one (below) worked North America's forests during the 1900s.*

THE CLASSIC *American caboose has a cabin on the roof for the crew.*

Italy to put the cab in front on coal-fired locomotives had produced some decidedly odd-looking machines.

America was also home to the "camelback" locomotive, in which the driver's cab was perched on top of the boiler. The fireman worked, often exposed to the elements, in the conventional position. This answered the need for a very large firebox to burn anthracite as fuel. Camelbacks, or "Mother Hubbards," were still used in the eastern United States until 1954.

STEAM AT SPEED

Steam engineers did not always give in easily to newer forms of power. The giant steam locomotives of the Norfolk & Western and New York Central produced some of their greatest performances in the face of the vaunted diesel. Much earlier, in 1903, England's Great Eastern Railway (GER) produced a steam engine specifically to counter the electric train.

The GER ran the world's most intensive steam passenger service out of Liverpool Street Station in London and built a unique three-cylinder 0-10-0 tank engine to demonstrate that steam could accelerate a 315-ton (321 t) train to 30 miles per hour (48 km/h) in 30 seconds. The Decapod achieved this and more, and electrification took another 56 years to come to the line out of Liverpool Street.

WORKING THE FORESTS

A long way from the bustle and grime of Liverpool Street, the lumbermen of America's Northwest were also served well by a distinctive engine type. This was the Shay, created to haul timber out of the forests on tracks that twisted and climbed.

Shays are flexibly mounted on four-wheeled bogies known as trucks. The cylinders are set alongside each other vertically on the engines' right-hand side and drive a horizontal crankshaft running the length of the engine, the drive applied by pinions slotted into beveled gears on the truck wheels. The crankshaft is made flexible by universal joints placed along its length.

Shays run at low speed, but in forest conditions line speed is subordinate to good articulation and the efficient transmission of power. Other geared locomotives followed, such as the Heisler and the Climax and, in the can-do world of the woods, to some fascinating derivations. Most extraordinary were those of the "bush" tramways in distant New Zealand, where engineers combined geared or chain drives with up to four bogies to build "lokeys" that were like nothing else on rail.

WHERE'S THE FIRE?

For industrial sites, such as gasworks, chemical plants, and paper and furniture manufacturers, where there is a risk of sparks or hot ashes or coals causing a fire, an unusual type of locomotive was invented. The fireless locomotive, as its name suggests, does not have a fire—though externally it still resembles a conventional locomotive (albeit without a chimney).

The "boiler" is merely a pressurized container, charged by steam at regular intervals from a high-pressure supply. The cylinders are conventional—in essence the locomotive is like a giant Thermos flask full of steam, on wheels, as this Cuban locomotive attests.

BUILDING *the* TRACKS

The first railway tracks often cracked under the weight of the trains;

today modern materials ensure ever-greater strength and durability.

A fundamental principle of railways is adhesion— flanged steel wheels will ride smoothly and efficiently on fixed guide rails, provided both are perfectly engineered and there are no steep grades. The condition of the track is all-important for every kind of train, from high-speed fliers to heavy freight trains.

Railway track is called "permanent way," the name originally used by Victorian engineers to distinguish be- tween the temporary lines laid by contractors and the finished product. Modern track has to be sophisticated because the trains that run on it are heavy, travel at high speeds, and must be 100 percent safe. This is a far cry from the earliest days,

TIES, OR SLEEPERS, *have been made of wood (above) since rail's beginnings, but today concrete is preferred for many heavy-haul and high-speed lines (below).*

when brittle cast iron rails laid on wooden baulks or crude stone blocks frequently broke under even the lightest loads.

RAIL MATERIALS

By the 1830s rails 18–20 feet (5–6 m) long were being rolled from more durable wrought iron, but a techno- logical breakthrough came with the invention of the Bessemer process of steel- making in 1857. The first

recorded use of a steel rail was in that year at Derby in England. The rail reportedly lasted more than nine years in a location in which an iron rail would have been worn out in weeks. As the cost of steel came down, steel rails became universal.

Many ingenious rail profiles were tried in the early years, but the world standard soon became the flat-bottomed, or Vignoles, rail that can be

AROUND AND ABOUT

Zig-zags (switchbacks) and spirals enable trains to climb mountains on adhesion, but at great cost to distance and journey times. The first mainline to use such an arrangement was the Indian Bombay–Poona line, which overcame a 1,831-foot (558 m) climb between Karjat and Khandaha with a 16-mile (26 km) climb up an average gradient of 1 in 37 (2.7 percent). The Bhore Ghat took seven years to build, from 1856 to 1863. Since then railway engineers have met similar challenges in the mountains of the Andes of South America, the Alps of Europe, and the Himalayas of central Asia, with ever more spectacular results.

spiked directly to the ties. The exception was Britain and some of its colonies; until the 1960s they retained the "bull-head" rail, a system supported by cast steel "chairs."

As train weights and speeds increased, so did the size of the rails the trains run on. Mainlines are often laid with rails of 132 pounds per yard (65.5 kg/m), strong enough to carry the fastest and heaviest trains. Dedicated coal and iron ore carriers can use rails of 155 pounds per yard (77.5 kg/m).

LAYING AND MAINTENANCE

Ties (sleepers in Britain) have traditionally been made of wood, resilient and durable, set in a fast-draining ballast of crushed stone. Many alternatives to timber have been tried, and in recent years prestressed concrete and steel designs have evolved and are now stronger and cheaper for the track beds of high-speed and heavily trafficked lines. On some high-speed lines, rails are laid on continuous concrete slabs. Though this form of track is expensive it is very low maintenance.

MAKING THE GRADE

The cog, or rack, railway is the engineering solution to steep gradients that cannot be negotiated by adhesion. It is a feature of the Swiss and Austrian Alpine railways. On the Pilatus Line (right) tourists ride gradients of up to 1 in 2, with horizontal cogwheels under the electrically powered cars engaging with toothed rails in the center of the track to ensure steady movement and prevent slipping (below right).

However, most rack railways use a differerent arrangement, invented by Roman Abt (1855–1933) in which the toothed rails and cogs engage vertically. The first Abt application was in the Harz Mountains of Germany in 1886, and it was soon widely adopted, in Switzerland in particular. A steam-operated Abt line has been restored for tourists in the remote southwest of Tasmania, Australia.

New lines for high-speed rail follow the same principles as expressway roads. Tunnels, cuttings, embankments, and bridges are used to keep the gradients favorable and avoid sharp curves, which slow down the train's progress.

Advances in track technology have also improved the turnout that takes trains from one track to another. Junctions on the latest high-speed lines can be taken by trains at 135 miles per hour (220 km/h).

Continuous rail welding has eliminated one of the major causes of rail wear, the constant movement of trains over the gap between short lengths of rail. This was the source of rail's once-familiar "clickety-clack" sound.

Track maintenance was heavy work until the 1960s: One length of rail weighed around a ton and took 20 men to lift it. Mechanization streamlined the process, with modern track machines able to renew half a mile (800 m) of prefabricated track in an eight-hour shift and replace ties at the rate of 15 a minute.

THIS MACHINE *checks and corrects the alignment of the rails, streamlining the job of track maintenance.*

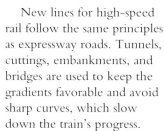

TRAIN CONTROL

A long way from oil lamps and semaphores, now computers guide the modern railroad.

Preventing train collisions relies on ensuring that no two trains are on the same track in the same place at the same time. Yet early railways had no signaling and only very basic control over trains. The ground-breaking Stockton & Darlington Railway in England's north simply told drivers which trains had priority. Should two trains meet on a single track the one without priority had to reverse to the last passing loop. Speeds were low, but the potential for accidents was still high.

The next stage was a time-interval system, with a policeman telling drivers how long it had been since the train in front had passed. If trains had been reliable, this might have worked, but breakdowns were frequent and time and again the failed train was hit by the one behind. Eventually, railways worldwide developed

COMPUTERS *at the Liverpool Street Control Center in London (above) have replaced manual systems such as block signaling, which designated line sections, as used in 1845 in England (left).*

signaling and control systems. Their basic principle was to divide the track into sections and arrange signal systems to prevent more than one train being in each section.

SIGNALING EVOLUTION

Early signals were colored flags, soon to be replaced by wooden boards which were less likely to blow away. The boards evolved into the semaphore signal, typically a long,

thin board pivoted at one end. When horizontal, it meant danger; at a 45-degree angle, it meant that the track was clear. At night, lamps and colored lenses conveyed the same messages. Catching sight of these often dimly lit oil lamps, especially on dark and windy nights, was never easy, and gradually colored electric light signals replaced semaphores. Bright enough to be seen in daylight, they made semaphore arms obsolete.

At first these new colored lights were arranged to give the same form and same meanings as the semaphores. But two distinct forms of signaling were developing. Great Britain opted for route-based signaling. The signals told the driver what route was set and he regulated the speed of his train accordingly. The United States and several

MODEL RAIL *was used in 1937 Britain as a training aid for railway signalers.*

European countries adopted a speed-based system. This told the driver the speed he should be doing as he approached the next signal.

Systems also evolved to prevent collisions on single lines where trains moved in both directions. On British-run railways, drivers were required to physically receive a token or "staff," which confirmed that theirs was the only train authorized to be in a particular section. In America telegraphic train orders were issued to achieve the same result, with a centrally located train "dispatcher" who might oversee many miles of track and numerous trains. From this evolved the system known as Centralized Track Control, in which the controller directs trains through lineside signals that may be hundreds of miles away from his desk.

Modern systems use no lineside signals at all. Instead, computers transmit speed commands straight to the cab. If the driver does not obey them, the computer takes control and stops the train at the right point. Some light railways have gone further and removed the driver altogether.

CENTRALIZED TRACK CONTROL *enables a controller to oversee many trains, directing them through lineside signals at great distances from the operating center.*

Computers work out the position of the train using satellite navigation technology. Elsewhere, electronics have taken over from mechanical signal boxes, allowing larger areas to be controlled—an obvious efficiency.

TRAIN ACCIDENTS

The early years of the railways were beset with accidents. Today, these mishaps are rare, but higher speeds and heavier trains mean that those that do occur can still result in the deaths of crew or passengers. The majority of accidents are either collisions or derailments. Improved signaling and train equipment have reduced the former, and track maintenance and driver training the latter. Many collisions in the past happened when signalmen allowed a train to move into a section of line when, often because of mechanical failure, there was already one there. As the reliability of trains has improved, so the number of collisions has fallen.

TOWERS AND SIGNAL BOXES

From the earliest days, gates and signals were permanently supervised by railway staff known as "constables," but their positions were without protection from the weather. It was not long before the railways provided them with special huts—the familiar signal boxes or signal cabins of Britain and Europe, or "towers" in America. They also housed equipment such as telegraph and block instrument apparatus. More than 150 years later the principles remain the same in modern, air-conditioned management centers filled with computer technology. The staff inside them might never see the trains but they still control them.

BRIDGES

At first, railway bridges were no different from road bridges. As the railways' needs changed, so too did railway bridge design.

Railway bridges come in all shapes and sizes, from the smallest arch over a stream to spans that march across canyons or rivers. Arched bridges have been used for hundreds of years. Normally made of brick or stone, the curve of the arch transfers the forces of gravity to the bridge piers.

The world's oldest railway bridge is the Causey Arch in Britain, a stone structure on the industrial Tanfield Railway, built in 1727. Apart from the fact that it carries a railway, it is almost indistinguishable from road bridges built in previous centuries.

NEW BRIDGE DESIGNS

As the railways developed, so bridge design became more ambitious. The design of Great Britain's Royal Border Bridge, carrying the London–Edinburgh mainline 100 feet (30 m) over the River Tweed at Berwick, is credited to the engineer Robert Stephenson. Opened in 1850, it comprises 28 massive stone arches, and is 720 yards (660 m) long. The limitations of arched bridges, not least their possible span,

A HUGE TIMBER TRESTLE *was combined with steel to build a bridge over Canada's Mountain Creek (above). The Royal Albert Bridge spans Cornwall's Tamar River (above left).*

were soon discovered. Hence, engineers resorted to other forms of construction, such as girder bridges, where a rigid iron or steel beam capable of withstanding adverse conditions, forms the span.

Perhaps the world's most famous rail bridge, the Forth Bridge, just north of Edinburgh, Scotland, opened in 1890. It is of cantilever design

KALKA–SIMLA

The 60-mile (100 km) line from Kalka to Simla in India climbs 5,000 feet (1,500 m). It has 107 tunnels, 2 miles (3 km) of viaducts, and 869 bridges. Built in 1903, the railcars on the line take five hours for the journey.

and is essentially built with steel girders. These are criss-crossed to allow the individual spans to stretch over longer distances with much greater load-bearing strength.

The Forth Bridge has three symmetrical cantilevers and, when including its approach viaducts, is over a mile and a half long (2.5 km) with 54,000 tons (55,000 t) of steel.

Swing bridges are used where railways cross water–

THE FORTH BRIDGE *in Scotland was the world's first structure made from steel.*

BRIDGE DISASTERS

Bridges have long been a cause of railway accidents. In December 1879 the 2-mile (3 km) bridge across the icy and turbulent River Tay in Scotland collapsed under a train in a storm. All 78 people on board died. Poor engineering was blamed and, although a replacement bridge opened in 1887, the old stumps are still visible at low tide, providing a sinister reminder.

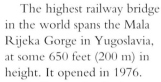

Such severe winds buffeted Ireland's Owencarrow Viaduct that trains were blown off it in 1906 and 1925. The viaduct stretched 380 yards (350 m) across a valley so exposed that no trees grew there. In the 1925 accident three coaches overturned, killing four people (above). After this, vehicles were weighted with concrete.

On Christmas Eve 1953, at Tangiwai in New Zealand, the bridge over the Whangaehu River was washed away. An approaching train then plunged into the water, killing all 151 people on board.

At Granville, Australia, the locomotive of a packed commuter train derailed on a curve in 1977. Traveling at around 50 miles per hour (80 km/h), the engine tore through the supports of a bridge over the line, which brought it crashing down onto the carriages, killing 83 people and injuring more than 200.

The highest railway bridge in the world spans the Mala Rijeka Gorge in Yugoslavia, at some 650 feet (200 m) in height. It opened in 1976.

Until recently, the longest railway bridge, at over 4 miles (6 km), was the Huey P. Long Bridge in New Orleans. In 2000 the sweeping Øresund Bridge opened, linking Denmark and Sweden. It is almost 5 miles (7.8 km) long.

The world's longest brick viaduct is the London & Greenwich Railway, which opened in 1836. It has 878 arches and is almost 4 miles (6 km) long. An even longer concrete viaduct links Brisbane airport with this Australian city's main rail system. It extends 6 miles (9.7 km).

ways close to the water. The span is balanced on a central pier, and rotates to open. Many swing bridges have a signal cabin above the pier, where the signalman can see both the railway line and the waterway.

Isambard Kingdom Brunel's 1859 Royal Albert Bridge on the Great Western Railway connects the English counties of Devon and Cornwall. The two spans are each 451 feet (138 m) long with an ellip-

tically shaped, wrought-iron tube from which the rail deck is suspended.

The Victoria Falls Bridge marks the border between Zimbabwe and Zambia, in southern Africa. Completed in 1905, the bridge has a single steel span of 500 feet (153 m), which carries the line over the Zambezi River 400 feet (122 m) below.

THOUSANDS OF CYCLISTS

cross the Øresund road and rail bridge before its official opening.

TUNNELS

*Where mountains, channels, or cities
must be crossed, tunnels offer the solution.*

The inability of trains to negotiate anything but shallow inclines means railways have a profusion of tunnels to take them through both mountains and urban areas. Simple shallow tunnels are often built using the "cut and cover" principle, whereby a cutting is dug and lined, a roof is built, and the area covered over again. Deeper tunnels in soft ground were initially dug out by hand, with wooden supports used to hold up the workings until a brick lining could be built. Tunnels through rock did not need a lining and were blasted out using explosives. Most tunnels are now dug using special boring machines and have a prefabricated concrete lining.

BEATING OBSTACLES

The steepest gradients require spiral tunnels, seen extensively in Switzerland and North America. A curved tunnel is dug inside a mountain, to emerge higher up the mountain.

In the days of steam engines, working trains through long tunnels, especially those on steep gradients, could be an ordeal for engine crews. Today the railways through most of the great tunnels are electrified, but some are not. In these the heat and fumes from diesel engines can be almost as big a problem as the smoke and steam of times past. Various devices are used to deal with this, including extractor systems and computer-controlled doors.

Japan has 1,200 miles (2,000 km) of railway tunnel, much of it under water. The 33.4-mile (53.8 km) Seikan

THE TUNNEL BORING MACHINE *dug the undersea Channel Tunnel (below). The entrance to an earlier trial bore near Dover, England, was photographed in 1957 (right). Tunnels and viaducts allow trains to traverse perilous terrain (above).*

Tunnel is the longest railway tunnel in the world, and about 14 miles (22.5 km) of it is 330 feet (100 m) below the seabed. Linking the islands of Hokkaido and Honshu, it opened in 1987 after 23 years of construction.

The Seikan's record will be eclipsed, however, on completion of the new 36-mile (57 km) St. Gotthard base tunnel from Switzerland to Italy. This will provide a more easily graded route under the Alps—the existing 1882 tunnel has very steep approaches on each side. Work started on the new tunnel in 1999, and trains should be running through it by 2011.

The previous longest tunnel, at 12 miles, 557 yards (19.8 km), was the Simplon, between Switzerland and Italy. It has two bores, the first opening in 1905 and the second in 1922. Construction took seven years, aided by a

LIGHT RAIL *also makes use of tunnels, as in Turkey.*

new rotary drill. Problems included extreme heat and water seeping into the workings—on one day alone 2 million gallons (9 million liters) were pumped out. The Simplon Tunnel became famous as being on the route of the *Simplon-Orient-Express,* which ran from 1919 to 1962 between France and Istanbul.

There are also remarkable tunnels on the Swiss narrow-gauge mountain railways, especially on the Rhaetian Railway. These include the Albula, Europe's highest, at 5,971 feet (1,820 m) and, opened in 1999, the 12-mile

(19 km) Vereina, which links Klosters with the Engadine Valley and St. Moritz.

The 31-mile (50 km) Channel Tunnel opened in 1994, almost two centuries after French engineer Albert Methieu first suggested a tunnel between Britain and France. Anglo-French wars and political misgivings halted progress until the 1880s, when trial tunnels were dug on both sides of the Channel before a nervous British Parliament blocked the scheme. Another atttempt after World War II met a similar fate, before being formally abandoned by Britain in 1974.

A proposal a decade later was successful and in 1987 work started. It took 15,000 workers seven years to build. The Channel Tunnel has the longest undersea section—23.3 miles (37.5 km).

THE NEW ST. GOTTHARD BASE TUNNEL *is due to open in 2011.*

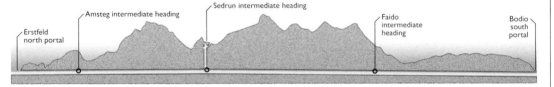

Erstfeld north portal — Amsteg intermediate heading — Sedrun intermediate heading — Faido intermediate heading — Bodio south portal

THE HEXTON SYSTEM

The Hexton tunnel system on the Cape Town–Johannesburg electrified mainline in South Africa is a complex of four tunnels. One is 8.4 miles (13.5 km) long with a passing loop inside and a maximum depth of 820 feet (250 m) below solid rock. The completed system opened in 1989.

Building the Hexton system had been proposed as far back as the 1940s to replace the steeply graded line through the mountains over the Hex River Pass, which had been a bottleneck on the mainline ever since it was built. The terrain made doubling of the track impractical, and the gradients

(up to 1 in 31) slowed trains to a crawl. Work started in 1948 but was abandoned two years later for financial reasons. A plan to revive the scheme in 1965 also failed.

Work started again in 1974 with the building of the first tunnel. Construction of the remaining tunnels began in 1981, and more than 1,200 tons (1,224 t) of explosive were used during the work.

The Hexton system saved a full four miles (over 6 km) and 472 feet (144 m) of climbing compared to the old route. Following the opening the original line over the Hex Pass was downgraded. Although it is still in place, no trains have used it since 1993.

REMARKABLE LINES

Some railway lines have grand bridges, others tunnels and steep grades.

And there are lines that are the result of remarkable engineering feats.

The spread of railroads saw engineers take the tracks to the most inhospitable places on Earth, over deserts, mountain ranges, and the widest rivers. Armies of laborers built their way across entire continents. Many were killed, but their efforts changed the world. The remarkable lines that they constructed are their epitaph.

THE LONGEST

At 5,777 miles (9,297 km), Russia's Trans-Siberian Railway connects Moscow to the Pacific and is the longest railway in the world. Starting in 1891, it took 10,000 men 13 years to construct the line across empty, wild terrain, where the winter temperature can drop to -40°F (-40°C).

The line has eight bridges more than 1,000 feet (305 m) long, massive cantilever structures considered of such importance they are guarded by soldiers. But by far the most difficult stretch to build was the Circumbaikal, skirting the 400-mile-long (644 km) Lake Baikal, the biggest freshwater lake in the world.

In the 50 miles (80 km) from Kultuk to Port Baikal, the track was built on the sheer cliffsides, and workers could only reach the building sites by boat. This one stretch alone, the last to be finished, contains 38 tunnels and more than 200 bridges. In 1904 the world's greatest railroad finally connected East and West.

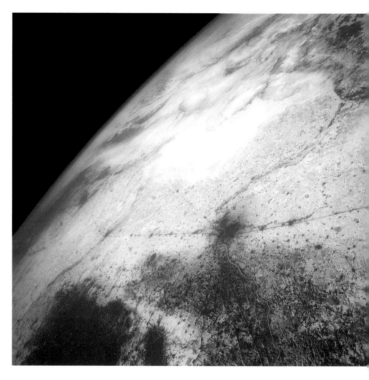

SEEN FROM SPACE, *the Trans-Siberian shows as a dark line against the snow, with the city of Omsk at the "hub." This view was taken from the shuttle Endeavor in 1994.*

THE HIGHEST

The Peruvian Central Railway is the world's highest. Its summit at Oroya is at 15,692 feet (4,783 m), and passengers can suffer altitude sickness, so the trains carry oxygen. The railway was begun in 1870, but it took 25 years to build because of Peru's poor economy. The line was laid out by dynamic American Henry Meiggs. It climbs 12,875 feet (3,924 m) in 75 miles (120 km) from Chosica, with grades as steep as 4.5 percent (1 in 22). The terrain forced curves of up to 330-foot (100 m) in radius and, at points where this was not enough, "switchbacks"

were built, whereby the train changes direction and "zigzags" up the mountains. There are 66 tunnels, including the ¾-mile (1.2 km) Galera Tunnel, inside which is the line's summit. The 59 bridges include the Carrión over Verrugas Gorge, named for Dr. Daniel Carrión. He died experimenting on himself while trying to find a cure for the *verrugas,* a mosquito-borne fever that killed thousands of railway builders.

THE STEEPEST

Switzerland's Pilatus line, a rack-and-pinion railway, opened in 1889, is the world's steepest railway. It is almost

IN ECUADOR *the mountainous line from Guayaquil to Quito, infamous for washaways, breakdowns, and derailments, was misleadingly nicknamed "The Good and the Quick."*

3 miles (4.6 km) long but has a staggering 50-percent (1 in 2) gradient. To stop trains lifting from the track, a new rack system was developed, whereby the train wheels grip the side and underneath of the central rack rail. Passengers ride in inclined coaches from Alpnachstad on Lake Lucerne up Tomlishorn to a station at 6,791 feet (2,070 m), 100 feet (30 m) short of the summit.

ACROSS THE ROCKIES

The Canadian Pacific Railway, engineered by William C. Van Horne, was the first to cross Canada and the Rocky Mountains. At 3,364 miles (5,414 km) it is still the world's third longest (after the Trans–Siberian and the Canadian National). In the 600 miles (966 km) over the Rockies, almost 300 miles (483 km)

INCLINED COACHES *compensate for the extreme gradient. on the Pilatus line.*

were blasted through solid rock. Rivers were diverted or crossed by trestle viaducts, and 14 tunnels were built. When the line opened in 1886, the grade of the steepest section was 4.4 percent (1 in 23); later tunnels reduced this to 2.2 percent (1 in 45). The first train ran in 1886; it took 139 hours to travel from Montreal to Port Moody, Vancouver.

OVER THE ALPS

The meter-gauge Bernina Railway from St. Moritz in Switzerland to Tirano in Italy is the highest railway to cross the Alps in the open. It peaks at 7,400 feet (2,256 m) and its gradients of 7 percent (1 in 14) are conquered without resort to cog-rail (rack) sections. The minimum curve is only 148 feet (45 m) in radius.

The severe winters and terrain meant construction could only take place in summer, so the 3½-mile-long (6 km) railroad took from 1906 to 1910 to build. It boasts numerous bridges and tunnels, but by far the most spectacular engineering feat is the Brusio spiral, where the line climbs over itself on a viaduct, gaining 60 feet (18 m). The line, now electrified, is part of the Rhaetian Railway. Snow on the Bernina Pass can be up to 20 feet (6 m) deep in winter, so special rotary snow plows are in service to cut through the snow and ice, keeping the line open year-round.

They [railway termini] are our gates to the glorious and the unknown. Through them we pass out into adventure and sunshine…

Howards End,
E. M. FORSTER (1879–1970), British novelist

CHAPTER FOUR

TRAINS *and* SOCIETY

THE SOCIAL IMPACT
of RAILROADS

The railroads not only gave people greater mobility, they also created towns, expanded industries, and enhanced communications.

Less than 200 years old, mechanized transport made its first startling impact in the form of the railroad. Riverboats and barges competed at the start, but it was the steam-driven train that created new towns and cities, fostered industries, and unified nations. The train brought people new kinds of produce and goods at prices they could afford. Rail travel broadened their view of the world and gave them an exciting new freedom—that of mobility.

The land grants that made railroad construction possible also enabled the settlement of the American West. On other continents railroads were similarly the key to colonization or had the effect of awakening communities from rural isolation.

The railroads' needs drove the 19th-century development of coal mining, engineering, and the iron and steel industries. The railroads supported the towns that grew around them, often on sites far from existing settlements. Birmingham in Alabama and Swindon and Crewe in England were industrial centers whose existence was due almost entirely to promotion by, or the growth of, the railroads. By the 1850s Chicago was the fastest-growing town in the United States, largely because of its position as the railroad city supreme.

WE ARE WHAT WE EAT
From the earliest days the railroads' ability to carry fresh produce faster and over longer distances than ever before changed people's lives in the most basic way—the food they ate. In the 1850s New Yorkers began to enjoy fresh milk brought in by train; the development of refrigerated boxcars soon afterward saw the start of a huge traffic in fruit and vegetables from Florida and California, and beef from Chicago.

Wine in France and beer in Britain widened their markets enormously. For the first time fresh fish became available in cities far from the sea, and in every case the volumes the railroads could handle meant that the goods could be sold at prices acceptable not only to the well-to-do but to the urban population as a whole.

Rail's ability to sustain such mass markets affected those who served them also. Farmers could now specialize in the crops and livestock best suited to their district's climate, instead of trying to supply all the needs of their neighborhood. This enabled them to grow more, giving them also the means of selling more.

On the largest scale, the prosperity of entire countries was linked with the coming of the railroad. Argentina and Australia, for instance, gained low-cost transport to their seaports, enabling them to

EMPLOYEES *often enjoyed company outings by train. This group in 1935 is setting off from London for Margate.*

CITY DWELLERS *gained easy access to the delights of the seaside due to the railways, which created resorts such as Dawlish in England's southwest, still rail-served today.*

become among the world's greatest exporters of meat, wool, and grains.

COMMUNICATIONS

As the railroads grew, they played leading roles in the development of other means of communication, ultimately affecting everyone. Standard time and time zone systems were adopted from the 1850s to meet the railroads' needs. From their earliest days they revolutionized mail services. A Travelling Post Office mail-sorting car ran in Britain from 1838 and the "Penny Post," pioneered there in 1840, relied on the speed of rail from the start. The railroads also gave people ready access to newspapers, putting copies into readers' hands in even distant cities just hours after publication. On many railroads the nightly newspaper specials became the fastest trains on the line.

The electric telegraph was also in railroad use as early as 1840, and most of the lines followed railroad routes. The railroads' almost universal use of the telegraph gave the fledgling industry widespread acceptance: In 1900 the citizens of Britain alone sent close to 85 million telegrams. Perhaps because of the railroads' use of the telegraph, they did not so readily adopt the telephone, patented in 1876, but before long railroads were also significant users of this device.

ULTIMATELY MOBILE

Above all, however, railroads brought to people the ability to move around, from workers who discovered that daily journeys by train let them live in more pleasant surroundings than crowded city centers, to migrants who could cross continents in search of a new life. People who wanted a better job, or who did not have one, could travel more easily than ever before to find one. And for the first time society began to embrace the concept of travel for pleasure.

THE RAILROAD EXCURSION

By the end of the 19th century millions were using the railroads to take vacations away from home. It is generally believed to have begun with a special train chartered one day in 1841 by Mr. Thomas Cook of Leicester, England. A thousand temperance reformers took an 11-mile (18 km) excursion, with tea and dancing included in the low fare. Employers soon organized private trains to give their workers a taste of fresh country air. The railways themselves saw the benefit of offering special low fares to encourage people to travel in their leisure time and ran seaside "holiday specials," such as this 1950s train (right).

THE RAILROAD BARONS

The building of the railroads across North America entailed more than great feats of engineering. It was big business.

Railroads in North America are big business and have always been dominated by big companies and men with big ambitions, most of whom built successful railroads; others simply manipulated shares for their own gain.

The first railroad baron was Cornelius Vanderbilt. Known as "the Commodore," he made a fortune as a New York ferry-boat operator and in 1863, at the age of 69, took control of the New York and Harlem Railroad, the only railroad that entered New York City. A wily and cunning collector of small

railroads, Vanderbilt, who disliked competition, created the New York Central System, which controlled railroads from New York to Chicago. He also helped build the cities along its length. He died in 1877 having amassed a personal fortune of more than $100 million (around $11 billion in today's terms).

One of the Commodore's rivals was the Erie Railroad, controlled by "Uncle Dan" Drew, Jay Gould, and Jim Fisk. These men were basically stock manipulators who accumulated Erie stock (and even created worthless stock), let prices rise, and sold

THE UNION PACIFIC RAILROAD

opened in 1869 with great fanfare. By 1897 it was broke.

out for a profit, only to repeat the exercise again and again. While they became wealthy, they did not build railroads, nor did they have much interest in operating them.

The other great Eastern railroad was the Pennsylvania Railroad, which tapped into the rich coalfields of the Allegheny Mountains. J. Edgar Thomson, a quiet, colorless businessman, built the Pennsy, which became the first great railroad

THE ORIGINAL *Great Northern Railway train of 1862 and a 1924 Oriental Limited, in the foreground, engaged on a transcontinental exhibition tour from Chicago to show the 60 years of progress since the establishment of the Great Northern Railway Co.*

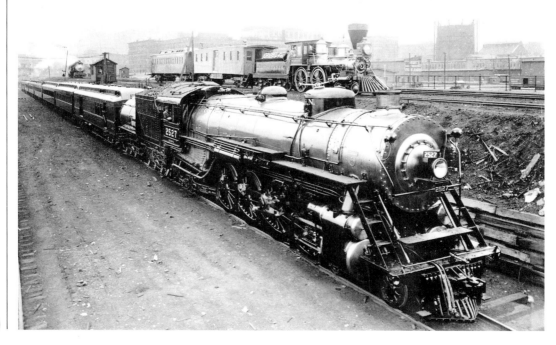

WILLIAM K. VANDERBILT *took over his father's railroad empire.*

network, and one of the first corporations of modern times. Thomson differed from the other barons in that he ran his railroad as a business, not as the exclusive preserve of the owner.

The Midwest was, and still is, dominated by two great railroads, the Santa Fe and the Union Pacific. When William B. Strong became General Manager of the Santa Fe in 1877 it had 780 miles (1,256 km) of track in Kansas but by 1889 it was a transcontinental railroad stretching from Chicago to California and to the Gulf of Mexico. While building his railroad from Colorado to New Mexico over Ralton Pass, Strong and his men had a shoot-out with builders of the rival Rio Grande Railroad to determine who got to build the line. Strong won.

BUYING AND SELLING
In 1897 sharebroker Edward H. Harriman bought the bankrupt Union Pacific Railroad (UP) at auction (he already owned Illinois Central). He injected fresh capital into the UP and also obtained a controlling stake in Southern Pacific. He was one of the best railroad operators in America, more as a rebuilder of railroads than a builder.

"Law! What do I care about law? Hain't I got the power?"

CORNELIUS VANDERBILT
(1794–1877), American railroad baron

The major railroad in California, the Central Pacific, which later evolved into the Southern Pacific (SP), was formed in 1863 by "the Big Four," Charles Croker, Mark Hopkins, Leland Stanford, and Collis P. Huntington. They formed a syndicate to build the western portion of the first transcontinental railroad. Huntington was the innovative, imaginative, and energetic leader, spending much of his time in lobbying for funds in Washington. The Big Four was a well-oiled machine and eventually the Southern Pacific ran from San Francisco to New Orleans. In 1901 the SP became part of UP but in 1912 the Supreme Court ordered the railroads be separated. In September 1996 Union Pacific again bought its southern counterpart.

Of all the barons it was James J. Hill who was known as "the Empire Builder." When the last spike on his Great Northern Railway was driven in 1893 he had built the only transcontinental railroad not subsidized by a land grant. His Great Northern, together with three other railroads he controlled, known as "the Hill Lines," developed the Northwest.

In 1881, as a director of the Canadian Pacific Railway, Hill recommended that William C. Van Horne of the Milwaukee Road become its new general manager. Van Horne's vision drove the Canadian Pacific across the Rockies, the longest and most expensive transcontinental railroad ever built. By linking British Columbia with eastern Canada, he united the country, which allowed the development of the western provinces of Canada.

One of Hill's backers was banker J. Pierpont Morgan. He also bought up railroads and consolidated them, stabilizing rates to ensure they made a fair profit. He understood the effects of cut-throat competition and took on the role of industry regulator, consolidating several railroads in the south to form the Southern Railway in the mid-1890s. The Southern was an industry leader for more than 50 years, with a succession of dynamic presidents, doing much to develop the South.

In the second half of the 20th century, the railroads still had their barons but they were professional managers operating efficient railroads rather than railroad builders. W. Graham Claytor Jr. of Amtrak and Stanley Crane of Conrail transformed a mishmash of systems and equipment into first-class railroads.

JAMES J. HILL, *founder of the Great Northern Railway Co.*

THE PULLMAN CAR

For more than a century the word "Pullman" has been synonymous with rapid rail travel in exquisite luxury.

The Pullman car story is the result of one man, George Mortimer Pullman, who was born in Brocton, New York, in 1831. He came from humble roots, training as a cabinetmaker before working as a construction contractor. Yet by the mid-1890s, when trains were a major means of transport in North America, Pullman controlled the entire railroad sleeping-car business.

In 1855 Pullman moved to Chicago, by then a major railroad metropolis, and he became interested in improving the then very rudimentary sleeping cars. Ten years later he launched his first coach, the sumptuously appointed Pioneer. It was not initially popular, being considered too big and heavy, but it gained fame when it was offered as a funeral car for the assassinated President, Abraham Lincoln.

Pullman cars were a forerunner (though a much more luxurious version) of the European couchette. They could be converted from day to night use by swinging down the upper berths, folding the seats to make them into lower berths, and separating them with curtains.

The Pullman Palace Car Company (later called the Pullman Company) began in 1867, south of Chicago. Pullman's firm built, staffed, and operated sleeping cars on all major United States railroads. By 1875, 700 Pullman sleeping cars were in service, followed by parlor cars and dining coaches. Pullman also invented a vestibule connection, enabling passengers to walk between coaches.

THE BUSINESSMAN

Pullman was extraordinarily successful as a businessman, though the growth of the business was not without incident. He built the town of Pullman to house company employees but, when fortunes declined in 1894 and Pullman slashed wages by 25 percent, he failed to lower rents or grocery prices in the company town. Workers were dismissed for protesting and a general railroad strike resulted.

A federal court ordered union leaders to call off the dispute. They refused. President Grover Cleveland sent troops to maintain law and order, but violence erupted

ORNATELY DECORATED *mahogany, English oak, and satin-wood adoms this 1887 Pullman car (right). Superb quality was the standard expected by George Pullman (above) in his coaches.*

TWO GEORGES AND TWO GREAT COMPANIES

The *Orient-Express* (the *Simplon-Orient-Express* from 1919) made its inaugural run in 1883. It was developed by Belgian businessman Georges Nagelmackers, a visionary whose Europe-wide organization stood the test of time, and survived two world wars.

He had visited Pullman's United States factory, and decided to introduce sleeping and other cars based on the Pullman principle to Europe, enlisting support from King Leopold II of Belgium. His company, Liège, known as Georges Nagelmackers et Cie, struck contracts with German, French, and Belgian Railways.

After the Franco-Prussian War Nagelmackers went into partnership with one of Pullman's rivals, Colonel William D'Alton Mann. The Colonel soon sold his share to Nagelmackers, who then set up the renowned Wagons-Lits company in 1876.

Pullman resented Wagons-Lits, which had contracts with all of the principal European railways, and financial links with French Railways. Though Pullman had a fleet of 20 sleeping cars on Italian Railways by 1876, he was unable to make any further expansion into Europe (with

the exception of Britain). But his Italian factory and cars were a constant thorn in Nagelmackers' side. Despite protracted negotiations, the two men were unable to do business. Pullman's price was too high and he wanted control of Wagons-Lits. In 1888 Pullman sold the Italian business to Wagons-Lits, which added the cars to its own fleet.

The best-known cars of that fleet were used on the *Orient-Express*, which ran from Paris to Constantinople (Istanbul) until 1977. James P. Sherwood of the Sea Containers Group revived the train as the *Venice Simplon-Orient-Express* in 1982. It earned much of its reputation from its British Pullman coaches and restored Wagons-Lits cars.

and much railroad property was destroyed. Strike leaders were arrested for refusing to return to work and all Pullman employees were ordered to sign a statement that they would never join a union. The government's actions ended the Chicago Strike, as it became known.

Pullman was so hated by his employees that, when he died in 1897, his heirs feared his body would be stolen and held for ransom. The coffin was enclosed in a room-sized slab of concrete and reinforced with railway sleepers.

THE LEGACY

Pullman's influence had spread to Britain by the 1880s and Pullman sleeping and, later, dining cars were often attached to crack express trains. By the 1920s, complete express trains were formed entirely of Pullman cars, built in Britain

under licence. They used the distinctive cream and brown livery until the 1960s, and some still survive on preserved railways and on the British leg of the *Venice Simplon-Orient-Express*.

The final all-new British Pullmans, which were modified air-conditioned carriages, were brought into service on the route from London to Manchester and Liverpool to coincide with electrification. They operated from 1966 to 1985, by which time standards of first-class travel had risen to almost equal those of Pullman travel. In 1981 Pullman's Chicago works produced its final coach, and the factory then closed. This marked the end of Pullman car production in the United States after a reign of 112 years.

BRITISH PULLMAN CARS *sporting brown and cream livery were built under licence. Some are still in service.*

GIANTS *of* STEAM ENGINEERING

The Golden Age of Steam created not only grand locomotives but also great locomotive building companies.

Several major schools of steam locomotive design evolved during the late 1800s: the British, American, German, and French, and that of the Austrian Empire. All produced highly distinctive locomotives of a discernible family appearance. Although many individual builders were engaged in these countries, their locomotives followed the national characteristics, both aesthetically and, generally, in mechanical design and principles, too. Japan, China, and Russia were also major locomotive producers, but their products tended to follow American practice.

THE BRITISH SCHOOL

It is widely accepted that the British school was the most elegant; there was at least one famous locomotive engineer who would permit no mechanical improvements lest they spoiled the engines' appearance. No fewer than 350 different builders are known to have produced locomotives in Britain, although inevitably the majority of these were small concerns that imparted little influence. There is a clear distinction between the British private locomotive builders, who provided some engines for the home railways and others for export, and the works of the home railway companies themselves, who, in general, built to their own

The VULCAN FOUNDRY LTD
Newton-le-Willows, Lancashire. England.

BEYER PEACOCK
(above left) and the Vulcan Foundry (left) were among Britain's most illustrious locomotive builders.

designs for their own use. It was these works that gave rise to the "railway towns," such as Crewe, Derby, Doncaster, and Swindon. By agreement, the railway companies' works would not build locomotives for other home companies or for the export market.

Perhaps the best regarded of Britain's private builders was Manchester-based Beyer Peacock, whose engines were strikingly beautiful, superbly crafted, and noted for their longevity. The company built close to 8,000 steam engines at its Gorton works from its formation in 1854 until its demise in the 1960s. Another renowned Lancashire builder was the world-famous Vulcan

Foundry. But the output of these two companies was eclipsed by the mighty North British Locomotive Company of Glasgow. Formed in 1903 by the merger of three legendary names, Dübs, Neilsens, and Sharp Stewart, the company had a combined output of 28,000 locomotives, of which some 18,000 were hoisted onto the decks of ships and exported to all parts of the world.

The Yorkshire city of Leeds also was home to four eminent locomotive builders who exported their products to every continent: Hudswell Clarke, Hunslet, Manning Wardle, and Kitson.

AMERICA AND EUROPE

In North America the railway companies in general did not build their own locomotives. This was left to the private builders, who also exported prolifically. By the beginning of the 20th century America's builders had evolved into

RAILWAY WORKSHOPS *needed heavy machinery to handle locomotive parts (left). Indian Railways' post-war WP Class Pacific, pride of the line, showed its American lineage (below).*

The distinctive French locomotives totaled 39,000 and the fine, handsome family of engines from the Austrian Empire some 15,000.

OTHER PRODUCERS

Russia, one of the world's great railway nations, produced some 50,000 engines, over 20,000 of which are believed to have remained in operation well into the 1950s. Their E Class 0-10-0, totaling around 13,000 examples, was the world's most numerous type. It was produced by 25 different builders across seven countries. Of the 16 builders active in Russia, the most prolific were Kolomna, with more than 10,000 locomotives, and Voroshilovgrad, with 9,500.

Kolomna's output alone equaled that of China, which is the only country where building continued into the 21st century, with occasional examples of the SY Class Mikado, for heavy industrial use, still emerging from its Tangshan works.

India built around 4,000 locomotives, many produced by the famous Chittaranjan Works in Bengal. The earliest of India's locomotives were of British lineage but the majority, which were built from the 1940s onward, were of pure American descent.

It has been reliably estimated that, worldwide, around 640,000 steam locomotives were built over the two centuries between 1803 and 2000, of which fewer than 4,000 remained active at the beginning of the 21st century.

three principal companies, the giant Baldwin Locomotive Works, the American Locomotive Company (Alco), and Lima. The "Big Three" absorbed many companies of high pedigree, including Brooks, Cooke, and Rogers, to name just three, enthralling the engineering world. The most celebrated was Baldwin, with more than 76,000 locomotives to its credit; Alco produced more than 50,000, and Lima upward of 8,000. In total, the United States produced 177,000 steam engines between 1831 and 1955.

Europe's greatest producer was Germany, with a total production figure of 155,000 recorded—against Britain's 110,000. German design exerted a significant influence on other European countries, from such eminent foundries as Henschel, Koppel, Borsig, and Krauss and Orenstein.

The man that drives the engine? Why, his smoke alone is worth a thousand pounds a puff.

Alice through
the Looking
Glass, LEWIS
CARROLL
(1832–1898),
English author

Great Railway Stations

Modern railway stations cope with enormous volumes of traffic,

but for the world's historic stations, architecture was the mark of greatness.

It is not known who first called the great Victorian stations "cathedrals of the railway age," but it is an apt comparison. These stations dominated the landscape, and they brought people together as the great churches did. But in steam days they were never havens of peace and tranquility; they were vibrant with hustle, bustle, and noise. When sunlight streamed through the steam and smoke the effect was arresting and exciting.

From the beginning, railway companies worked to combine the fundamental of protecting people from the weather with the desire to establish themselves as new, progressive, and substantial institutions. In doing so they set great challenges for both engineers and architects; the one to address the practical need to shelter an increasing number of people, platforms and tracks, the other to give the terminal a fitting identity and presence.

BUILT IN 1839 *London's Euston Station entrance (left) was demolished in the 1960s.*

Engineers pioneered the construction of the cavernous train sheds that in the 19th century became railroad status symbols. The soaring roofs were not just for effect—their height was needed to let the smoke and fumes from steam engines disperse. Building them demanded new methods and materials. The earliest of these relied on the skilful use of wood, like Brunel's 1841 hammerbeamed roof at Bristol Temple Meads Station in the west of England, but a break-through came with the use of iron. The wondrous glass-and-iron Crystal Palace, built in London in 1851 for Queen

Victoria's Great Empire Exhibition, showed the way. Its innovative use of transverse glazing, iron vaulting, and new techniques of prefabrication led directly to the design of the magnificent roof of Paddington Station in London. Completed in 1854, it featured three huge arches spanning 240 feet (73 m). And across the Channel, the Gare de l'Est in Paris, with its huge circular "rose" window high-lighting the curve of the iron roof, owed a similar allegiance, as did many more built over the next six decades.

Bigger stations demanded even bigger multi-arched roofs, such as the five parallel spans built in 1888 at Frankfurt in Germany. But the engineers' aim was to achieve the widest possible arched span, leaving platforms and tracks uncluttered by pillars. A single iron span of 211 feet (64 m) was achieved at Birmingham New Street Station, England, as early as 1851;

THE WATERLOO EUROSTAR TERMINUS *in London is noted for its interesting multi-level design and the quality of its finishes. It exploits the use of large glass panels to create a cheerful, light-filled environment for its crowds of travelers.*

THE GARE DU NORD *in Paris, built in 1864, features a grand triumphal arch and statues that represent the towns served by the Nord railway line.*

other great spans followed in Europe (Hamburg) and the United States (the first Grand Central in New York), and culminated in 1893 with the spectacular 300-foot-wide (91 m) arch over Philadelphia's Broad Street Station.

ON A GRAND SCALE

The Victorian architects' approach to railway stations has been called "picturesque eclecticism." With no secular precedent, and often seeking to dramatize as much as to meet functional needs, they produced many extravagant buildings that today—where they have survived—can only be marvelled at. The idea that the railroad terminal was a gateway produced the colossal Grecian portico of the 1839 Euston Station in London and other grand interpretations worldwide. In contrast, 30 years after Euston was built, St. Pancras and its associated

Grand Hotel rose up nearby with an exuberance of Victorian Gothic ornamentation and scant acknowledgment of its railway origins.

Unrestrained city development in the 20th century meant that many notable railroad edifices, like the 1910 Pennsylvania Station in New York, are gone. But many do remain, including the biggest of all, New York's Grand Central. While long-distance trains no longer leave from the terminal, commuter trains do, and above the platforms the beautifully renovated 1913 buildings are now a retail center. More than half a million people still pass through Grand Central every weekday. Leipzig Station in Germany, one of the country's busiest terminals, has been completely

renovated. Other historic structures, such as the elegant Gare d'Orsay in Paris (now a museum), and romanesque St. Louis Station live on in non-railway use.

And new railroad stations are still being built. Some are sparsely functional but others have given designers every chance to be as innovative as the Victorians were 150 years ago. Stations such as Waterloo International in London, built between 1990 and 1993 for the Channel Tunnel *Eurostar* trains, and Olympic Park in Sydney, Australia, make the most of modern materials and technology—not cathedrals, but in keeping with the new railway age.

MYTHOLOGICAL FIGURES *grace Grand Central Station in New York.*

RAILWAY PEOPLE

The railways have always been a demanding employer. A skilled workforce committed to high standards has been the outcome.

I n the early, primitive years of the world's first steam-worked railway, the 1825 Stockton & Darlington, the drivers of engines hauling coal trains on the single track often settled right-of-way arguments with their fists. Doubling the line solved this problem, but working on steam engines was always a tough life.

Until well into the 20th century British locomotives with more than rudimentary cover for their crews were the exception rather than the rule. American engines had substantial cabs much earlier. The physically hard, demanding work of preparing, oiling, and cleaning steam engines was often carried out in the open in all kinds of weather. Working hours were extraordinarily long—in Britain up to 98 hours a week, according to evidence given to a parliamentary inquiry in 1890.

Unsurprisingly, engine drivers were among the earliest to be organized into powerful unions, yet even the most militant displayed the distinctive characteristics of railroaders everywhere—pride in the job and loyalty to their line. Everywhere the railroads went, their people formed closely knit groups. The apparent security of railway employment with regular payment made railroad jobs highly sought after, and led to the emergence of "railway families," in which sons followed fathers in railway work. All expected to stay with the railway for the whole of their working lives, and many did.

Whole "railway towns" evolved, and in smaller communities a job on the railroad was equally something to aspire to. Railroaders in senior grades became figures of great respect. In the United States in 1900, more than a million people worked for the railroad companies.

As employers, the railroads demanded high standards, which also contributed to the status of railway people. From the earliest times, workers likely to come into contact with passengers had to be able to read and write—not by any means universal skills in the mid-19th century—and be capable of acquiring increasingly encyclopedic knowledge of rules and regulations, rates, schedules, facilities, and so on.

The major British railways required station staff to qualify in a wide range of duties, in some cases including the use of the electric telegraph after this became widespread in the 1840s. At the smallest stations in America the depot agent, similarly, was expected to

WOMEN WORKED *for the railways in a wide range of jobs during World War II (right). An 1888 engraving (above) shows a despatcher in an American freight yard.*

DRIVING TRAINS *was once the preserve of men, but roles gradually changed in the rail industry as more women entered the workforce.*

look after everything to do with running the trains and keeping the customers happy. At the other end of the scale the man in charge could have a staff of hundreds.

RAILWAY DISCIPLINE

Running an organization as complex as a railway calls for high degrees of discipline. To achieve this many railways imposed military or quasi-military standards. British railway signalmen are still colloquially known as "bobbies" (slang for policemen), because that is exactly what the earliest signalmen were. Uniforms provided to passenger train guards and station staff were often of military style and the wearers were expected to maintain military smartness. Whatever their railway rank, they could consider themselves to be symbols of authority. In continental Europe, notably in Germany, where the railroads were treated as a strategic arm of the army, this reached its highest levels.

MILITARY STYLING *is the favored look for the early 20th-century British uniform (far right) and the Japanese ones of the 1980s (right).*

Military officers were directly involved in railroad organizations and railroad jobs were reserved for ex-soldiers. It is easy to suspect that the high presentation standards of German, Swiss, and other European railroads today owe much to this history.

Women have always found work on the railways, though not in any great number until World War I, when they quickly showed their ability to take over jobs that were by tradition held by men. Before then there had been women bookkeepers, booking clerks, and, especially, telegraph and telephone operators, as well as the large staffs of railway refreshment rooms and hotels.

Railroads in the 21st century are much less a

"private world." The dynastic, routine-based disciplines that were their strengths prior to World War II became weaknesses after it, when they had to face up to competition from the far more adaptable road and air transport industries and, more importantly, the private automobile.

Responding to this, the railroads have changed their structures and their style. In the process, many traditional railroad jobs have disappeared, overtaken by technology, and many long-serving railroad people have gone with them.

In their place are people with new skills but, overall, the number working on the railroads is a fraction of what it once was. Those who work for today's railways, however, have the same responsibilities, the same challenges, and hopefully the same incentives for success, as their predecessors.

TRAIN DESIGNS

Trains of today continue a winning tradition, as designers match functionality with style.

Trains can be very beautiful creations. Historically, many designers have taken immense pride in the aesthetics of their subjects. The potential for exciting concepts exists whatever the type of train, and many of the trains of recent years are, in their own way, every bit as imposing as the classic trains of the steam era.

The definitive Americanstyle 4-4-0s of the early years of railroading were sensuously beautiful creations, with their balloon-stack, spark-arresting chimneys, clanging golden bells, ornate headlamps, colorful cowcatchers, wooden cabs and buffer beams, and

THE GREAT WESTERN RAILWAY'S *King locomotives were totally at home in the English countryside, replete with polished brass and copper-capped chimneys.*

glorious eight-wheeled bogie tenders flamboyantly bearing the name of the railroad company. The sonorous, moaning whistles of these steam trains epitomized freedom and a spirit of adventure—the opening up of a new continent. These engines captured the world's imagination and filmmakers took any opportunity to feature them. American steam locomotives possessed a very distinctive family resemblence, just as the trains of each of the main train-building countries had their own unmistakable collective likeness.

America's later steam locomotives were rugged and very often brutish. Period after period, particularly at the end of steam, they were bigger than those produced by any other country. Their styling was not confined to the United States, however, as the vast American export market took their aesthetic to the world. A synthesis of styles occurred when other nations built in a similar manner.

THIS SUPERB BRAZILIAN *4-4-0 passenger engine was exported from Scotland in 1862 to work the meter-gauge Mogiani Railway.*

BRITISH STYLES

American locomotives contrast vividly with the softer and gentler lineage of the British tradition, which, at its best, was capable of producing locomotives that were truly elegant. Patrick Stirling's 8-foot-gauge Singles, introduced in 1870 for the Great Northern Railway, were masterpieces. The copper-capchimneyed Great Western Star, Castle, and King were created for the soft English countryside through which they ran; they enhanced and invigorated the landscape. The large-boilered Claughtons of the London, Midland & Scottish (LMS) line were harsher and more angular but they had a symmetry of form and rhythm reminiscent of great architecture. It did not need much imagination to be overwhelmed by them.

Many of the basic forms of engine, such as Pacific 4-6-2s and Atlantic 4-4-2s, were naturally harmonious in their own right, and all the major building traditions played tantalizing variations on them. The LMS Pacifics that worked the *Coronation Scot,* built in the 1930s, and the

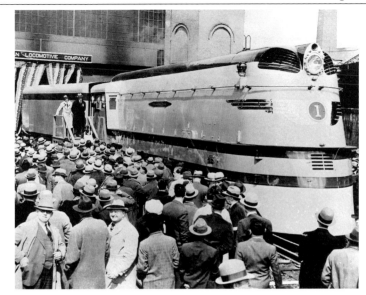

Hiawatha Atlantics of the Chicago, Milwaukee, St. Paul & Pacific Railroad were two among many locomotives that reached visual perfection.

EMBELLISHMENTS

It is fascinating to see how potentially ugly ironmongery, such as windshields, feed-water heaters, brake pumps, and external pipework and fittings, was harmoniously incorporated into the overall design. In Britain many such elements were absent. In France, in true Gallic fashion, they were fully embraced, resulting in bold machines of extraordinary complexity that were still astonishingly stylish. A prime example were the famous Chapelon Pacifics.

Even finer examples could be found in the locomotives created by Karl Golsdorf for the Austrian Empire. This great engineer produced more than 50 different designs from 1891 to 1916, all with a vivid family likeness. To the un-initiated, Golsdorf's engines were hideous angular monsters. But connoisseurs with a seasoned palate could appreciate the stark grandeur of their arresting shapes. These, too, were engines of their environ-

This snorting little animal, which I felt rather inclined to pat.

FANNY KEMBLE, British actress, when shown a steam engine by George Stephenson in 1830

ment, in this case the rough, mountainous terrain through which they traveled, radiating their sheer beauty—the finishing touch being the gold band around their chimneys.

THE 20TH CENTURY AND BEYOND

There were instances of railway companies commissioning the leading designers of the day, especially during the 1930s, the "Age of the Streamliner."

One was artist and designer Otto Kuhler, who created the

Hiawatha, but even more dramatic were the creations of Raymond Loewy. His belief that the beauty of technical objects came from improving their functionality and appearance was encapsulated in the title of his autobiography, *Ugliness Does Not Sell.*

The slump in American railroad fortunes during the 1930s Depression, following the stockmarket crash of 1929, prompted the Pennsylvania Railroad to commission Loewy to design aerodynamic casings for their K4 Pacifics. This association culminated in Loewy's handsome GG1 electric locomotives and the incredible T1 4-4-4-4s, which were introduced in 1941.

The first Japanese "Bullet Train," some 20 years later, was a continuation of these sleek, aerodynamic design principles. These are being boldly followed to this day in such masterpieces as the French *TGV*, British *Eurostar*, and even the comparatively humble *Gatwick Express*, which entered service at the beginning of the 21st century between London's Victoria Station and Gatwick Airport.

WEST JAPAN RAILWAY'S *JR 500* *"supertrain" was built in the 1990s to aerodynamic design.*

INTERIOR DESIGN

As passenger travel increased, the appearance and comfort level of train interiors were upgraded.

How railway coach interiors looked, and the ambience they generated, were governed at first by necessity and happenstance. Later, as passenger railroading became a more sophisticated affair, the décor and style of rail vehicles—not only the original day coaches but also sleeping cars, dining cars, club cars, lounges, dome cars, observation cars, and variations and combinations of all these—reflected the tastes of the moment. Over time, this would range from the excesses of the Victorian era to the clean-lined, stylized look of art deco.

The first passenger carriages were Spartan in the extreme, with some lacking even the basic comforts of seats and roofs. Where there were seats, they were often of unpadded wood. In the United States, many of the first cars looked like round-sided stagecoaches, not surprising given that they were built by stagecoach manufacturers who worked from the only models they knew. The cars that began service in 1831 on New York's Mohawk & Hudson, are a good example of these stagecoach-like vehicles, which boasted springs and upholstered seats, but the carriages were very cramped. Passengers could not get up and take a walk around—an opportunity that railcars, which were far less restricted by weight than stagecoaches, would soon provide.

CLASS AND CLASSES

Railway car builders began seizing on the advantages of this mode of transport. The coaches grew in length and, since the tapered sides needed to accommodate road vehicles' large wheels were unnecessary on rails, coaches then became wider and more spacious.

Carriages for daytime travel became increasingly comfortable, but evolved in very different directions in Britain and America. For one thing, British carriages became hierarchical, with two or three classes of travel that varied substantially in comfort and style, from the amount of seat padding to elegance of finish. Related to this was the British and European penchant for compartment travel on trains. For many years entry to these compartments was from outside the car, with no provision for passing through the car.

In North America the day coach evolved as a single open space filled with rows of seats. This gave access to washrooms at the end of the car, essential on the longer journeys typical in America. Also, it may have

EVEN MENUS *were stylish in design on the* 20th Century Limited *(right).* First Class, *painted in 1855, depicts mid 19th-century opulence (above).*

THE EASTERN & ORIENTAL EXPRESS *lounge car (right) was built in the 1990s, but it evokes the luxurious style of an earlier era. More workaday modern coaches (below right) often use big windows and bright colors to give a sense of spaciousness.*

allowed for a gregariousness that was developing in the American character. The coaches were also only one class. However, train travel in North America was not without its class distinctions. These came with the establishment of sleeping-car, or Pullman, services. In time, club cars—also generally operated by the Pullman Company—would offer first-class daytime travel.

THE DESIGNER TOUCH

It was in these extra-fare sleepers and club cars, along with diners and lounges, that interior design reached its most notable expression. By the 1870s "Palace sleeping cars" were the vogue—plush, exquisitely ornamented vehicles that exemplified the Victorian style. These cars featured clerestories of stained glass, carved wood accents, kerosene and later gas light fixtures of polished brass, patterned fabrics, tasseled drapes, and intricately painted berths.

As wooden cars gave way to composite and then steel cars, décor became simpler, reflecting the different tastes of the Edwardian era. From the 1930s, when lightweight streamliners replaced heavyweight steel cars, an entirely new aesthetic came into being. The new look was clean-lined and "moderne," with art deco accents. Industrial designers had immense influence, and trains were among the many objects that felt their touch.

In 1938 Henry Dreyfuss styled a new *20th Century Limited* for the New York Central, and it is considered one of the most beautiful trains ever created—cool, contained, understated, elegant. Meanwhile, using a brighter color palette, rival Raymond Loewy designed a new *Broadway Limited* for the Pennsylvania Railroad. Although Dreyfuss and Loewy also dressed the trains' exteriors, their main contributions were inside: fabrics, furniture, fixtures, and myriad details, even down to menus and matchbooks.

In Britain and Europe, Edwardian aesthetics lingered, especially in the British Pullmans. Even after World War II, these luxury

RAYMOND LOEWY

was a leading designer of streamlined train interiors and exteriors.

day cars were being built with wood-paneled interiors featuring exquisite inlays. But the top trains of today—Britain's *InterCity 225*s and cross-Channel *Eurostar*s, and the French high-speed *TGV*s—offer a pleasant but plain décor. The look is businesslike, as are the trains themselves, more fast-track than frilly.

CRIME *on the* RAILROAD

Trains were soon used to shift large sums of money and precious cargo, as well as transporting wealthy passengers, making them easy targets for daring robbers.

From the railways' earliest days the most affluent people traveled by train, and were potentially easy pickings for criminals. The railways soon began to carry valuable cargo such as gold bullion and payloads, providing new opportunities for crime.

Despite their attraction for criminals, trains were not generally a grand harvest for robbers. Stagecoaches, the railways' predecessor, were easy to stop and rob; stopping a train was a different matter.

Some daring robberies have made their way into romantic folklore. American outlaws took advantage of long, unprotected railroads on the frontier transporting people, money, and goods. Among the best known were Sam Bass, Butch Cassidy and the Sundance Kid, the Dalton Gang, and Jesse James.

THE JESSE JAMES GANG
Tiring of raiding banks, the James Gang decided to turn to robbing trains. On July 21, 1873, the gang robbed a train on the Chicago, Rock Island & Pacific Railroad at Adair, Iowa, having learned that a large consignment of gold was to be on board. They derailed the train, killing the driver,

THE RAILROADS *began to offer rewards for the capture of outlaws such as Jesse James (above).*

but the treasure was not there. In frustration they robbed the occupants. Now train crews and passengers alike were concerned for their safety.

On January 31, 1874, one of the most famous train robberies occurred on the St. Louis, Iron Mountain & Southern Railroad mainline north of Piedmont, Missouri. The James Gang planned to hold up the train to kill detective Allan Pinkerton, who had been hired to apprehend or kill James. The masked marauders arrived at Gads Hill Station and herded passengers and the station manager into a storeroom. Having stopped the train by altering the signals, the bandits robbed the passengers on board. Pinkerton, however, was not among

them. Despite having a price on his head, James retired from crime in 1881, moving to St. Joseph, Missouri, under an assumed name.

ROBBERIES IN FILM
These stories provided good material for fledgling movie companies. One of the most famous early films is *The Great Train Robbery*, made in 1903 by director Edwin S. Porter. It contains many of the elements of the classic hold-up story: a daring robbery involving violence and death, a posse being hastily formed, plus the final flight and showdown in the woods.

The original—and most audacious—great train robbery took place in England in 1855. A dapper gentleman

THE ORIENT-EXPRESS

The famous *Orient-Express*, the train favored by aristocrats that began running between Paris and Turkey through central Europe in 1883, was also a favorite of smugglers. The lure of a reliable route for the 1,700 miles (2,737 km) between Istanbul, Turkey, and Western Europe saw a steady trade in hashish, fine art, and doubtless much more.

The train was also the scene of a crime that never actually happened. In Agatha Christie's book *Murder on the Orient Express*, murder is committed on the train while it is stuck in a snowdrift. Hero detective Hercule Poirot, played by Albert Finney (above) in the 1974 film of the best-selling classic, unraveled the mystery.

THE WILD BUNCH *poses for a portrait in 1900 (above). Seated left to right are Harry Longabaugh (Sundance Kid), Ben Kilpatrick (Tall Texan), and Robert LeRoy Parker (Butch Cassidy); standing are Bill Carver and Harvey Logan (Kid Curry). Train-robber Ronald Biggs (right), lived in Brazil for 30 years until his return to Britain and jail in 2001.*

thief, Edward Pierce, set his sights on a consignment of gold en route from London to the Crimea. He gained access to the bullion van by hiding an accomplice in a coffin.

Pierce's mistress turned informer, however. He was tried and sentenced to death by hanging, but in a final twist he escaped, never to be recaptured. The story was fictionalized by the novelist Michael Crichton, also as *The Great Train Robbery*, in 1975. In 1979 it was made into a film starring Sean Connery.

MODERN CRIMES

Yet more was to come. On August 8, 1963, an armed gang daringly stole £2,600,000 ($50 million in today's values) from the Glasgow–London Royal Mail train. Bruce Reynolds, a known armed robber, led the gang of 15 men, assisted by two accomplices.

They stopped the train by obscuring a green signal and turning another to red using batteries. During the robbery the driver was beaten, suffering serious head injuries. The gang then took their hoard by trucks to a farmhouse.

The police were soon on the trail, and found all of the gang members, of whom 12 were convicted and jailed.

One, Ronald Biggs, escaped in 1965 and fled first to Paris, then to Australia and on to Brazil, where he remained until he was convinced to return to Britain in 2001.

Today, railway crime takes some interesting forms. In 1999, 51 people were arrested on charges of hacking into a Chinese railway's computer system. Cheap tickets had been purchased and, by tampering with the reservation computer, upgraded to more expensive express train tickets.

A man who has never gone to school may steal from a freight car; but if he has a university education, he may steal the whole railroad.

THEODORE ROOSEVELT
(1858–1919), 26th President
of the United States of America

Above all, the railways were an instrument of liberation, a breaking of the customary bonds of the past.

The Victorian Railway,
PROFESSOR JACK SIMMONS (1915–2000),
British historian and author

RAILROADS *in the* AMERICAN CIVIL WAR

Military control of America's railroads, which could move

troops and supplies quickly, proved a decisive weapon.

The war between the states—the Civil War —is often cited as the first great railroad war. It is a fair judgment, though trains had earlier played small roles in the Mexican and Crimean Wars. The North's railroad superiority was a significant factor in its eventual victory. And there was to be a further outcome, as the Civil War had a major impact on the subsequent expansion of the railroads in America—and, particularly, on the transcontinental railway reaching the West Coast.

UNION GENERAL JOHN POPE'S ARMY *destroyed locomotives and track during their retreat after the Bull Run Campaign. This train was wrecked in Virginia in 1862.*

THE CONTROL FACTOR

When Confederate forces fired on Fort Sumter in April 1861, beginning the war, the railroads of the North were stronger than they had ever been. By then they completely dominated the region's transportation scene.

The Depression of the late 1850s had slowed route expansion, but this had the salutary effect of redirecting energies to consolidation and improvement of existing lines and operations. Though there were still multiple gauges in use, the vast majority of the Northern railroads were of standard gauge. In the South more lines than not were 5-foot gauge, complicating the interchange between the states. Many Northern railroads also had grown into trunk lines that ran over considerable distances.

The industrialized North, not the agrarian South, had the lion's share of the manufacturing of locomotives, cars, and rails. Southern railroads had preferred British over American rails, and the Northern blockade of shipping cut off this supply. Compounding this, Tredegar Iron Works in Richmond, the South's major locomotive builder, had switched to manufacturing armaments at the war's inception. The result was that rail mileage and the vital supply of rolling stock and locomotives were hugely disproportionate in favor of the North.

By far the most famous railroading story to come out of the Civil War is that of the Andrews Raid in April 1862, often called "the great loco-

motive chase." The subject of two movies, this piece of Southern lore recounts how a group of disguised Yankees stole a train at Big Shanty, Georgia, on the Western & Atlantic, planning to steam on to Chattanooga, destroying the railroad behind them as they went. The locomotive they commandeered was a 4-4-0 named *The General*. The raid was foiled when the Confederates took chase with another locomotive, *Texas*. Both of these engines, built in Paterson, New Jersey, have been preserved—*The General* at Kennesaw (formerly Big Shanty) and *Texas* at the Cyclorama Building, Atlanta.

Both sides benefited, at different times, from the railroad's ability to transfer troops and supplies rapidly from one theater of war to another, with the South holding the advantage early in the war. General Bragg moved his Army of Tennessee by rail to Chattanooga and claimed victory there. Later, troop movement by rail played its part in victory at the Battle of Chickamauga. But the Union ultimately made the better use of the railroads. It formed the United States Military Railways (largely composed of routes that Union troops had captured) under the direction of Daniel C. McCallum, the former superintendent of the Erie Railroad. McCallum ultimately rose to the rank of general. Also in the field was Herman Haupt, a man skilled at bridge building and other railroading arts.

Getting there firstest

with the mostest.

Attributed to an American Civil War general who knew the value of the railroads.

The Civil War devastated the railroads of the South, with bridges destroyed, rails irrevocably twisted, and crossties burned, and it took as many as five years after peace had been restored for some to be rehabilitated. On a national level, however, the war gave railroading a great boost and launched the industry into its greatest years.

Such Northern railroads as the Erie and Pennsylvania

prospered greatly as a result of wartime traffic. At the height of demand, Paterson, New Jersey, with three locomotive builders, was producing a locomotive every working day. The war pushed railroads into conversion from iron to steel rail, and from wood to coal as locomotive fuel.

ACROSS A CONTINENT

The Civil War was also the cornerstone on which the great transcontinental railway was built. The engineers and foremen who led the project had learned or bettered their skills in the war. The laborers who laid tracks were, in many instances, men used to taking orders in the army—and who were looking for work when the war ended. The cohesive sense of purpose that had won the war was responsible for the completion of that epic railroad, among the greatest American accomplishments of the 19th century.

THIS RAILROAD YARD *at Manassas, Virginia (below), was devastated by Confederate General Stonewall Jackson's troops. Confederate shells were blamed for damage to the Fred Leach (left).*

RAILWAYS *in* WORLD WAR I

The Great War in Europe saw rail transporting troops and supplies.

Warring countries built lines as part of their battle strategies.

The lessons of the American Civil War were not lost on army planners on the other side of the Atlantic, as Prussia showed in its successful war against France in 1870 to 1871. Prussia then, and the German Empire after 1871, treated the railways as a military asset. They built lines to frontiers for strategic reasons, on routes approved by the military, with high-ranking officers assigned to rail transport roles. When war broke out, the railways enabled the Prussians to assemble 384,000 men at the border in less than two weeks and effectively defeat the less-organized French army. The Prussians then used the French railways to reach Paris, and besieged it into submission.

Over the next four decades Germany, France, Austria, and Russia were in a railway race, each building new lines as much to military require-

ments as for peacetime needs. By 1914 Germany, with potentially hostile powers on either side, controlled a net-work of strategic railways in East Prussia, as well as 13 double-tracked mainlines to its western frontier. Russia and Germany also understood the value of standardization—the Prussian State Railway built

RAILWAY WAGONS *were adapted as armored vehicles, such as these German cars mounted with machine guns.*

more than 3,500 of one type of 4-6-0 passenger locomotive, and Russia had 8,000 standard 0-8-0 freight engines, which were used by most railways. French railway companies, characteristically, were individualists, making coordination far more difficult when war came.

Each country had its own deployment plan, based on railways, to be triggered in the event of war. In August 1914 most of these strategies worked smoothly, although the Nord Railway of France quickly lost large numbers of trains to the German advance. But, while the war dragged on,

REBUILT TRACKS *often took the most direct route, even through buildings, to get troops to the front.*

LONG-RANGE, HEAVYWEIGHT GUNS *on rail chassis were used by both sides in the war. The Germans used the notorious rail-mounted* Big Bertha *to shell Paris from 60 miles (100 km) away. Here German artillerymen prepare to fire a 280 mm cannon.*

the colossal consumption of supplies and munitions, and constant movement of troops and armed forces personnel, put an enormous burden on the railways. About 200,000 tons (204,000 t) of freight, mostly ammunition, needed to be delivered to the British army alone each week at the peak of the war. Rail tracks were constantly extended to keep up with the movement of the front lines, and steel rails had to be shipped to France from Britain, Canada, and even from Australia.

Outside Europe

Since the battlefields of World War I were in continental Europe, Britain's railways were shielded from the direct impact of war (apart from the first startling experience of air raids). But Britain still faced an immense transportation task. The government assumed control of private railway companies, for the first time operating as a 20,000-mile (32,000 km) national system. This was successful—one company alone was calculated to have transported more than 20 million men in the four years of war—but the price was high in terms of deferred maintenance and worn-out engines and rolling stock.

In America, President Wilson took a similar step at the end of 1917, when the railroads were struggling to handle the wartime traffic. The government created the United States Railroad Administration to exercise control. It reduced restrictive practices, cut unproductive train mileage, addressed wagon shortages, and adopted standard locomotive and rolling stock designs. Not for the last time in that century, the railroads rose to the wartime challenge.

GETTING TO THE FRONT

In the terrible deadlock of trench warfare, both sides made great use of narrow-gauge light railroads to transport men, supplies, and munitions between standard-gauge railheads and the front. The lightweight tracks were of 600-millimeter gauge (1 foot 11½ inches), and the little trains were operated by army engineers in appalling conditions, usually at night and often under shellfire. By 1918 a network of more than 800 miles (nearly 1,300 km) had spread throughout the fighting areas; 125,000 men were engaged upon it on the Allied side alone. The typical German Feldbahn locomotive (left) was an 0-8-0T. British and American builders produced great numbers of 4-6-0Ts and 2-6-2Ts, and gasoline-engined locomotives were also used. Many of these locomotives passed into industrial use after the war ended, some as far from the grim battlefields of Europe as the sugarcane tramways of Australia and India.

AMERICAN RAILROADS *in the* GREAT DEPRESSION

The Depression took its toll on the railways but also gave birth

to the design innovation of streamlining and established an American icon.

Since they first became a significant factor in American life in the mid-19th century, railroads have both reflected and affected the country's economic condition. Never was this more apparent than during the Great Depression, the protracted period of economic stagnation and devastating unemployment that followed the Wall Street stock market crash of October 24, 1929—"Black Thursday."

A 1935 POSTER *representing the Roman god Mercury delivers the message that express trains mean speed, to promote rail travel during the Depression.*

COMPETITION BEGINS

During the decade leading up to the crash, the nation's railroads were still in their heyday, though they had begun to feel the impact of highway competition. During the "Roaring Twenties" the American railroads had largely recovered from the stresses World War I had placed on them, and from management constraints that flowed from their control by the U.S. Railroad Administration.

However, though passenger travel and freight shipment by train remained the norm, the winds of change were already blowing. The very prosperity of the 1920s, which had bolstered the railways and made possible their postwar recovery, had actually been kinder to the competition. With money plentiful, private ownership of automobiles soared, and the federal gov-ernment was by then solidly in the highway-building mode. The railroad industry had stood by naively—even supportively—as highways were constructed that would allow trucks as well as automobiles to eat into railway passenger miles and freight tonnage. For a time railroads actively assisted road building on the misguided premise that trucks would be a valuable feeder of freight to the rails, not a serious competitor for long-haul business.

THE EMERGENCY ACT

While competition from roads and the fledgling airlines was initially muted by general prosperity, they intensified the negative impact of the Depression, which by 1932 had left 13 million Americans, roughly a quarter of the workforce, unemployed. Railroad statistics echoed these numbers. From 1930 railroad passenger service recorded annual losses. Rail revenues in general dropped to pre-1915 levels, and from 1932 to 1934 the industry ran net deficits.

These conditions led the Interstate Commerce Commission to recommend and Congress to pass, in 1933, the Emergency Railroad Transportation Act, which created a Federal Coordinator of Transportation. During the three-year term of the Act, he was to oversee the elimination of redundant services and facilities and generally reduce expenses—a mission that was largely a failure. Rail management remained skeptical (and thus generally uncooperative) and a key provision of the Act, that rail employment could not be reduced, was hugely limiting.

THE HOBO: AN AMERICAN ICON

Among the most persistent images to emerge from the Depression is that of the hobo, bindle stick over his shoulder, waiting in a railroad yard to hop a freight train (top). It is, at heart, a romantic concept: the independent wanderer answerable to no one but himself (or herself, as some women also rode the rails). The staying power of this American icon is underlined by the existence today of a National Hobo Association.

Hobos, essentially migrant workers using freight trains for free, if illegal, transportation (not to be confused with tramps or bums, who didn't work), existed long before the Depression, of course, but the hard times of that era hugely expanded their population. In 1934, the U.S. Bureau of Transient Affairs put their number at 1.5 million; other estimates easily doubled that.

The reality of life in the often violent "hobo jungles," or camps was, no doubt, more harsh than romantic. Hopping freights was physically dangerous, even in the days when empty boxcars ("side-door Pullmans") were easily found. Railroad "bulls" (detectives) were always on the prowl to send those caught on their way (right), and train crews were often unfriendly. Still, the unfettered freedom of the hobo is a peculiarly American ideal.

For all the stresses that the Depression placed on railroading in America, it actually was not without its long-term benefits, forcing the railroads to move in some constructive directions more rapidly than they might have otherwise done. Certainly the passenger train, buffeted mightily by the decline in travel caused by the Depression and the growing attraction of motoring, was among the beneficiaries as the railroads sought ways to restore its cachet. The primary tool was streamlining, an aesthetic as well as practical innovation promoted by new professionals called industrial designers.

In 1934 the Union Pacific introduced its M–10000, the *Streamliner,* later named *City of Salina,* and the Chicago, Burlington & Quincy brought out its *Zephyr.* Both were lightweight streamliners. Before the decade was over railroads across the country had rolled out their own versions of these forward-

looking trains. While drab Pullman-Green "heavy-weight" conventional cars hauled by black steam locomotives seemed hopelessly passé to the public, no match for the silvery sleekness of airplanes or the liberating independence of the automobile, colorful streamliners, often pulled by new-fangled diesel locomotives, spoke of speed and a better future.

THE ROLE OF DIESELS

The diesels themselves were an important innovation that gathered momentum during the Depression. Steam locomotives lingered through the

1950s, but the ability of the diesel to dramatically cut operating costs, demonstrated most flamboyantly by some of the early locomotive designs, helped the railroads survive the Depression.

Though the Depression saw railway mileage reduce dramatically (and railway employment even more so), the industry was no doubt toughened by adversity and forced to be more efficient. All too soon this toughness and efficiency were severely tested, however, as America's railroads were asked to meet the unprecedented demands of World War II.

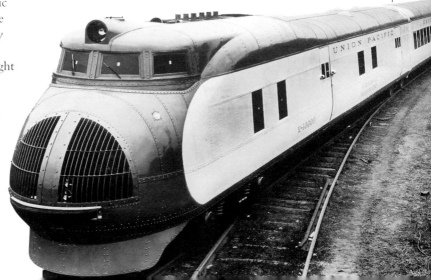

CITY OF SALINA, *an aluminum-alloy streamliner, was built in 1934.*

EUROPE *between the* WARS

Challenges to rail's future between the two World Wars resulted in government intervention and technical advancements.

Physical damage to Europe's railways in World War I was not extensive, except in northeast France, Belgium, and western Russia. Many railways were rundown, however, and Germany was required to give up 5,000 locomotives as war reparation. More significantly, the 1920s was the decade in which railway managers met real competition from road transport for the first time, as army-trained drivers and mechanics came home and went into the haulage business, some with great success.

RAIL'S RESPONSE

After the war, rail's share of freight traffic, high-value freight in particular, began to fall in almost every country. The problems were compounded by the Great Depression in the 1930s. Some governments, notably those of Germany and France, tried to protect their railway revenues by regulating road transport to limit its growth. Elsewhere, railway companies bought out truckers with the aim of developing coordinated services—most of which ultimately worked more in favor of road than rail. All faced a huge challenge to make rail services, passenger as well as freight, more competitive. A consequence of the commercial pressure was the increase in government control of European rail.

Germany's new constitution nationalized its railways as Deutsche Reichsbahn (DR) in 1919. In 1924 Austria completed the nationalization of its system, and Belgium formed Belgian National Railways (SNCB) in 1926. The French mainline companies sank heavily into debt during the Depression and were taken over by the state in 1938, creating the Société Nationale des Chemins de Fer (SNCF).

During the war, the British public had seen how well a unified, centrally controlled system could work and there were calls for full nationalization there too. The outcome, however, was a compromise, with the formation of four new railway companies on January 1, 1923. Each was given essentially a territorial monopoly but also inherited many inefficiencies.

TECHNICAL ADVANCES

Against this unpromising background, European railways nevertheless made substantial achievements in the 20 years before the next war. Much freight traffic in the 1920s was still highly labor intensive until the railways invested in mechanized handling devices. The first demountable containers appeared, to handle anything

DUCHESS OF GLOUCESTER *was a Princess Coronation Class locomotive built in 1937 for the high-speed service from London to Scotland.*

MUSSOLINI'S MILANO CENTRALE *station at Milan, Italy, was a product of the 1930s.*

from furniture to fish. Marshaling yards, which were traditionally bottlenecks in the rail freight business, began to be automated in order to keep the freight trains moving.

Electric traction had been technically feasible before 1914, but now became more widespread. London, Berlin, Paris, Budapest, and Moscow were among the cities that greatly expanded their electrified suburban railways in the years between the wars, while the first mainline electrification schemes took shape in France and Italy; the latter had the greatest electrified mileage in the world in 1939. By the end of the 1930s mountainous Switzerland was well on its way to total electrification.

In Europe the diesel engine made its mark in lightweight passenger railcars. Germany's *Flying Hamburger* made the headlines in 1933 with its 100-mile-per-hour (160 km/h) speed record, and its successors took Germany to the top of the European speed tables. By 1938 some 650 railcars were in use in France (including rubber-tired cars and the stylish Bugatti streamliners), and Denmark had fast *Lyntog* (Lightning) diesel-electrics running on all main routes.

But, above all, the 1930s are remembered as the peak of steam locomotive development in Europe. Power outputs were revolutionized by the work of French engineer André Chapelon. Applying his principles, British designers such as Nigel Gresley of the London & North Eastern Railway and William A. Stanier of the London, Midland & Scottish set out to show that steam could outperform the diesel trains then available. The result was the *Silver Jubilee*, *Coronation*, and *Coronation Scot* streamlined trains and, ultimately, the 126-mile-per-hour (203 km/h) world speed record for steam achieved by Gresley's *Mallard*.

In a Europe that had just emerged from the Depression, such trains were not only commercially successful but a public relations triumph, too.

LUXURY IN THE FACE OF ADVERSITY

Challenging the Depression, the *Golden Arrow* was introduced in 1929 as the British link in a luxury service between London and Paris. It was joined in 1936 by the *Night Ferry*, whose blue and gold Wagons-Lits sleeping cars crossed the English Channel aboard ship, thus conveying their passengers in comfort for the entire journey between the British and French capitals.

RAILWAYS *in* WORLD WAR II

IN WAR AND PEACE
WE SERVE

GWR · LMS ⊠ LNER · SR

During the conflict railways once again played a vital role, shifting troops, supplies, and evacuees.

The colossal burden of war fell again on the world's railways on September 3, 1939. At least the Allies were better prepared than in 1914. On the first weekend of the war, Britain's railways ran 1,577 special trains to evacuate more than 600,000 children from London in anticipation of air attacks. In France the railways handled mobilization equally smoothly and efficiently.

Railways were not to be the dominant factor they had been in World War I, largely because the conflict in World War II was far more mobile. But some campaigns would have been very different without the railways. Converting broad-gauge Russian mainlines to standard gauge was the key to the German invasion of Russia, because the Germans could keep their armies supplied. British and American army engineers ran

supplies to Russia through the perilous mountains of northern Iran. A fragile line along the North African coast supported the advancing Allied armies in 1942, while Japanese troops depended on the railways for their supplies in the jungles of Thailand and Burma. In the United States, the railroads had unprecedented freight and passenger traffic volumes.

IS YOUR JOURNEY REALLY NECESSARY?

In Britain the railways again came under government control. Passenger services were decelerated and civilian travel was discouraged. Contingency plans, improvization, and flexibility were a feature of service as was demonstrated in May 1940 when the Southern Railway transported 225,000 troops of the British Expeditionary Force rescued from the beaches of Dunkirk.

An immense build-up of freight traffic continued for

the duration of the war despite disruptions from air bombardment in 1940 and 1941 and the German rocket attacks three years later. In 1943, in the lead-up to the invasion of Europe, freight haulage was 46 percent higher than in the year before the war.

The United States Office of Defense Transportation coordinated the movement of 50 percent more freight during each of the war years than in 1918, despite having many fewer locomotives and employees. The task began with the movement of supplies to the East Coast in 1940; after Pearl Harbor the flow was reversed, with massive loads of men and materials traveling west. Extraordinary efforts were made to meet such challenges. Centralized Traffic Control was installed to prevent bottlenecks along hundreds of miles of transcontinental mainline. New locomotives were rushed into

BRITAIN'S RAILWAYS *proudly proclaimed their war effort in posters (above), which included the evacuation of children from London to the safety of the countryside (right).*

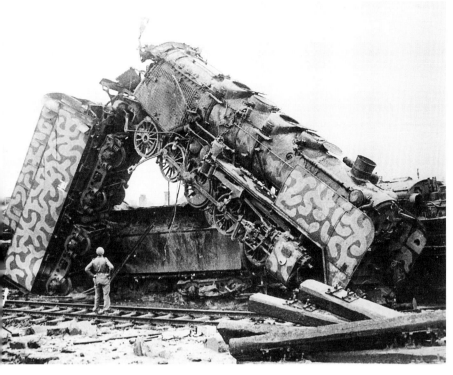

GERMAN TRAINS
*were attacked by
Allied "train-
busters." This
locomotive was
found by Allied
forces entering
Münster in 1945
(left). Adolf Hitler
traveled on his own
"Führer Train"
(below left). Fully
equipped hospital
trains traveled
thousands of miles
during the war,
carrying wounded
soldiers from the
front lines (below).*

service, most spectacularly Union Pacific's gigantic Big Boys. These could wheel 3,000-ton (3,060 t) refrigerated fruit expresses (the famous Californian "Vitamin C" trains) at close to passenger train speeds.

To cope with the movement of many thousands of personnel, sometimes from coast to coast, the Pullman Standard Car Company built special "troop sleepers." Trains of 20 or more such sleepers carried up to 39 GIs in each, with regular Pullman porters providing service.

American locomotive builders produced thousands of steam and diesel engines for export to Europe and the Far East during the war. The standard-gauge lines of Europe received the United States Army Transportation Corps' S160 Class 2-8-0, while a versatile meter-gauge 2-8-2 locomotive known as the "MacArthur" went to the Far East, Africa, and India.

THE DESTRUCTION OF VITAL LINES

In the war zones railways were always prime targets. The steam locomotive, with its trailing smoke by day and firebox glow by night was vulnerable to warplane attack, but in fact railways were hard to put out of action. Plain track damaged by bombs was easily repaired, and marshaling yards could be quickly back in business unless the bombers destroyed complex switching layouts or control centers.

In continental Europe, air forces and resistance fighters attacked bridges, viaducts, and tunnels, but engineers were quick to restore the damage or bypass the ruins. It was only the overwhelming force directed at the railways of northern France and the key German rail centers that decisively destroyed those vital lines of communication.

RAILWAYS *in* CHINA

Time and again, China's railway development has been thwarted; today, things have never looked better.

LOCOMOTIVE CREW *at Mukden (Shenyang), which has always been an important center for China's railways.*

Railways came to China very late; early attempts by the British had been resisted on the grounds that the railways were a tool of colonial powers. The first permanent line opened in 1881 and coincided with the 100th anniversary of George Stephenson's birth. The first locomotive was given the nickname "Rocket of China" by British engineers.

The development of China's railways took place spasmodically. Concessions were granted to a number of foreign powers, including Russia, Britain, Belgium, and France. By 1903 Vladivostok, at the eastern end of Russia's Trans-Siberian route, was linked with Harbin, Mukden (Shenyang), and the strategic Port Arthur (Dalian) on the Yellow Sea coast. These

concessions, along with railways built by the Chinese government, formed the outline of a national network, but by 1912 only 6,000 miles (9,650 km) had been built, a very low figure in such a huge country. The establishment of a new republican government in that year brought plans for a nationwide railway system. The revolutionary leader Sun Yat-Sen envisaged a state-run network of 100,000 miles (161,000 km), with links into central Asia and Europe.

This grand vision was thwarted by the Chinese Civil War. By the mid-1930s a mere 10,000 miles (16,100 km) of railway was in operation, much of it in the east and in the Japanese-controlled region of Manchuria. The Sino-Japanese war of 1937 inflicted further damage on China's

railways. In 1945, at the end of the war, barely 1,000 miles (1,610 km) of railway were operable, when the United States, roughly the same size as China, had more than 200,000 miles (322,000 km) of active railroad routes.

REBUILDING BEGINS

The absence of a properly functioning railway network was a serious impediment to China's progress. Massive aid came from United Nations Relief & Rehabilitation, including steel rails and locomotives. Again, plans were drawn up for a national system. Again, they did not get beyond the drawing board. In 1946 civil war broke out and more destruction followed.

However, since the time that the fighting ended, in 1949, China has been avidly making up for lost time. Great progress was made, initially with Russian support. New lines were built and existing ones upgraded. This involved many spectacular engineering feats, in the form of massive cuttings, long tunnels, high fills, and soaring bridges.

China's railways have a distinct American character. They were derived largely

BRITISH MANUFACTURER, *the North British Locomotive Company of Glasgow, exported this steam locomotive being unloaded at a Chinese dock.*

CHINA RAILWAYS *diesel-electrics head a freight train over the Changchun-to-Jillin line in 1993.*

from Japan and Russia, whose railways were themselves American oriented.

Until the 1990s, there was a policy of steam continuing as the principal form of locomotive power, with some 10,000 active steam engines. But in the last few decades no country has developed its railways with the commitment that China has shown.

EYES TO THE FUTURE
China is the world's third largest country, after Russia and Canada, in terms of land mass, and the largest in terms

of population. When the People's Republic of China was established in 1949, it had only 13,544 miles (21,800 km) of railways. But whatever difficulties China Railways (CR) may have had in the past, rail investment is now at an all-time high. A $32 billion plan covering the period 1998 to the end of 2002 represented five times the funds invested between 1993 and 1997.

By 2000 CR was operating trains over 36,000 route miles (nearly 58,000 km), and the expansion continues. There are plans to add 6,830 miles

(11,000 km) of additional track. More than a quarter of the railway has now been electrified and work is being accelerated on international rail corridors to central Asia and Europe, with top priority given to a line on the historic "Silk Road" route through Kyrgyzstan into Uzbekistan and Kazakhstan. No other country is building or electrifying railroads on this scale.

Among the many exciting projects is the electrification of the 589-mile (948 km) Harbin–Dalian line through the industrialized region of Manchuria. Equally thrilling is a proposed high-speed line between Beijing and Shanghai, and work began in 2000 on a new east–west trunk route.

Tilt–train technology is high on the agenda, and all principal routes are planned to offer high-speed passenger services, using locally built diesel and electric locomotives and multiple-unit trains.

A STANDARD SY CLASS MIKADO *2-8-2, some 1,750 of which were in service, worked at the vast open-cut coal mine at Manzhouli in northeastern China.*

DEVELOPMENT *in* INDIA *and* PAKISTAN

Founded in imperialism, today the subcontinent's rail networks are modern and expanding. Founded in

The British Raj introduced many things to India, but possibly none was more beneficial than the railway. Under British rule the entire subcontinent was linked by an intricate network of railways that embraced four gauges: 5 feet 6 inches, meter, 2 feet 6 inches, and 2 feet.

The railway provided an important infrastructure and a foundation that was to help both India and Pakistan in their efforts to modernize and unify their respective nations. The subcontinent's railways mirrored Great Britain's, at least up until World War II. What was good for Britain was also considered good for the British Empire.

The subcontinent's first railway opened in 1853, many years after those in Europe and America. This vast region extended from Afghanistan in the west to Thailand and China in the east, and from the Himalayan range and Kashmir in the north to the tropical Indian Ocean and Ceylon (now Sri Lanka) in the south. All types of physical terrain were embraced, while the sparsely populated rural areas contrasted with crowded towns and cities. Before the railway networks, the slow, creaking ox cart was the main form of transport; proper roads were non-existent and systems of communication poor.

BUILDING THE LINES

The building of the first Indian railways is a tribute to the aspirations of Victorian Britain. To vest a distant land with such superb technology, prevailing over every obstacle that nature could throw in the way, is the stuff of legend. By 1870 more than 5,000 miles (8,000 km) of railway had been opened. Development was then rapid.

The many engineering feats included the Bolan line in the far west, which climbs to 5,874 feet (1,792 m) above sea level. In other areas of vast

IN STEAM DAYS *the pride of Indian railroaders showed in highly decorated locomotives such as this WP Class 4-6-2.*

plains and deserts, the railway was laid level and straight for miles on end. Mighty rivers were spanned by imposing viaducts, some up to 2 miles (3 km) long. During torrential monsoonal rains, rivers could change their course and wash away sections of the railway; these were rebuilt. There were tunnels 2½ miles (4 km) long and adhesion-worked gradients of 1 in 25.

The railways established lines of communication for trade and development, as well as providing the British with a means of moving troops to areas of strategic importance to control the local population and to put down uprisings—the great Indian Mutiny of 1857 underscored this. Railways were invaluable for moving food to areas where drought and famine occurred. As the writer Paul Theroux has stated, "The railway was the bloodstream of India."

As in Britain, a number of celebrated railway companies evolved, including the Great Indian Peninsular Railway, the East Indian Railway, the Madras and Southern Mahratta

CROSSING INDIA'S WATERWAYS *required long bridges and viaducts, such as that over the Godravi River in Andhra Pradesh (above). A modern diesel locomotive pulls out of a suburban station in India (left). Mumbai (formerly Bombay) Railway Station epitomizes the grandeur of the Raj (below).*

Railway, and the Bengal and Nagpur, among many others. State ownership began during the 1920s and, after independence and partition in 1947, the entire system came under government control in both India and the newly formed Pakistan. At this time the total mileage was 43,000 miles (69,230 km) of track.

MODERN NETWORKS

The capital outlay in building India's railways had all been repaid by the time of partition, and India and Pakistan took over the property free of cost. But British personnel continued to play a leading role in railway operations.

A strong railway culture developed with a powerful sense of unity, dedication, and pride of service—as it had done when the great British companies ran the railways.

As the 20th century drew to its close, Indian railways each day ran 11,000 trains, over a distance of more than 633,000 miles (1.2 million km), which is equivalent to three and a half times the distance to the Moon. The railways are still the main form of transport in India and Pakistan and, in their 150 years of evolution, have grown into modern networks. India alone now has more than 38,500 miles of railway track (62,000 km) and 7,000 stations. Every day the railway carries more than 10 million passengers and a million tons of freight.

Conversion of many of the meter-gauge lines to 5 feet 6 inches is well under way. In

spite of India being romantically associated with steam trains, electrification began in 1925. Today the seven trunk routes that connect Mumbai (formerly Bombay), Calcutta, New Delhi, and Madras are all electrified, with lengthy stretches cleared for 100-mile-per-hour (160 km/h) running. Steam operation ceased on the mainline network in 2000.

India's rich railway heritage is preserved in the National Railway Museum in New Delhi. It is one of the finest railway museums in the world, its creation fittingly inspired by British engineer Mike Satow.

RAILROADS *in* AFRICA

Built by Europe's colonial powers, much of Africa's once-extensive rail network is now gone, with some notable exceptions.

Colonial administrations, in the main, developed Africa's railroads, with strategy dictated by local need, either for military purposes or in order to exploit mineral resources. There was no basis for a pan-African overview. The gauges varied, 83 percent of the continent using smaller than standard gauge, usually 3 feet 6 inches, meter, or narrower.

COLONIAL BUILDERS
British engineers built the continent's first railway in 1854 between Cairo and Alexandria. As in many other parts of the world, Great Britain was to the fore in such areas as Egypt, Sudan, Gold Coast, Uganda, and South Africa. The coming of the railway actually created one nation, Kenya. The French

built superbly engineered standard-gauge systems in North Africa. In contrast, the Italians were active in Ethiopia, Somalia, and Libya, bequeathing lines that spiraled over the spectacularly rugged terrain. German interests held sway in Tanganyika (Tanzania), South West Africa, Cameroon, and Togoland. Belgium built in the Congo; while Portugal vested its colonies of Angola and Mozambique with valuable railway networks. In all, some 50,000 route miles (80,500 km) of railway served the continent.

Historically, Africa has had many highly efficient railway operations. Had they been treated as a high-priority investment during the post-colonial era and been extended with continental interests in mind, Africa

would today have a bedrock for economic wellbeing.

THE LOCOMOTIVES
During one and a half centuries some 13,000 steam locomotives were active on the African continent, toiling through deserts, jungles, and mountainous escarpments, and across savannahs teeming with wildlife. More than 20 African countries operated Beyer-Garratt locomotives. Their light axle loading and articulation proved ideal for the lightly laid lines that twisted their way through the rough undulating country.

BRITAIN BUILT THE FIRST *African railway. This line in Johannesburg, South Africa (left), was under construction in 1895. East Africa Railways operated this 2-8-2 (above) in the days of steam.*

DIESEL TRAINS *have taken over in Africa, as in many other areas of the world. Here, a diesel crosses a bridge on the mainline from Windhoek, Namibia, to South Africa.*

Here railroads were built to go over obstacles, rather than through them, in order to contain building costs in un-developed regions. Classics among the many Garratts were Kenya's 246-ton (250 t) meter-gauge "Mountains," which operated the 332-mile (535 km) line from Mombasa on the Indian Ocean to the Kenyan capital, Nairobi. Algeria even had a 75-mile-per-hour (120 km/h) express passenger version.

Most of the continent's railway systems have declined over the last 30 years. Rail-roads are, by very definition, capital intensive and prove difficult for emergent countries to maintain.

The road-based economies of Western countries have created the illusion that roads are essential, modern, and progressive. Road transport, however, offers only a quick-fix alternative. Though there has never been a shortage of ideas for potential extensions to the railway networks, they are hardly relevant when even the status quo cannot be adequately maintained.

Signs for the Future

One exception has been the building of the Tanzam Rail-way to connect the port of Dar es Salaam in Tanzania with the Zambian copper belts. An extension will join Malawi with southeastern Zambia for agricultural use.

But Africa's railway heyday died with the age of steam. Although extensive moderni-zation in the form of diesel traction has taken place, much of this new equipment is liable to have a short life due to its complexity and the need for expensive spares. Many of the continent's networks are but a ghost of their former selves—Zimbabwe, Sudan, Ghana, Kenya, and Uganda, to mention but a few—while damage and closure through civil wars have been all too common. Paradoxically, although most of the decline is through poor economic circumstances, South Africa, the economic high spot of the continent, has also decimated its once comprehensive rail-way network. Following the deregulation of freight opera-tions during 1980, heavy trucking became predominant, while buses took the long-distance passenger traffic. Many branchlines were then closed. However, the Richards Bay coal railway and Sishen-Saldanha iron ore systems remain as spectacular rail-roading operations.

At the start of the new century there were some signs that railways have a meaning-ful future in Africa. In 2000 the first direct investment in Africa by an American rail-road company was made, to run the Malawi rail system. Libya signed contracts for construction of a long-awaited rail link between its capital, Tripoli, and the border of Tunisia, and unveiled plans for a 1,850-mile (2,980 km) network. Swaziland launched a rail upgrading program and sought backing for a direct rail link to Johannesburg in South Africa. Mozambique was to reopen a line that had been closed for 17 years. And more will undoubtedly follow.

RAILWAYS *in* AUSTRALASIA

Australian and New Zealand railways today are progressive systems,

actively seeking freight business and running passenger schedules.

At least once every day a long freight train leaves Sydney on Australia's Pacific coast on a 2,430-mile (3,910 km) transcontinental journey to Perth, the capital of Western Australia, on the Indian Ocean. Rolling across the legendary Nullarbor ("treeless") Plain at 70 miles per hour (115 km/h), the train will usually be a mile or more long, carrying double-stacked containers or loaded truck trailers. It will maintain a coast-to-coast delivery schedule that would have been thought impossible not so long ago.

THE GAUGE QUESTION

Crossing Australia by train was not always so simple. In the early days Australia's scattered colonies were as independent in their approach to building railways as in most other things. What mattered in the 1850s was providing transport to open up the inland, rather than building railways to a common gauge to connect one colony with another. When the trans-continental link was finally completed in 1917, a journey from Cairns in Queensland to Perth in the west, freight or passenger, involved at least eight changes of train, running on three different track gauges—a marathon of about 4,100 miles (6,600 km) from the northeast of the continent to its southwest corner.

The gauge question bedevilled Australian railway operations for more than a century and to an extent it still does. Although all of the mainland state capitals have been connected by standard-gauge mainlines since the 1990s, many rural routes are still unconverted. Queensland remains a narrow-gauge state except for the short section of the Sydney–Brisbane mainline north of the border.

That has not stopped Queensland Rail (QR) from becoming one of Australia's most progressive systems. The key has been coal, which is freighted from open-cut mines in the state's interior on purpose-built lines, many of them electrified and able to carry 8,000-ton (8,160 t) trains. The proceeds of this traffic have funded a massive upgrading of QR's coastal mainline. Australia's first high-speed tilt trains now run on this line—electric between Brisbane and Rockhampton, and diesel north to Cairns.

PRIVATIZING THE LINES

State governments in the 1990s embraced privatization and either sold off their rail assets or installed "open access" regimes. New South Wales locomotives appeared on coal hauls in South Australia; private operators' liveries brightened grain trains in Victoria and container freight trains in Tasmania.

PILBARA IRON ORE in Western Australia is hauled by giant diesels.

AUSTRALIA'S FIRST *high-speed electric tilt train (below) runs between Brisbane and Rockhampton.*

CANE RAILWAYS

Visit coastal Queensland between July and November and there is a good chance you'll meet a different kind of freight train, smaller in scale but no less impressive than the heavyweights on the mainlines. It is sugar harvest time, when 23 sugar mills bring in the cane on private rail lines—2,500 miles (4,000 km) of them, and most are 2-foot gauge. Queensland's sugar mills were once home to a charming collection of vintage steam locomotives. Now many mills have 40-ton (41 t) diesel locomotives that haul cane in trains of 1,200 tons (1,224 t) from fields up to 75 miles (120 km) away. This converted ex-Queensland Rail DH locomotive (above) is operated by the Isis sugar mill in Childers.

The famous *Indian Pacific* and *Ghan* passenger trains have also passed to private operators. Ultimately, except in Queensland, it seems likely that the vital but perennially loss-making commuter networks of the state capital cities will stay under government control, but little else.

It is intended that private enterprise will join with government to build the new Alice Springs–Darwin railway in the Northern Territory, the biggest rail project on the continent in decades, across 930 miles (1,500 km). The new line will link the existing railway between Alice Springs and Adelaide to give a north–south route through Central Australia. This will also allow Darwin to be developed as a major freight port.

And in the northwest of Western Australia, in the dry and dusty Pilbara region, the greatest trains of them all are found. Here the railways carry iron ore from inland mines to the export terminals. They are American-style in everything but location, with state-of-the-art 6,000 horsepower diesel locomotives hauling trains that weigh up to 25,000 tons (25,500 t). The world's longest and heaviest train ran on the Mt. Newman ore railway in the Pilbara in 1996—10 locomotives moving 56,500 tons (57,630 t) of ore in a 540-wagon train that was almost 4 miles (6 km) long.

NEW ZEALAND RAIL

Across the Tasman in New Zealand, the trains are smaller but no less distinctive. After some false starts New Zealand opted for the narrow 3-foot-6-inch rail gauge to traverse its green but mountainous islands; its mainlines are mostly single track and often tortuous. Privatization reinvigorated rail operations in the 1990s. The railways reclaimed freight traffic lost to road and gained long-term contracts for coal haulage, and passenger trains in both the North and South Islands are rating well in the travel plans of tourists.

RAIL TRAVEL *is being revitalized in New Zealand where much fine scenery is accessible by train.*

THE DECLINE *of* STEAM

The world's love affair with the steam locomotive has been

a passionate one; today, however, steam power is all but spent.

The disappearance of steam traction was heralded in the 1940s and 1950s, when North America's railroads turned to diesel and, to a lesser extent, electric traction. Other Western countries followed suit, albeit at a more leisurely pace.

During the transition, many railway officials championed steam for its simplicity, cheapness of construction, ability to consume locally produced fuel, and availability in times of war. Even developed countries such as Britain continued to build mainline steam locomotives until as late as 1960.

But steam was becoming increasingly costly to run—largely on account of its being highly labor intensive—and laborers able and willing to tolerate the harsh working conditions were difficult to find. The relentless competition from road and air travel forced the railways to streamline their operations. Pollution was another decisive factor, with steam locomotives becoming widely regarded as survivors from the smokestack age. If the railways were to compete they had to be socially acceptable—modern, clean, and fast.

BEGINNING OF THE END
Throughout the industrialized world, anywhere that was anywhere had a steam railway, and in the early 1950s there were at least 150,000 active steam locomotives. By the year 2000 fewer than 4,000 remained, which indicates the massive revolution that has taken place, not just in motive power but also in modes of transport. Many railways have been closed as governments encouraged the development of roads and road traffic.

For the developing world, steam was ideal "intermediate technology," particularly as it could be kept running with a bare minimum of available resources, whereas diesel and electric trains demand more complex facilities. However, developing countries have followed the advanced nations and have begun to move away from steam. This trend has been exacerbated by the fact that, once the principal locomotive exporting countries switched their production lines to other forms of motive power, that was what they wished to sell.

It is a great tribute to the steam locomotive that it survived so long. After all, electric traction was a practical proposition a century ago. Electric locomotives were working on the City of London tube railway in 1890 and in Baltimore in the United States in 1894. And the Chief Mechanical Engineer of Britain's mighty London and North Western Railway, F. W. Webb, had claimed before 1900 that within 15 years Britain's West Coast mainline between London and Scotland would be electrified, with trains traveling at 100 miles per hour (160 km/h). This did not happen until 1966.

The first type of steam trains to disappear under modernization were the suburban passenger workings around the world's big cities. The frequent stops and starts, often with

BUILT IN 1919, *this Baldwin 0-4-0 ST locomotive survives in sugarmill service in Cuba.*

A MOBILE STEAM CRANE *coals up a 2-8-0 in Calcutta, 1981. The 1924 locomotive is no longer in service.*

heavy trains, favored electric or diesel traction, while the pollution in heavily built-up areas became a contentious issue which the railways had to address. The busiest main-lines, especially those over shorter distances, merited the cost of electrification, and steam was largely relegated to secondary lines, lesser freight trains, engineering works trains, and industrial service.

Steam trains ended regular mainline service in North America in the 1950s, in Britain in 1967, in Western Europe and Australia in the 1970s, and in South Africa and most of Eastern Europe in the 1980s.

END OF THE BEGINNING

As the 21st century dawned, steam vanished in India, so ending a one-and-a-half-century tradition that many believed would last forever. China was then by far the biggest user, with several thousand steam locomotives active. Building continued prolifically through the 1980s, then at an ever-decreasing pace in the 1990s. Once Chinese engineers convinced themselves that the steam engine could not be practically developed any further, the decision was taken to phase it out as quickly as possible.

Dwindling pockets of industrial steam are likely to survive around the world for some years to come. Thus the working life of the steam loco-motive as a form of motive power will have spanned more than two centuries. Its global influence could never have been imagined when Richard Trevithick built that first example at the Coalbrookdale Ironworks in Britain in 1804.

THE LAST GREAT STEAM MAINLINE

The journey from Shenyang to Harbin, in China, is 339 miles (546 km) through the heart of industrialized Manchuria. In the 1930s it was the route of the streamlined, air-conditioned *Asia Express*; in the 1980s and early 1990s it was famed among railfans as one of the world's last great steam-worked mainlines. Sujatan engine terminal at Shenyang (below) was home to more than 100 locomotives.

Changchun, the City of Eternal Spring, had another massive steam allocation and a workshop where steam locomotives were built and repaired (right). Harbin, where winter temperatures drop to -22°F (-30°C), echoed to steam working around the clock in vast marshaling

yards, the staccato exhaust beats of the switch engines punctuated by the booming voices of the yard controllers. To travel the line in steam days was to see a freight train flash by the window every few minutes, massive QJ 2-10-2 locomotives shunting wagons at wayside stations, and, if lucky, even a rare and handsome American-inspired Mikado 2-8-2 on heavy switching in a yard.

Today, the masts and wires of electrification have come to the Shenyang–Harbin line, but it will be remembered as one of the special scenes before steam's final demise.

GRAVEYARDS *of* HISTORY

Most relics of the steam age meet their fate

in a breaker's yard, but some are just left to rust.

THE BOSTON & MAINE RAILROAD
of Massachusetts abandoned this tower (above). A rail graveyard in Thessaloniki, Greece (below), includes 2-10-0s of Austrian Empire lineage and some of Major Marsh's S160s from World War II.

The steam age has left behind a legacy of rusting hulks. Many of these locomotives were originally set aside in railway yards as standbys. During the Cold War, for example, many thousands of steam trains were spread throughout Russia for use should there be a national emergency. Today, more than 30 years later, the locomotives are beyond repair.

Ultimately, many of the abandoned engines scattered around the world will be broken up for scrap, but a few survive intact, isolated and forgotten after the railway was demolished around them.

The brooding atmosphere of a locomotive graveyard can be positively haunting. Gone are the sulfurous smells of the locomotives' oily emanations and the noise of the pounding engines. As with graveyards of another kind, the silence is punctuated only by birdsong and the hum of insects. Not much changes except for the shadows and the seasons.

What a contrast to the breaker's yard, where the wrenching sound of tearing metal and the bitter stench of acetylene gas predominate. The timeless shadows of the graveyards dissolve into a frenzy of activity while huge piles of metal build up and are depleted in a constant state of flux. The different grades of metal will be resold, with piece after piece being dis-sected from the great beasts.

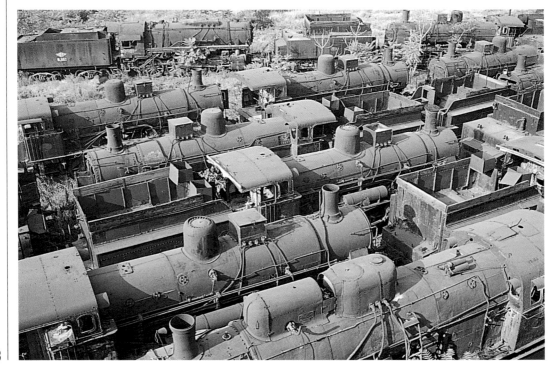

DISPLACED *in the early 1900s, locomotives from New York's elevated line were sold to an Alaskan railway and now lie derelict on the Arctic tundra (above).*

The old roar and knock

of the rails / Melts in

dull fury.

From "The Night Ride"
KENNETH SLESSOR (1901–1971),
Australian poet

THE END OF THE LINE *for one of Indian Railways' mighty XE 2-8-2s (above) as fire takes hold of it at Jamalpur Works. The metal is sorted and sold for scrap. A legacy of Britain's colonial rail building history (right). The remains of the* Prince of Wales, *a Ghana Railways 4-8-2, lie in a scrapyard.*

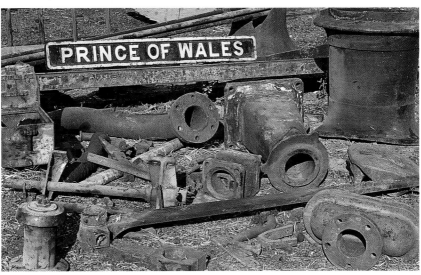

139

RAIL'S FUTURE ROLE

Railways can meet our transport needs with minimum effect on the environment; are they the key to our future wellbeing?

The impact of cars and heavy trucking was increasingly felt in Western countries from the 1960s onward, precipitating the closure of many branch and secondary railroads. The most dramatic closures took place in the United States, where the 210,000-mile (338,000 km) network of the 1930s had been reduced to around 100,000 miles (about 160,000 km) by the end of the 20th century.

Perhaps the most publicized example of the philosophy of abandoning railways was Great Britain's infamous 1960s Beeching Plan, under which more than half of the nation's rich railway infrastructure was shut down. Many felt the plan was ill-conceived, badly structured, and gave no thought at all to what would ultimately happen if everyone owned a car and all freight, in an ever-growing economy, was moved by road. Some of Beeching's actions have been redressed by the reopening of some branch lines, while mainlines, such as the Great Central and the Waverley Route in Scotland, are constantly reviewed for reopening. The massive amount of money that had to be spent on the road system, and its appalling environmental effects, never entered the Beeching equation. For all the money that has been spent, traffic congestion is still

an irredeemable scourge in Britain and, indeed, in all Western countries.

CLOSING THE LINES
The developing world seems irresistibly attracted to the ways of Western society—and transport is no exception. As recently as the mid-1980s, many of China's cities were virtually traffic-free; today, those cities are groaning under the strain of constant jams. This was also the case in neighboring India, where inadequate roads are packed with every conceivable type of vehicle, from bullock carts to juggernaut trucks. Nearby Pakistan has recently witnessed a program of railway closures. No one in India or China appears concerned for the day when each individual of those vast nations aspires to car

A SIGNAL BOX *stands redundant (above left), but Winslow Station (left) on the Oxford–Cambridge line in England may yet reopen.*

ownership. Sadly, the lessons of Western countries have still not been learned.

Until the fall of communism, the economies of Eastern European countries were rail-based, but in recent years these have also begun to fragment under freer economic policies. At the beginning of the 21st century Poland's rich railway network was under threat from a massive program of closures. Railway contraction has also occurred in many parts of Latin America, while in some developing nations the value of railroads is clearly not recognized; neglect comes all too easily. Paraguay's tracks lie moribund and Sierra Leone has abandoned its railways completely. Even the once-fabulous network in South Africa is today a shadow of its former self.

THE LONG TERM
The severing of a railway network inevitably weakens any section that remains. It isolates districts from railway connections, increasing the need for adequate road infra-

RUSH HOUR *in many cities around the world sees millions of cars take to the roads, but trains are a more efficient and less stressful form of transport.*

structure. And, in a road-based economy, the most prized developments are those adjacent to the motorways, thus rendering the railway increasingly irrelevant.

Such foreboding needs to be seen in perspective. The railway has made massive progress in high-tech passenger trains, which have proved more than a match for many airlines. At the same time, the clogged roads have drawn people back to the railroads; no longer are trains seen as unfashionable. Even Amtrak

in the United States carried a record 22 million passengers in 1999—a heartening contrast to the 1960s, when the end of long-distance rail passenger travel in America was widely predicted.

Railways are a very precise discipline, quite capable of fulfilling our transport needs in an ordered way. But the road lobby is powerful. Few politicians seem to understand railways—at worst they see them as a drain on the economy; at best they regard them as a relatively marginal

industry. A report in Britain's *Daily Telegraph* newspaper during a fuel crisis, when blockades closed most of the nation's gas stations, summed up an ideal, lost world that railways could well revive: "The capital has never seemed more beautiful; it was all but empty of cars but London was not asleep. All shops, libraries, restaurants, and clubs were open, all that was absent was the great curse that blights all modern cities: the traffic."

PRESENT MEETS PAST *(left) as an InterCity train passes model rail lovers. The Pendolino tilt train (above) is the face of the future. Its design allows increased speed on Italy's railways.*

Rumbling under blackened girders,
Midland bound for Cricklewood,
Puffed its sulphur to the sunset...

Parliament Hill Fields,
JOHN BETJEMAN (1906–1984), English poet

CHAPTER SIX

PRESERVATION *and* HOBBIES

THE FASCINATION *of* TRAINS

*From knowledgeable devotees to children waving at a passing
train, the magic of the railroads captures everyone's imagination.*

What is it about a train that has always turned heads, that has enchanted children, especially little boys, and captured the imagination of adults? What is it that has given myriad song-writers a perfectly syncopated subject, led generations of men to make small-town depots the gathering places of choice, and given rise to countless societies and publications for the seriously entranced, who call themselves "railfans" in North America, "enthusiasts" in the United Kingdom?

"Big things that move," is one answer, suggested by American columnist Don Phillips, who links trains with ships as the largest things built that are capable of motion, giving them a substantial majesty. An aura of majesty, and of motion too, attends the steam locomotive particularly, seen today largely only in preservation. But when one chugs past on a museum line or, more specially, races by at speed on a mainline

CHARTERED SPECIALS *in the 1950s visited countless lines before "rationalization" closed them forever. These enthusiasts, like many others, shared a passion for trains.*

excursion for fans, it's easy to see what has made countless small boys dream of becoming locomotive engineers.

OF STEAM AND DIESEL

The vitality of a steam loco-motive is palpable. It is a machine that appeals to many of the senses. There is the smell of steam, hot grease, and coal smoke; the sound of the whistle (so different in North America from the typically shriller shrieks of British and European steam) and the rhythmic beat of exhaust; plus the arresting image of flailing siderods, dancing valve

BRITISH TRAIN-SPOTTERS *treasured their lists of locomotive numbers and names.*

gear, and smoke boiling from the stack as the locomotive hustles by. Engineers of the steam era typically spoke of their locomotives as having souls and personalities, and the casual observer at track-side could sense some of that anthropomorphism. Who wouldn't be fascinated?

Diesel trains, although routinely disparaged by steam fans upon gaining ascendancy on the rails in the 1950s in the United States, and a decade later in Great Britain and Europe, have a commanding presence of their own. For those who grew up after the fall of steam, diesels are a main focus, with their own appeal to the senses. Certainly the first-generation units that took over from steam, now almost vanished themselves, are widely revered by fans. Diesels are the major presence

names as colorless and unromantic as CSX. Yet still Americans watch. They count the cars of mammoth freight trains at rail crossings, perhaps ruing the lack of the charismatic caboose—once the train's traditional punctuation. They cling to the idea of a national rail service in Amtrak, though relatively few actually ride its trains. They visit rail museums and tourist railroads and flock to trackside to see a passing steam excursion.

What is the hold? "Big things that move," is a good answer, but clearly not the only one. Certainly nostalgia plays a role, a yearning for a past when the pace was slower and machinery gave up its secrets less grudgingly than technology does today. For many people, it's far simpler to understand how a steam locomotive works than to decipher a computer program.

THE WORLD WATCHES

It is unsurprising that this worldwide fascination with trains is particularly strong in Britain, the birthplace of the railways, and in the United States and Canada. These countries embraced the railways with an unprecedented vigor and were literally built and given their current shapes by trains. But go to Australia, or South Africa, or Brazil, or Norway, or countless other countries and you'll find rail museums, steam excursions, train societies, and magazines —all there to serve those whose pulse quickens at the sound of a diesel horn or a steam whistle in the distance.

in *Trains Magazine,* the hobby's flagship publication, founded in Milwaukee in 1940 by A. C. Kalmbach. They are also well represented in a flood of books and videos about trains.

THE PUBLIC FIXATION

This fascination with trains goes well beyond the hobbyists who model, study, or photograph them. Even today, when railroads play a much smaller role in contemporary culture than they once did (a change less marked in Europe than the rest of the world), the public pays attention to news of trains, if only to lament their perceived decline.

It cannot be denied that, despite a substantial rebound in the health of freight railroading, trains today have a presence in the American cultural landscape that is

drastically smaller than a century ago. Back then, in railroading's heyday, they directly touched the lives of most citizens. Trains served some 140,000 communities, and 95 percent of the population lived near a rail station. Since that time, many secondary lines and branches have been abandoned, and most passenger trains discontinued. A seemingly endless array of evocatively named railroads have been merged and compacted into a few giants with

I have seldom heard a train go by and not wished I was on it.

The Great Railway Bazaar,
PAUL THEROUX (b. 1941),
American novelist

THE BRITISH ART *of* TRAINSPOTTING

Most people share a fascination for trains, but in Great Britain
the railways gave the nation a whole new pastime.

The magic of train-spotting was once all-consuming. In the 1950s, when a rare Scottish-based Jubilee-class steam locomotive worked south-ward through Rugby in the English Midlands, the gathered spotters cheered wildly from the tracksides, with pens, engine number booklets known as ABCs, notebooks, and sandwiches flying into the air amid the uninhibited enthusiasm.

A NATION ENTRANCED
By the end of the 19th century Great Britain's railway system was built, and the populace soon realized what a fascinat-ing industry had been created. The railway was the nation's lifeblood, industrially, com-mercially, and socially. It abounded in mechanical and civil engineering wonders, and both railway professionals and people at large followed developments keenly. Britain was also railway builder to an empire and the world; vast systems were conceived, financed, built, exported, and operated by the "sceptered isle" as it spread its industrial revolution worldwide. The popular *Railway Magazine* began publishing in 1897 and remains on sale today, along with many other glossy rail-way periodicals.

Seen in this perspective, it is easy to understand how this

A YOUNG TRAINSPOTTER, *photographed in 1952, consults his notepad as he stands between two steam locomotives.*

nation responded to the rail-ways' fascinations. Many popular activities grew around the railway, such as modeling, while the pleasure of watching trains and appreciating the complexity of their operation absorbed generations of rail-way enthusiasts, and continues to do so. Railway photog-raphy, which was pioneered

by the legendary names of the late 19th and early 20th centuries, such as E. Pouteau and F. E. Mackay, rose to become an art form in its own right. Steam trains are both sensual and beautiful, eminently suitable for the medium of photography. By the mid-20th century, a poignancy was added as the

TRAINSPOTTERS RECORD *locomotive numbers and classes in ABCs, in a bid to "collect" engines, much as birdwatchers note the species they've seen.*

passing parade of trains brought the chance of spotting rare and exotic engines. In summer at the famous trainspotting places such as Rugby, Crewe, Doncaster, and Carlisle, the grass would be worn off the embankments, grandstands to the finest unfolding dramas. As in any great sport, the thrill of the unexpected loomed behind every quiet moment.

Interest in railways still flourishes, with many people regarding them nostalgically as being part of a quieter, slower, and less confusing age. Others still pursue the art of trainspotting, viewing the high-tech railway of today as a benchmark of true civilization—the way we ought to be and the true antidote to the brash inefficiencies of automobiles and heavy trucking.

thrill of innovations contrasted with a need to capture the multitude of veterans that were rapidly disappearing. Today the greatest railway photographs combine animation and atmosphere in a stimulating historical context.

The artistry involved is akin to the hobby of railway modeling, which covers a vast field of creativity. It began with steam-driven examples in the 19th century and grew to detailed operational layouts of great authenticity. This has blossomed into building full-size mainline replicas of extinct types. Britain leads vigorously in this field, the latest project being the construction of a 160-ton (163 t) LNER A1 Class Pacific for eventual use on the mainline.

WHAT DO THEY SPOT?

Perhaps the greatest example of the railways' popular appeal, though, is trainspotting, which for several decades from the 1950s assumed the proportion of a national sport. It is hardly an exaggeration to say that some boys liked trains, some liked football, and others both! The fact that trainspotting today is often ridiculed by the media and comedians, perhaps reflects a society whose sense of adventure and outgoing spirit has been battered by

television, videos, computer games, and the internet.

Britain had 30,000 steam locomotives. The engines formed hundreds of different classes with an amazing variety of geographical and historical backgrounds. Trainspotting provided romance, color, and excitement. The aim was to see all members of every class and mark off the number in the ABC. Some classes consisted of one or two engines, often localized; others ran into hundreds and roamed Britain.

Trainspotting was proactive and intensely competitive. It opened young eyes to the country's geography, giving incentive to travel; it revealed industrial history; it developed the eye for detail and aesthetics, the mind for numbers and statistics; and it broadened comprehension of distribution and purpose, cause and effect. Those who understood the railways had their finger on the nation's pulse. Spotting trips to faraway places contrasted with the events of the local lineside, where the

CLAPHAM JUNCTION *in London, one of the world's busiest rail junctions, is still a popular venue with trainspotters.*

RAILWAY MUSEUMS

Railway museums worldwide maintain fascinating collections of historical locomotives that would otherwise have been lost forever.

Around the world thousands of historic locomotives, rolling stock, and items of railway equipment have been preserved both in static museums and at "live" locations where they can be seen replicating the duties they were built for.

A mix of governments, private organizations, and individuals supports them, and the end of steam power has done little to slow the speed of collecting. The word "preserved" means different things in different countries. At the lowest level are the many redundant steam locomotives to be found, weather-worn and neglected, outside railway stations or in public parks. Enthusiasts are now reclaiming many of these engines, working wonders to restore rusted hulks to mint condition and often to full running order. At the other extreme are the professionally

RARE VINTAGE steam engines are on display at the California State Railway Museum in Sacramento (above). A Canadian National 2-8-2 dominates a Baldwin 0-6-0 switcher at Steamtown in Scranton, Pennsylvania (below).

maintained rail museums of countries that seek to give their railway heritage the recognition it deserves.

Although Britain claims to have the first locomotive to reach 100 miles per hour (161 km/h) in the 1903 Great Western 4-4-0 *City of Truro*, there is one contender in

the Museum of Science & Industry in Chicago, Illinois. This is the home of No. 999, an 1893 New York Central 4-4-0 that is said to have reached 112.5 miles per hour (181 km/h) at Batavia, New York, in 1893. Here also is the *Pioneer Zephyr*, the first streamlined diesel-powered

THE GREAT HALL
*of Britain's National
Railway Museum at
York (left). This replica
of Der Adler (below),
is usually held at the
German railway
museum in Nürnberg
but here is being
exhibited at the
Verkehrshaus in
Lucerne, Switzerland.*

passenger train built for the
Chicago, Burlington &
Quincy Railroad. Some
30 locomotives are housed at
the Scranton, Pennsylvania,
Steamtown National Historic
Site. Some are put through
their paces on a three-hour
excursion on the 56-mile
(90 km) line to Kingsley.

A rare 1944 Southern
Pacific Baldwin 4-8-8-2
articulated locomotive, with
the driver's cab at the front,
dwarfs the other exhibits at
the California State Railroad
Museum at Sacramento,
which stages a Railfair every
10 years, attracting visitors
from all over the world.

ACROSS THE ATLANTIC

The British National Railway
Museum (NRM) at York
claims the title of world's
largest. There are almost 100
steam, diesel, and electric
locomotives in the collection,
along with a wide selection of
coaches, many of them Royal
saloons. The star attractions
include the original *Puffing
Billy* of 1813 and *Mallard*, the
locomotive that in 1938 set
the world speed record for
steam of 126 miles per hour
(203 km/h). Among its many
supporting activities the NRM
maintains a collection of more
than 1.4 million fascinating
historic photographs.

The principal
German collection
is located at the
Bavarian city of
Nürnberg, from
which the country's
first steam train
departed for the
neighboring city
of Fürth in 1835.
Great public interest
in an exhibition in
1882 led to the foundation of
the museum, now managed
by German Railways. Among
the exhibits is a replica of the
first German locomotive,
Der Adler (The Eagle). The
museum's various high-speed
machines include a 4-6-4
steam engine and a 1930s
Flying Hamburger express diesel.

Mulhouse is the location
of France's railway exhibition
center, with more than 100
exhibits. The most venerable
locomotive is the 1843-built
No. 33-111 *St. Pierre*, but one
of the most popular exhibits
is the No. BB9004, which,
on March 31, 1955, gained
the world speed record for
electric traction of 206 miles
per hour (332 km/h).

While a steam presence
is actively maintained on the
Swiss narrow-gauge mountain
railways, attracting great
tourist interest, the national
Verkehrshaus museum of
communications at Lucerne

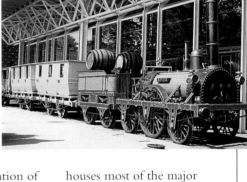

houses most of the major
exhibits. Those in working
order run public excursions
at weekends, and the electric
locomotives are sometimes
used on everyday freight
trains to keep the engines
in good working order.

CELEBRATING RAILWAYS

The Austrian state museum
in Vienna was enlarged to
celebrate the country's 150th
railway anniversary in 1987.
The Railway Museum (Das
Heizhaus) is located in the
former locomotive depot of
Strasshof. There are 24 steam
locomotives and one diesel on
show, and some are turned
out for special duties.

Netherlands Railways
manages a recently expanded
museum near its headquarters
at Utrecht. The relative lack
of domestic designs exhibited
there attests to the country's
reliance on imported locomotives, most from Britain.

MODEL TRAINS *for* ALL

From tiny miniatures in painstaking detail to massive track layouts, model railroading is an enthralling pastime.

A RARE PLATINUM MODEL *train was displayed by Hanz Zink of the German toy manufacturer Märklin at the German Toy Fair in Nuremburg (above). The City of Truro locomotive, built in 1903, is rendered in perfect detail in model form (above left).*

Model railroads are as fascinating to train enthusiasts as the real thing. Crowds flock to model train shows that bring the railroad world to life in miniature. Railroad modeling as a hobby has been around almost as long as the railway itself, and it continues to have a huge following despite the advent of the computer and other demands on leisure time.

Model railroad clubs flourish, but the hobby is a personal and wonderfully diverse one. To the "rivet counters" it is the challenge of building the most accurate replicas possible of favorite locomotives, rolling stock, or structures. To others it is using artistic and engineering skills to reproduce a piece of the railroad in the landscape. To many more it is creating something that, faithful to a prototype or not, just captures the railroad atmosphere.

Fine metal etching and casting, resistance soldering, and other modern techniques are put to good use by skilled modelers today. At the same time, manufacturing advances have vastly improved the quality of mass-produced model trains. Today's models are a far cry from the printed tinplate, often clockwork-powered models of the 1930s and earlier; these now-sought-after collectables bring huge prices at auction.

Some fine models, in fact, were available as far back as the 1880s, many of them powered by miniature steam engines. "Live steam" is still a well-supported branch of the hobby, especially for garden railways, with radio control adding an exciting dimension.

The first "train sets" were offered in the 1890s by the German firms Bing and Märklin. They developed a track gauge of 1¼ inches (32 mm) known as "0 gauge" that became a standard to be followed by manufacturers such as Ives and Lionel in the United States and Bassett-Lowke and Hornby in Britain.

The smaller, H0 ("half 0") scale, best known today, had its beginning in 1922, again from Bing, which offered

THIS 1928 MODEL *of an Atlantic locomotive took two years to construct.*

MODEL BUILDERS *create whole working rail systems, including signals, stations, and other rail equipment, as well as the locomotives.*

"the world's smallest clock-work railway" with a track gauge of 16.5 mm and a scale of 3.5 mm to the foot. Easily accommodated on a table-top, Trix Twin electric train sets to this size followed from Germany in 1935. Three years later the British Hornby-Dublo trains debuted and became immensely popular. They were realistic and sturdily built, running on 12v DC electric current, which was double the voltage previously used and provided more reliable performance. Electrically operated signals were among the accompanying accessories.

Today the aspiring model railroad builder has a wide range of choices, from tiny N gauge that reproduces "big" railroading even in modest space to the giants of G scale and Gauge 1. Many American modelers devote hundreds of hours to building pikes with maximum track footage and spectacular scenery. Across the Atlantic the faithful copy of a rustic branchline terminal can be a gem of painstaking detail.

SCALES AND TRACK GAUGES

Model railway scales are an odd mixture of metric and imperial dimensions. The most popular scale, 1/87, is defined as 3.5 mm to the foot and known as H0 when used with 16.5 mm track, which exactly represents the prototype 4-foot-8½-inch gauge.

Scale	Defined as	Track gauge	Prototype gauge	Known as
1/13.5	22.5 mm:foot	45 mm	2 ft 0 in	G
1/19	16 mm:foot	32 mm	2 ft 0 in	SM-32
1/29	10.5 mm:foot	45 mm	4 ft 8½ in	G
1/30.5	10 mm:foot	45 mm	4 ft 8½ in	Gauge 1
1/32	⅜ in:foot	¾ in	4 ft 8½ in	Gauge 1
1/43.5	7 mm:foot	32 mm	4 ft 8½ in	0
1/43.5	7 mm:foot	33 mm	4 ft 8½ in	Scaleseven
1/45	¼ in:foot	1¼ in	4 ft 8½ in	0
1/64	³⁄₁₆ in:foot	⅞ in	4 ft 8½ in	S
1/64	³⁄₁₆ in:foot	16.5 mm	3 ft 6 in	Sn3½
1/76	4 mm:foot	16.5 mm	4 ft 8½ in	00
1/76	4 mm:foot	18.2 mm	4 ft 8½ in	EM
1/76	4 mm:foot	18.83 mm	4 ft 8½ in	Protofour (P4)
1/87	3.5 mm:foot	16.5 mm	4 ft 8½ in	H0
1/87	3.5 mm:foot	12 mm	Meter	H0m
1/87	3.5 mm:foot	12 mm	3 ft 6 in	H0n3½
1/102	3 mm:foot	14.2 mm	4 ft 8½ in	Scalethree
1/102	3 mm:foot	12 mm	4 ft 8½ in	TT3
1/160	2 mm:foot	9 mm	4 ft 8½ in	N

DINNER-TABLE RAILWAYS

A farmer in Vermont once built a little railway to bring dishes to his dinner table so that servants would not interrupt the meal. But the most famous railway of this kind belonged to the Maharajah of Gwalior, a great Indian prince in the glittering days of the British Raj. An electrically powered silver train on a silver track brought fruit, sweets, wine, port, and brandy to each distinguished guest in turn.

THE PRESERVATION MENTALITY IN BRITAIN

The railway preservation movement began in Britain,

the birthplace of the railways.

Britain's railway preservationists unwittingly created a major tourist industry that attracts millions of visitors each year. They also created a blueprint for the rest of the world.

It is appropriate that Great Britain, the mother nation of railways, leads the world in railway preservation. Steam trains have been an intrinsic part of the British way of life since their inception, and there are now over 100 preserved lines across the country, many of which connect with the national railway network. These lines attract visitors of all ages and backgrounds, providing them with firsthand experience of the magical age of steam.

The first railway to be reopened by enthusiasts was the Welsh narrow-gauge Talyllyn line in 1951. It opened

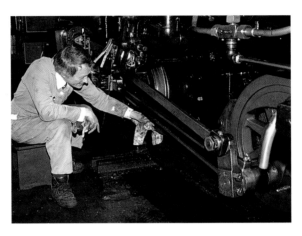

UTTER DEVOTION *British enthusiasts began their quest to preserve lines and locomotives in the 1950s.*

amid considerable opposition since it was widely claimed that enthusiasts did not have the expertise to run a railway. But the volunteers persisted and the Talyllyn set a precedent for other schemes, notably the Bluebell, opened in 1960, the first standard-gauge line to be preserved.

THE "BEECHING AXE"

By the early 1960s British Railways was rapidly phasing out steam operations in deference to diesel and electric trains, casting aside class after class of the country's

incredibly rich locomotive heritage. The government did earmark a number of exhibits to be preserved in museums, but the millions of people who revered working steam were not prepared to see it vanish. Innumerable organizations sprang up to preserve lines, locomotives, carriages, wagons, signal boxes, and historic "railwayana." They later unified under the Association of Railway Preservation Societies (ARPS).

With the concurrent vast increase in road transport and the beginning of the national network of motorways, the railway inevitably began losing money. In 1962 the Tory government selected Richard Beeching, from multinational

NOT STEAM ALONE *Early diesel and electric trains are also being saved for posterity. Here a prototype of Britain's HST—in its day the world's fastest diesel train—contrasts with a treasured Stanier Class 5 4-6-0, built for the London Midland & Scottish Railway less than 25 years before.*

SMALL MUSEUMS *such as this one (left) at Shackerstone Station, in Leicestershire, preserve many items of railway history. Volunteers (below) are the heart of the preservation industry.*

ICI (Imperial Chemical Industries), to chair the Railway Board and rectify the situation. This resulted in the infamous "Beeching Axe," which closed more than 40 percent of Britain's railways. This did release a vast number of branch lines, however, many of them scenic, and some became the subject of preservation bids.

In the meantime, hundreds of engines had accumulated in the yard of scrap dealer Dai Woodham, in Barry, South Wales, and the ARPS entered into negotiations with him to place a hold on these until funds could be raised to purchase them. Over a 20-year period, the preservationists rescued more than 200 locomotives from Woodham's yard, many of them among the best-known and most-loved examples now running.

Railway preservation is not restricted to operating lines; many centers house static displays of locomotives, with only limited steam operation.

Some also provide major overhauling facilities for other lines. In addition, there are regional and privately owned museum collections.

In all, Britain has over 2,000 preserved steam locomotives, some used to run "specials" over the national network, including engines from the National Railway Museum at York.

The preservation business continues to grow, as the first generations of diesels have now joined the steam fleets, and preservation societies actively seek extensions to many of the preserved lines. The most ambitious is the Great Central Railway's (GCR) planned extension.

Currently running between Leicester and Loughborough in the English Midlands, the GCR's northward extension to Ruddington will give a total of 16 miles (26 km) of superbly engineered railway. This line, closed under Beeching, was originally the GCR mainline between

Manchester and London. Opened in 1899, it was built to the European loading gauge, because it was originally intended to connect Britain's industrialized northern cities with Europe via a tunnel under the English Channel, a concept that was first proposed in 1881.

A SAVING GRACE

The preservationists' motives might be questioned: Many simply want to play trains and relive their childhoods; and an insularity exists, with many individuals focused on their own schemes, remote from the railway as a total system. But perhaps this is essential to their success.

The sheer awe, fascination, even trepidation that a first encounter with live steam can produce makes it immediately evident that, whatever their motives, the preservationists have, in all of their diversity over the latter half of the last century, achieved nothing short of a miracle.

PRESERVATION *around the* WORLD

Governments, private companies, and individuals are recognizing the value of preserving railway heritage.

Railway preservation in North America consists of a multitude of individual efforts, following the agenda of many different organizations, and has no distinct national plan.

At the end of the steam age, North America had 60 class-one railroads; some of these, notably the Southern Pacific (SP) and Union Pacific (UP), had an enlightened policy toward preservation; others, like the Erie Road and the New York Central, tragically preserved nothing.

In the UP roundhouse at Cheyenne, Wyoming, a number of classic locomotives remain to this day but there is no public access. However, one of these, the 4-6-6-4 Challenger, has received a

massive overhaul and can run at mainline speeds of 70 miles per hour (113 km/h). Though this is primarily a public relations exercise to promote the UP to its potential clients, the engine is available for rail tours and is occasionally used to haul freight trains.

Much more of the leading railroads could have been preserved if North America had possessed an army of railway enthusiasts as Britain did. Trainspotting, so popular in Britain, was not practiced in America; the size of the country and relative sparcity of railway operations in any given area was not conducive

to it. The railway did not have an impact on the young. Also, the United States was the first country to dispense with steam: It had virtually all gone before the preservation movement began in the 1950s.

However, much has been achieved and some 1,500 steam locomotives exist, with around 100 in running order at any one time, and some of these operate rail tours over the mainlines. America has some lines that are dedicated to steam. These are widely celebrated, such as the Cumbres & Toltec that runs across Colorado and New Mexico. Owned by the state,

PRESERVED TROLLEY CARS, *such as the one above, have great appeal. So, too, do steam engines such as Old Tucson (below), one of many classic restored United States. locomotives that now run on the Reno Steam Railroad.*

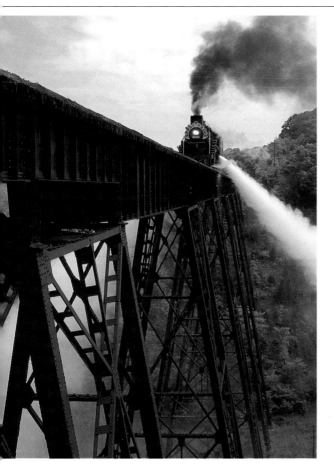

TRACKS AND BRIDGES *must be preserved, as well as engines. A Mikado traverses the Boone and Scenic Valley line, Iowa (left). A rail enthusiast works on a Baldwin 0-6-0 (above).*

this line is contracted to an operator who is supported by volunteer enthusiasts. The Durango & Silverton, also in Colorado, did not actually close but was sold to be run as a business for tourists.

There are a number of fine museums in North America; some are state run, some are private, and others are operated by donations. Of note are the Railway Museum of Pennsylvania, and Baltimore & Ohio Museum, Sacramento. There are also around 100 preserved railways of differing lengths and in various stages of restoration. Many of these are enthusiast led.

Train rides are popular with the American public but, for many visitors, the ride is more important than the motive power, and the use of diesels, for simplicity and cheapness, is increasing. There are also locomotives saved as static exhibits in many towns,

especially in the Midwest and Far west. In all, there are over 200 railway preservation sites in the USA and the country is second only to Britain in the extent of its achievements.

ON THE CONTINENT

In Europe, the preservation movement is also firmly established; most countries have excellent rail museums, although many remain in the early stages of development. Steam rail tours are frequent and attract much interest, as do special gala events. Most impressive is the Polish State Railway's initiative in running steam over a section of its network. Based in Woltzyn, these trains are operated in association with enthusiasts from other countries and it is hoped that steam might survive here indefinitely.

But the laurels go to Russia for operating the world's most spectacular rail tour, when a

group undertook a 10-day itinerary covering 3,523 miles (5,672 km). It involved an incredible 28 different steam locomotives. Many of these engines were taken from the nation's strategic reserve of mothballed locomotives, which had been set aside for emergency use during the Cold War.

Russia, in common with most countries around the world, has no tradition of railway enthusiasm, but in recent times government and tourist authorities worldwide are recognizing that heritage railways attract visitors.

In much of the developing world these endeavors are inevitably state inspired but some also attract widespread recognition. India's Darjeeling and Himalayan Railway, for example, is known as one of the world's great rail journeys, as well as being a magnificent preserved railway line.

A class K36 2-8-2 steam locomotive on the Durango & Silverton line

Colorado's Narrow-Gauge Railroads

Durango & Silverton and Cumbres & Toltec, United States of America

Though narrow-gauge railroads were once scattered across America from Maine to California, no state had more than Colorado. In their heyday, these charismatic little lines—particularly those of the Denver & Rio Grande (D&RG)—knitted together the state's mountain reaches with a tangle of routes, probing wherever gold or silver was discovered. Happily, significant remnants of that 3-foot-gauge network today survive to haul tourists and train buffs through some of North America's most head-turning scenery.

The D&RG's San Juan Extension, a line from Antonito, Colorado, via Chama, New Mexico, and Durango, arrived at the boom town of Silverton in 1882, when the narrow-gauge empire was approaching its maximum dimensions of more than 1,800 route miles (2,900 km), reaching from Salt Lake City to Santa Fe. Though the D&RG (which became the Denver & Rio Grande Western in 1921 in a reorganization) was the giant, Colorado had other important 3-foot-gauge lines as well.

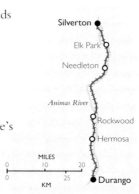

Silverton
Elk Park
Needleton
Animas River
Rockwood
Hermosa
MILES
0   10   20
0   25
KM
Durango

These included the Colorado Central (part of which survives as the Georgetown Loop Railroad, its spectacular curved High Bridge reconstructed in 1984), the Florence & Cripple Creek, and the Rio Grande Southern. Much of this slim-gauge network was built in the Rockies, since that is where the precious metals were. Because narrow-gauge trains could thread through tighter spaces than their standard-gauge counterparts, construction costs for tunnels, fills, and grading were all significantly lower.

The D&RGW's Silverton Branch—which has been the Durango & Silverton Narrow Gauge Railroad since 1981, when D&RGW sold it into private ownership—is a 45-mile (73 km) route replete with breathtaking scenery. Leaving Durango, the train chugs easily through the broad meadows. Here the Animas River Valley, which the railroad follows all the way to Silverton, is wide and gentle, but at Rockwood topography changes. The rails thread a deep gorge, then burst out onto the spectacular High Line, where the locomotive tiptoes along a

The Durango & Silverton follows the gorge of the Animas River

An engineman hoses down his K28 Mikado in preparation for departure from the mining town of Silverton.

The Silverton train's steam locomotives are of two classes, K28 and K36, all Mikados by virtue of their 2-8-2 wheel arrangement. Built in the 1920s, they feature an unusual "outside frame" design, which places the driving wheels inside the locomotive frame rather than outside, and is a device used on big engines that run on narrow-gauge track. Passengers ride in old-fashioned coaches

narrow ledge hacked from sheer cliff. The Animas is a boulder-fractured torrent running 400 feet (122 m) below. For the remaining 27 miles (44 km) to Silverton, the railroad runs through mountain wilderness, the 2-million-acre (810,000 ha) San Juan National Park. At Needleton or Elk Park the train is likely to stop to pick up or drop off back-packers, since the area has no roads. Silverton is a classic Victorian mining town, so special that it became a National Historic Landmark in 1962 (just five years before the railroad that serves it gained that designation). However, at midday, when as many as four trains arrive in town, the scene is frantic.

crossing sign decorates a building

FIELD NOTES

DISTANCE 45 miles (73 km)

BEST TIME TO TRAVEL Open May to October

GETTING THERE Durango is 350 miles (564 km) southwest of Denver on US 160/550; regular air services from Denver

A pair of 3-foot-gauge Baldwin 2-8-2s wait at the Cumbres & Toltec terminal in Chama, New Mexico.

The 64-mile (103 km) C&TS (which straddles the Colorado–New Mexico border) traverses classic Western landscape, from sagebrush-arid out of Antonito to evergreen-alpine at 10,015-foot (3,052 m) Cumbres Pass. The grade eastbound from Chama to Cumbres is a backbreaking 4 percent, making for some exciting railroading. Other highlights of the line include precipitous Toltec Gorge, and Whiplash and Tanglefoot Curves, broad loops the railway uses to gain elevation.

Chama, the western end of the C&TS and a division point in D&RGW days, is a modest and traditional railroad town caught in a time warp. The main street stretches the length of the railroad yard. Facing it (and the tracks) is Fosters Hotel, dating from 1881, just after the railroad arrived, where the bar and restaurant have resisted gentrification. Other buildings lining this quiet thoroughfare look hardly newer, in marked contrast to Durango, which has become a major tourist center.

Presided over by a tall wooden coaling tower, the Chama yard is an icon of old-time steam railroading, at first preserved by benign neglect

(wooden cars dating from the 1880s or steel replicas) or canopied gondolas. A single train each day carries an extra-fare parlor car, "Alamosa," and private cars are available for charter as well. One to four trains run daily (depending on the season) from May through October, and the trip, including a layover in Silverton, takes all day.

The Durango & Silverton is among the few preserved lines to offer a substantial journey. Another is its neighbor, the Cumbres & Toltec Scenic (C&TS) Railroad—the other surviving piece of the D&RGW's narrow-gauge empire. While the two obviously have similarities, they also have marked differences.

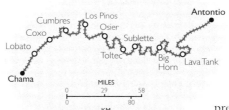

Cumbres
Coxo
Lobato
Chama

Los Pinos
Osier
Sublette
Toltec
Big Horn
Lava Tank

Antontio

MILES
0   29   58
0   80
KM

A rotary snow plow throws sheets of snow from the tracks

(in the 1960s the D&RGW was eager to abandon the entire line) and later by intent. The rambling board-and-batten station, the sandhouse, where the sand that will help provide traction for the struggle upgrade is stored and dried: It's all there. In Durango, the D&S recently opened a museum in its roundhouse (built in 1990 to replace the original, lost in a fire). But in Chama, the whole place is a museum, and visitors are welcome to wander around.

The C&TS exists thanks to the foresight of the states of Colorado and New Mexico, which bought the best portion of the Antonito–Durango line in 1970, two years after D&RGW finally received the Interstate Commerce Commission's permission to abandon it. (A natural-gas boom in New Mexico had given the antiquated narrow-gauge a surprising late-career traffic base that had made it hard to kill off.)

C&TS motive power is cut from the same cloth as D&S's engines: some K36s, a K37 (slightly larger, built in the 1930s from a standard-gauge 2-8-0), and a K27—called a "mudhen" for the way it waddles down the track. All surviving D&RGW passenger equipment was long ago moved to the Silverton Branch, so C&TS has created its own coaches, the earliest being converted from box cars.

Trains run May to October, leaving each end of the line for all-day traverses of the entire route, meeting roughly midway at Osier, where lunch is available. From there it's possible to return to the originating end or continue on, with a bus connection back.

> **FIELD NOTES**
>
> DISTANCE 64 miles (103 km)
>
> BEST TIME TO TRAVEL Open May to October
>
> GETTING THERE Antonito is about 260 miles (419 km) southwest of Denver on the Colorado–New Mexico border (US 285)

A plow train pauses at dusk at Cumbres Pass, the highest point on the Cumbres & Toltec Scenic Railroad.

Southbound at Willaha, on the Grand Canyon Railway

The Grand Canyon Railway

Arizona, United States of America

In 1901 the first passengers on the Grand Canyon Railway (GCRY), part of the far-flung and feted Atchison, Topeka & Santa Fe, arrived at the South Rim of the Grand Canyon, effectively opening that now world-famous attraction. Trains would bring in visitors, workers, and water—all essential for developing this natural wonder into the magnet for travelers that it has become. In time, however, transportation patterns changed with the automobile's ascendancy, and Santa Fe ran its last passenger train to the South Rim in 1968.

But 88 years to the day after the rail was inaugurated, on September 17, 1989, there was a second inauguration, with trains returning under the banner of a new Grand Canyon Railway. These trains, made up primarily of traditional "heavy-weight" coaches dating from the 1920s, are pulled from June through September by vintage steam locomotives. Historic diesels do the honors at other times.

The 64-mile (103 km) ride from Williams, Arizona,

Grand Canyon
Coconino

MILES
0   17   34
0   40
KM

Willaha

Quivero

Red Lake

Williams

traverses pleasant, if somewhat unexceptional, Southwestern scenery—high desert plains scattered with sagebrush and Ponderosa pine, backed by views of distant mountains. The line's highlight, which comes near the end of the two-hour northbound trip, is the winding 4-mile (6.5 km) Coconino Canyon. But the real highlight, of course, and the objective of the journey, is the Grand Canyon itself, where the train pulls right up to the South Rim, in the heart of historic Grand Canyon Village. Just a short stroll from the 1910 depot, a handsome two-story log structure, is the vast colorful chasm.

Tourism at the South Rim was developed by the Santa Fe in conjunction with lunchroom and hotel impresario Fred Harvey, who staffed his establishments with the famous Harvey Girls—prim in their black dresses and white aprons. Harvey did much to settle and

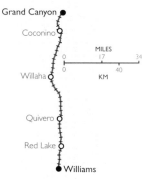

No. 4960 entered GCRY service in 1996, after a three-year rebuilding.

Coach-class travelers ride in an authentically restored 1923 Harriman coach with windows that open.

FIELD NOTES

DISTANCE 64 miles (103 km)

BEST TIME TO TRAVEL Operates vintage steam locomotives daily from June through September; vintage diesels at other times, except December 24 and 25

GETTING THERE Williams depot is off Interstate 40, about 30 miles (48 km) west of Flagstaff; Amtrak's Southwest Chief also stops at Williams

civilize the West. The Williams depot (on the National Register of Historic Places, as is the depot at the South Rim) once contained the Fray Marcos, a Harvey House. There's a museum in the former lunchroom.

Today's Grand Canyon Railway began operation with No. 18, a 2-8-0 built in 1910 by the American Locomotive Company, one of three similar engines that had served Michigan's Lake Superior & Ishpeming Railway hauling iron ore. Now No. 18 alternates with No. 4960, a 2-8-2 from the Chicago, Burlington & Quincy.

No. 20, sister to No. 18, is currently displayed at the Williams depot, while the slightly larger and older No. 29 is being readied to steam again. The diesels, FPA-4s and an FPB-4, were built in 1959 for Canadian National.

Standard accommodation on the GCRY is in 1923 Harriman coaches—classic cars that have an authentic old-time ambiance and windows that open. One has been upgraded to Club Class, with the addition of a bar. The train also features a café car, two dome coaches, and an open-platform ex-Canadian National business car rebuilt as a "Luxury Parlor Car." At whatever level of luxury, the ride is a pleasure and the destination unbeatable.

161

■ No. 9, Waumbek, built in 1909, is coaled up at Marshfield

Mount Washington Cog Railway

New Hampshire, United States of America

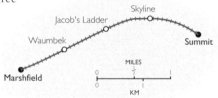

Opened in 1869 after three arduous years of construction, the Mount Washington Cog Railway is a remarkable survivor, doing today exactly what it was built to do all those years ago: haul tourists to the top of the mountain. Curious little steam locomotives still storm up the steep grades (with boilers tilted to keep them level), pushing coaches of sightseers ahead of them. The engines roar and pound furiously, and fragrant coal smoke pours from the stacks.

The Mount Washington Cog Railway is the oldest rack-and-pinion mountain railroad in the world. In 1858, when it was first proposed by retired meat packer Sylvester Marsh, the concept seemed ludicrous to most. In fact, when Marsh approached the New Hampshire legislature for a charter, one wag among the lawmakers apparently suggested that they might as well charter a railway to the Moon. However, this once outlandish concept not only succeeded but was often replicated, particularly in Alpine European countries.

And the original is still going strong. From the end of April to the end of October trains leave the Base Station (called Marshfield for the railway's founder) for a 3-mile (5 km) climb to the summit. "Train" almost seems a misnomer, for it's always a single locomotive pushing a single coach.

The average gradient is 25 percent, or one foot up for every four ahead. The maximum grade is an astounding 37 percent—the second

An original locomotive pushes a car up "Jacob's Ladder," a section of trestle on the Mount Washington Cog Railway.

The whole line is built on a trestle that often sits flush to the ground

steepest in the world, exceeded only by Switzerland's Pilatus Bahn. This is reached on a stretch of high, curved trestling appropriately called Jacob's Ladder. The entire line, in fact, is built on a trestle, though it often lies virtually flush to the ground.

FIELD NOTES

DISTANCE 3 miles (5 km)

BEST TIME TO TRAVEL Open late April to late October

GETTING THERE In northern New Hampshire, Marshfield is reached from US Highway 302

What makes the operation possible at all is the cog rail, a sort of horizontal ladder in the middle of the track with "rungs" up which the 19 teeth of the gears aboard the locomotive can "climb." The locomotive always operates on the downhill end of the coach, for safety, whether it is ascending or descending the steep grade.

A round trip, made at roughly the pace of a brisk walk, takes approximately three hours, including 20 minutes at the summit of Mount Washington to take in the spectacular view. The climb is around 3,600 feet (1,100 m), to an elevation of 6,288 feet (1,918 m), making it the tallest mountain in the Northeast. Its moonscape topography is both spectacular and daunting, and the summit's fickle weather is said to be the worst in the United States.

On the upbound journey, the train stops at Waumbek Tank, where the engine takes on water—of which it will use about 1,000 gallons

The horizontal "ladder" of the cog rail sits in the middle of the track. The engine's gear teeth then climb the "rungs."

(4,550 l) on the climb, along with a ton of coal. Then comes Halfway House, a shelter for skiers and hikers, with the timberline not far beyond.

The railroad operates seven steam locomotives, six built between 1875 and 1908, and the seventh in 1972. The coaches include five wooden cars, lookalikes to the originals but built in the 1990s, and a pair of less attractive aluminum models from 1958 and 1961.

Showman P. T. Barnum once called the Cog Railway "the second greatest show on Earth," and that remains a fair description.

163

■ A steam locomotive pulls into historic Orbisonia Station

The East Broad Top

Pennsylvania, United States of America

Located in the mountains of south-central Pennsylvania, the steam-powered, 3-foot-gauge East Broad Top (EBT) Railroad is perhaps the most complete and authentic preserved railway in the United States. In any case, it is the most surprising, since a scrap dealer made it happen.

When the 33-mile (53 km) line opened in 1873, it hauled both iron ore and coal; by the early years of the next century, the iron was gone but the coal continued to flow—as it did until 1956, when the mines played out and the railway finally shut down. Kovalchick Salvage Company, Pennsylvania's largest scrap dealer, then bought the whole operation: locomotives, cars, shop buildings and stations, right-of-way, company houses, and thousands of acres of coal lands.

That, it seemed, was the end of the EBT story. But not so. Owner Nick Kovalchick scrapped essentially nothing—just some branch-line trackage and mining machinery. In 1960 the Lions Club of Orbisonia (site of the EBT's headquarters) asked Kovalchick if he'd help the town celebrate its bicentenary. He agreed to fix up 5 miles (8 km) of line, as well as a

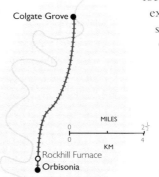

Colgate Grove

MILES
0   2½
0   4
KM

Rockhill Furnace
Orbisonia

locomotive and some coaches for an excursion train over a pleasantly scenic stretch from Orbisonia to Colgate Grove—part way to Mount Union, where the EBT once interchanged with the standard-gauge Pennsylvania Railroad. Trains have been running on summer and early autumn weekends ever since.

Today's East Broad Top is a nearly perfect slice of 1920s narrow-gauge steam railroading, preserved as if in amber. Four of the six surviving narrow-gauge steam locomotives have been restored and alternate in service. (All are Mikados, with a 2-8-2 wheel arrangement, and all were built by the Baldwin Locomotive Company between 1911 and 1920.) Coaches, cabooses, and freight cars remain, along with a 1927 gas-electric car.

The clapboard two-story station, with

carriage heater

A train bound for Rockhill Furnace approaches McMullen's Summit

Baldwin-built 2-8-2s get steam up at Rockhill Furnace during a "Fall Spectacular."

belt-driven shop machinery. It's the totality of the preservation that is so remarkable: cars, engines, structures, the whole set-up. The four decades of preservation have not always been easy for the EBT, designated a National Historic Landmark in 1964. The Kovalchicks—the late Nick, and now his son Joe, recently joined by *his* son Nathan—have had to sell off land and other ancillary assets to keep the railroad going.

general offices upstairs, still stands at Orbisonia, along with a brick roundhouse and "armstrong" (manually spun) turntable.

Perhaps most remarkable of all, and also most vulnerable, is the rambling shop complex. This cluster of red-painted wooden buildings—the blacksmith shop and foundry, the pattern house, car shop, boiler shop, machine shop, carpentry shop, and lumber shed—is crowned by a pair of soaring silver-painted smokestacks for the 1911 Babcock & Wilcox boilers that provided steam to power the

Once a year, on the Saturday and Sunday of Columbus Day weekend in early October, the EBT holds its Fall Spectacular. Typically all four locomotives are in steam, gas-electric M-1 is cranked up, and the shop complex is open for tours.

FIELD NOTES

DISTANCE 5 miles (8 km)
BEST TIME TO TRAVEL Columbus Day weekend, early October, but runs summer to early autumn
GETTING THERE About 18 miles (29 km) from Pennsylvania Turnpike (exit 14), southeast of Altoona

165

Cass Scenic Railroad

West Virginia, United States of America

In railroading's heyday, certain lines played specialized roles quite different from the industry's bread-and-butter work of hauling freight and passengers on the mainlines. One of those niche roles was logging—going into the woods for felled timber and bringing it to a pulp mill or sawmill.

Cass Scenic Railroad, in West Virginia State Park, preserves the intertwined histories of logging and railroading from the early to middle years of the 20th century. Beginning in 1900, West Virginia Pulp and Paper (WVP&P) developed the mill town of Cass, as well as the railroad and mill itself. The logging railroad climbed up Cass Hill, using 8.7 percent grades and two switchbacks to probe the remote stands of timber.

This dramatic line survives, along with some of the Shay-type geared locomotives that served it over the years. Invented by Ephraim Shay and patented in 1881, these vertical-cylindered engines ride on trucks,

much as freight and passenger cars do, rather than on driving wheels like other steam engines. This allows them to negotiate the often temporary marginal tracks laid down by logging operations, their gearing giving them great pulling power up steep grades. Shays were built exclusively by Lima Locomotive and Machine Works (later Lima Locomotive Works) by agreement with the inventor.

The Cass Scenic roster includes seven of these locomotives, of which six are operable. Two of them hauled logs over the tracks where they now haul tourists. No. 5 was built in 1905, today making it the second-

Shay No. 5 was built in 1905 for the Greenbrier & Elk line, the original name for the WVP&P railroad operations from Cass.

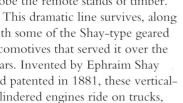

oldest surviving Shay. The collection also includes the last and largest Shay ever built, the 1945 Shay No. 6, which originally toted coal on Western Maryland Railway's Chaffee Branch in West Virginia. Two of the Shay's competitors, a Climax (unserviceable) and a Heisler, which runs regularly on the line, share the Cass property.

The Cass Scenic Railroad has steam up from the end of May through September and offers additional trips on weekends in late October. There is a choice of two excursions. The shorter is an 8-mile (13 km) round trip of one and a half hours through the two switchbacks on the way to Whittaker, the site of a 1940s logging camp recreated by the volunteers of the Mountain State Railroad and Logging Historical Association. The camp features loggers' living quarters and a Lidgerwood tower skidder, which was used to haul logs to a central point for loading onto flatcars.

The longer jaunt is a 22-mile (35 km) round trip to Bald Knob, which takes four and a half

FIELD NOTES

DISTANCE 8 miles (13 km) or 22 miles (35 km)

BEST TIME TO TRAVEL Runs from the end of May to September, plus weekends in late October for autumn colours

GETTING THERE Cass is deep in the Appalachian Mountains; airports at Charleston, WV, and Roanoke, VA, are a 3-hour drive away; Pittsburgh is a 5-hour drive to the north

hours and offers spectacular panoramas from the peak, which, at 4,228 feet (1,289 m), is the second highest point in West Virginia. This trip covers the last trackage laid by the Mower Lumber Company before it shut down operations in 1960. (The company had purchased the railroad and mill from WVP&P in 1942.)

The restored line opened for tourists as the Cass Scenic Railroad in 1963 and has been going strong ever since, with geared locomotives storming up the steep grades taking excursionists through some fine Appalachian countryside.

This four-wheel "bobber" caboose is typical of those used by the logging railroads of West Virginia, which now cater to tourists.

A pair of diesels crosses the trestle spanning Glacier Gorge

White Pass & Yukon Route

Alaska, United States of America, and British Columbia
and Yukon Territory, Canada

A product of the Klondike Gold Rush of 1898, the 3-foot-gauge White Pass & Yukon (WP&Y) Route has survived a century of ups and downs as dramatic as the steep grades it climbs. The line connects the Alaskan port city of Skagway with Whitehorse, 111 miles (179 km) away and capital of Canada's Yukon Territory since 1955. Soon after the WP&Y began operations in 1900, the gold played out and the population of the Yukon plummeted. But as early as the 1920s the railroad was successfully promoting tourism to this beautiful area. Because of the WP&Y's strategic location, the United States Army took it over during World War II, and in the 1950s

railroad business boomed with a broader traffic base, including silver, lead, and zinc. During that period WP&Y began the first ship–train–truck container operation, the world's first "intermodal" containerization operation, forerunner of one of modern railroading's greatest successes.

But in 1982, when mining company Cyprus Anvil closed its huge open-pit operation, the railroad closed with it. The line reopened in 1988, when area tourism, largely through cruise ship calls at Skagway, had burgeoned to the point where hauling people could be profitable.

In 1988 the WP&Y carried 39,000 passengers on 40-mile (64 km) round trips from Skagway to White Pass summit. In a dozen years, that count grew to 290,000, and more of the line reopened. In July 2000 the railroad celebrated its centennial at Carcross, a remote settlement in the Yukon Territory, 68 miles (109 km) from Skagway. The line from Carcross to Whitehorse is not yet in service, but a regular Carcross–Lake Bennett run began in 2001.

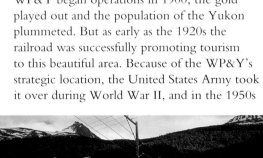

General Electric diesel locomotives haul the train most days. This one is running through Broadway Street in Skagway.

The Yukon Route traverses the snow-covered peaks of White Pass

An excursion ran from Skagway to White Pass in 1899, before its official opening.

The WP&Y offers three different excursions, the one from Carcross and two from Skagway. The original and still most popular run is the shortest, climbing 2,685 feet (819 m) from sea level to White Pass over 20 miles (32 km). This round trip takes three hours and runs from May through September. The train battles the steep grades up the canyon of the Skagway River, crossing dramatic bridges in the process. Snowcapped mountains loom all around.

Four days a week from June through August, there's a longer run, 41 miles (66 km) each way, from Skagway to Bennett Station (built in 1903 and thoroughly restored) on the shores of Lake Bennett, British Columbia. This is an all-day trip, with a two-hour stopover for a walking tour of the historic townsite. On Saturdays, the Lake Bennett train is hauled by Mikado No. 73, built by Baldwin Locomotive Works in 1947 and the WP&Y's last steam engine purchase. It was restored in 1982 and ran briefly before the shutdown. In 1999 the railroad acquired a lease from Colorado's Georgetown Loop Railroad on a second steamer, a 2-8-0 built by Baldwin for service in Guatemala. Diesels do the honors on the other days. Most are unusual shovel-nosed units built by General Electric from 1954 to 1966, now repainted in their original green-and-yellow color scheme. Joining them are three chop-nosed diesels from Montreal Locomotive Works (1971), all that remain of the original 10. More than half of the 45 passenger cars in the fleet date back to the 1920s and earlier, many to before 1900.

FIELD NOTES

DISTANCE 111 miles (179 km)

BEST TIME TO TRAVEL Runs May to September for Skagway–White Pass; June to August for Skagway–Lake Bennett and Carcross–Lake Bennett

GETTING THERE Skagway is served by Alaska Marine Highway ferries and local air service, and is on the Klondike Highway, as is Carcross

The Esquel Branch

Patagonia, Argentina

I n 1979, Paul Theroux published his *Old Patagonian Express,* an account of his journey, mostly by train, from Boston to Esquel, deep in Argentina's Patagonia region and the southernmost point reachable by contiguous rail in the Americas. He treated his steam-hauled journey on the 249-mile (401 km) Esquel Branch, the end of his long trek, as something of an ordeal, but many rail aficionados following in his footsteps have taken quite a different view. In any event, Theroux's book gave the little railroad some fame—and a popular, if ironic, moniker (it runs at far from "express" speed).

For something that looks like an antique, the 750-millimeter-gauge (about 2 ft 6 in) Esquel Branch is actually quite young, not completed until 1942. The equipment—creaky wooden coaches (most built in Belgium by Famillereux) and steam locomotives—dates largely from the 1920s, however, when the government of Argentina projected and began an extensive network of lines crisscrossing Patagonia. Though

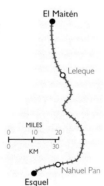

El Maitén

Leleque

MILES
0   10   20
0   30
KM

Nahuel Pan

Esquel

most of these lines were never built, 80 steam locomotives were delivered, far more than was needed at any one time to operate the Esquel Branch, so there have always been plenty of spares. Some of the fleet of oil-fired 2-8-2s, 25 of them built in the United States by Baldwin and 50 built in Germany by Henschel, are still in service today. (Henschel also supplied five tank engines, long since out of use.) At present only the southern 103 miles (165 km) of the branch are in operation. On Tuesdays the train runs south from El Maitén, the railroad's head-quarters and site of extensive repair shops, to the line's terminus at Esquel, returning on

Esquel is the southernmost point in the Americas reachable by a continous railway line, and the final destination of what author Paul Theroux dubbed the Old Patagonian Express.

Double-headed 2-8-2s, built in Germany, work south toward Esquel

Wednesdays. On Saturdays, a short tourist excursion runs just 12 miles (19 km) from Esquel to Nahuel Pan and back.

The northern end of the line, which connects at Ingeniero Jacobacci with the broad-gauge (5 ft 6 in) mainline between Buenos Aires and San Carlos de Bariloche, a resort town near the Chilean border, has been out of service since 1996 (except for some specials for enthusiasts).

The entire branch, which, along with the Buenos Aires–Bariloche route, had been the government-run Ferrocarril Nacional General Roca, was shut briefly in November 1993, a product of unacceptable deficits and a country-wide railway privatization initiative. Within three months trains were running again south-ward from El Maitén, under the auspices of the Provincial Government of Chubut, and three months later the entire line was reopened, though only for a few years.

The *Old Patagonian Express* chugs through country reminiscent of the North American

FIELD NOTES

DISTANCE 103 miles (165 km)
BEST TIME TO TRAVEL Spring or autumn, though winter snows can be spectacular
GETTING THERE In Patagonia's Chubut Province, about 995 miles (1,600 km) southwest of Buenos Aires, Esquel is accessible by road and air from Bariloche, a resort city 150 miles (240 km) to the north

West: brown hills where sheep and cattle graze, backed by soaring mountains that are often crowned with snow. Human presence is limited in this empty, desolate, though exhilarating country. With its 1920s equipment (plus a diner and first-class coaches built in the 1960s), its tenuous narrow-gauge track winding through wild and in-hospitable country, this little line is like a time machine returning the traveler to the days when steam trains served outposts of civilization around the world. The line is revered by the people of the region, who fittingly call it La Trochita, the "Little Branch."

Inside the log station at Leleque, an operating telegraph key and sounder are survivors from an earlier era of railroading.

The Great Central Railway

Leicestershire, Great Britain

Britain's Great Central Railway opened in 1899, the last mainline to reach London. It was formed with the extension of the Manchester, Sheffield & Lincolnshire Railway southward from Annesley in Nottinghamshire to Quainton Road in Buckinghamshire, joining the Metropolitan Railway and proceeding over shared tracks to London, where the Great Central (GC) built its own terminal station at Marylebone.

This extension provided the new railway with a mainline from Manchester and Sheffield to the capital, and, apart from its prestigious passenger trains, which were elegant, fast, and renowned for their onboard services, the route also served some of Britain's most industrialized regions, carrying a huge amount of freight.

GC chairman Sir Edward Watkin intended to link up with the South Eastern & Chatham Railway in order to operate through trains into Europe via a tunnel under the English Channel, upon which work had already begun. So the extension from Annesley was engineered to Continental standards. However, it was almost a century before Britain's railways were connected with those of the European mainland via the

Loughborough

Quorn

MILES
0   1   2   3
0   KM   4

Leicester North

Channel Tunnel and, ironically, it was long after the GC was closed in 1969.

The present-day GC operates over an 8-mile (13 km) preserved section of the original line from Leicester North to Loughborough. A planned extension north from Loughborough will involve building a new viaduct over the Midland mainline— the original was demolished after the line was closed. The GC's ultimate intention is to connect the outskirts of Leicester and Nottingham, two of Britain's biggest cities, with a fully operational double-track steam mainline, in accordance with the company's stated aim to "recreate, for present and future generations, the experience of British mainline railway operation during the best years of steam locomotives."

The locomotive shed and works are located adjacent to Loughborough Central Station, and the atmosphere is an experience to savor—like stepping back in time to be immersed in the legends of the steam age.

Steam services operate daily throughout summer and on weekends and bank holidays during winter. The line passes through rolling

Locomotives arrive at and depart from a busy scene at Quorn Station

FIELD NOTES

DISTANCE 8 miles (13 km)

BEST TIME TO TRAVEL Steam services operate daily through summer and on weekends and bank holidays during winter

GETTING THERE Both Loughborough and Leicester can be reached by train from London's St. Pancras Station and by road from the M1 Motorway

LNER Class V2 No. 60800 Green Arrow, normally based at York, hauls a train over Swithland Viaduct on a visit to the GC.

English farmland and includes two viaducts over Swithland Reservoir in the Charnwood Forest. Some of the special dining-car trains stop on one of the viaducts for passengers to see the rich variety of birdlife, including ducks, waders, and wintering swans.

The GC has many fine engineers, and one of their greatest achievements was the restoration of the unique Pacific locomotive 71000 *Duke of Gloucester*. More recently the sole surviving Robinson O4 Class mineral-hauling engine has been restored to full working order. The GC was an important carrier of coal, and these beautiful engines, introduced in 1911, operated extensively on the line for most of its existence. An unusual attraction is an invitation to don the company's overalls and, for a modest fee, "Fulfill your dreams and drive a locomotive of your choice on the mainline."

The original GC route is the subject of other exciting possibilities. Central Railway, a consortium of business operators, intends to reopen other sections of the original GC route as part of an international freight link from Liverpool to Lille in France, so echoing Sir Edward's vision. In addition, Chiltern Railways, which operates local services from Marylebone, has announced its long-term intention to reopen the GC line to Leicester for passenger traffic.

The sole surviving Gresley B12, built in 1928, crosses Victoria Bridge

Severn Valley Railway

Bewdley, Worcestershire, Great Britain

The Severn Valley Railway is the "Premier Line" among Great Britain's heritage railways. It is located within easy reach of the West Midlands, one of England's most populated areas, and is linked to the national rail network.

This is a former branch line of the old Great Western Railway (GWR) and retains the distinctive GWR station architecture, footbridges, and signals.

Upon leaving its connection with the national railway at the historic carpet-making town of Kidderminster, the Severn Valley line follows the course of the Severn River for 16 glorious miles (26 km) to Bridgnorth. Near Bewdley, an ancient riverside town noted for its

Restoration-period and Georgian houses, the line skirts the edge of the huge West Midlands Safari Park. Just before Arley the trains cross the elegant Victoria Bridge, built by engineer John Fowler in 1861, with its single 200-foot (61 m) span rising high above the river. This is one of the railway's many famous photographic spots and is also a popular location for anglers.

The railway continues past the village of Arley, set on the riverbank, through Highley and Hampton Loade, and on to the medieval market town of Bridgnorth, where the main locomotive shed and works are situated. The journey provides views of the ancient Wyre Forest and passes through lush coppices and water meadows.

The line's six stations are magnificently restored and feature carefully tended gardens. Each station is also the hub of a network of public walking trails, and the frequent train service enables visitors to traverse the line in stages, exploring the many places of interest along the route.

Many visitors combine a trip to the Severn Valley with a visit to the nearby Ironbridge Gorge museum complex, heralded as the

station lanterns

A 2-6-0 and a 0-6-0 pass Hampton Loade

The Severn Valley Railway has faithfully restored many locomotives and carriages, used in special events.

birthplace of industry. One of the earliest steam locomotives was built here at Coalbrookdale Ironworks and the museum houses a magnificent working replica.

Around 20 locomotives run on the Severn Valley line at any one time; various engines work at different times in association with other organizations, not least the National Railway Museum in York. The works at Bridgnorth can undertake major restorations as well as full locomotive overhauls.

In the spring of 2000, as part of its 30th anniversary of running trains, the Severn Valley held a Branch Line Gala, which was reminiscent of life on the railways 75 years ago, a more tranquil and romantic age. Nine steam locomotives operated five separate passenger trains plus a freight train and an "Auto Push and Pull" set (which can be driven in either direction). This anniversary coincided with the opening of a spectacular new carriage shed at Kidderminster, built with a grant from the heritage lottery fund. The four-track building is 984 feet (300 m) long and holds 56 coaches.

Like all preserved railways, the Severn Valley Railway relies heavily on its volunteers and could not function without them. The railway has 14,000 members and almost as many shareholders. With this support, it is able to present an enormous range of attractions, including "vintage vehicle" days, World War II nostalgia events, excellent dining car services, train hire for corporate events, locomotive driving courses, and, for the enthusiast of tomorrow, Tank Engine Thomas weekends and the much-loved Santa specials during the Christmas season.

FIELD NOTES

DISTANCE 16 miles (26 km)

BEST TIME TO TRAVEL June to October

GETTING THERE The national rail network joins the Severn Valley Railway at Kidderminster, which is conveniently reached by rail from Birmingham and Wolverhampton; Bridgnorth Station is on the A442 road

Meadows and moorland make the NYMR one of Britain's most scenic lines

North Yorkshire Moors Railway

Yorkshire, Great Britain

This line was engineered by George Stephenson, Britain's "Father of Railways," as part of the Whitby & Pickering Railway that opened in 1835. It was a flourishing route during the steam age, carrying traffic to and from the historic port of Whitby. But in the years after World War II, the onslaught of motor traffic gradually reduced revenues and its closure came in 1965.

There were many who felt passionately that this line, with its proximity to the eastern coast of England and unrivaled access to the North Yorkshire Moors National Park, had a viable future. A preservation society was formed, receiving strong local and national support, including that of the North Yorkshire County Council, and a section of the line was reopened by the Duchess of Kent in 1973. Three years later, the full 18-mile (29 km) stretch between Pickering and Grosmont, the North Yorkshire Moors Railway (NYMR), was restored.

Soon after leaving Pickering, the line enters Newton Dale, a huge glacial overflow channel, which for 10 miles (16 km) forms a natural cutting for the railway. This section of the National Park is very remote, and during severe winters the trains have provided an emergency service when snow has rendered the roads impassable.

Gradients as steep as 1 in 49 occur in the gorge and as the line climbs to a summit 532 feet (162 m) above sea level, the heavy bark of the toiling locomotives reverberates throughout the surrounding hills. Nearby is the Fen Bog, which is 40 feet (12 m) deep and noted for its rich variety of bird and plant life, including remnants of the birch, alder, and willow forests

Grosmont

Goathland

MILES
0   4   8
0   10
KM

Pickering

Diesel-hydraulic D821, Greyhound, leaves Grosmont for Pickering on the North Yorkshire Moors Railway.

that grew here 10,000 years ago. From the summit the line drops 500 feet (153 m) to its terminus at Grosmont in the Esk Valley. On the way it passes Goathland, where a magnificent camping coach is available for hire for the ultimate holiday experience.

At Grosmont the line connects with the mainline from Whitby to Middlesborough. The locomotive shed is also at Grosmont, where a splendid signal box was built in 1996 using original bricks from a similar 19th-century signal box at nearby Whitby.

The 25 or so locomotives that travel the line are extremely varied and include a trio of celebrated war engines from the early 1940s: an American S160 2-8-0, of which some 2,300 were built for service in many parts of the world; the British War Department 2-10-0 *Vera Lynn;* and a Hunslet Austerity 0-6-0 ST, of which almost 500 were built. There are also former LMS Black 5

FIELD NOTES

DISTANCE 18 miles (29 km)

BEST TIME TO TRAVEL June to October

GETTING THERE Connects with the national railway system at Grosmont, on the Whitby–Middlesborough line; Pickering Station is on the A170 road between Thirsk and Scarborough

4-6-0s, of which 842 were built, Southern and LNER Pacifics, and classic North Eastern Railway 0-6-0s and 0-8-0s, which for many years provided a valuable service hauling that railway's heavy coal traffic.

A trip on this beautifully preserved railway is a wonderful experience. The line embraces some of Britain's finest countryside with charming historic stations and halts that provide easy access to the many walking trails of the National Park.

No. 92220 Evening Star *leaves Whitby on its way to the NYMR.*

A locomotive approaches the crossing at Horsted Keynes

The Bluebell Line

Sheffield Park to Kingscote, Sussex, Great Britain

The Bluebell was the first standard-gauge passenger line to reopen following closure by British Rail (BR), and it quickly proved that enthusiasts could run a full-size railway. The line was originally part of the Lewes and East Grinstead Railway, which opened in 1883. Set amid the glorious Sussex countryside, the line served villages and agricultural needs and brought passengers from far afield to social functions at stately homes along the route.

The line is named after the bluebells that grow in profusion along the embankments and in the woods through which the line passes. For those who savor the heady combination of magnificently restored Victorian steam trains and the sheer beauty of the English countryside, the Bluebell is unsurpassed.

The locomotives, rolling stock, and stations are impeccably restored to their former glory, the staff dressed in period attire, and most of the trains are authentic to the line's history.

The railway runs for 9 miles (14.5 km) from Sheffield Park to Kingscote, from which an extension to East Grinstead will be opened in 2002. This extension will connect the Bluebell

with the electrified mainline. Upon leaving Sheffield Park, the trains begin climbing to Horsted Keynes. This section includes the renowned photographic location of Freshfield Bank. Here many of the smaller locomotives work at full throttle, often with two or three engines on a train, and enormous columns of exhaust pour from their chimneys.

The line continues through wooded country inhabited by many pheasants before arriving at Horsted Keynes. From here, a future branch to Ardingley and Haywards Heath swings away to the southwest. The country junction atmosphere at Horsted Keynes is perhaps the best on any preserved railway—even when the trains are not running.

After leaving the junction, the trains pass through the half-mile (0.8 km) Sharpthorne Tunnel, the longest on any preserved railway. During winter huge icicles form inside the tunnel from water dripping through the roof, and a shunting engine has to pass through the tunnel to break them off before passenger services can commence.

Kingscote Station, which was in ruins when the line was obtained from BR, has been

Map labels:
Kingscote
Sharpthorne
Horsted Keynes Station
Sheffield Park
MILES 0 1 2 3
KM 0 4

A locomotive pulls out of Sheffield Park Station ready to embark on the climb to Horsted Keynes on the Bluebell Line.

7.30 p.m. and, during dinner, makes two return trips over the line.

The Bluebell has attracted many television and film companies to shoot on this scenic line. In the 1990s this included the remake of the much-loved movie *Railway Children*, which starred British actor Richard Attenborough.

The Bluebell receives 180,000 visitors per year and is now firmly established as a British institution, with 30 steam locomotives and 100 carriages and wagons.

painstakingly restored over many years and finally reopened in the mid-1990s. The extension from here to East Grinstead will include an elegant six-arch viaduct.

The locomotive fleet is extremely varied, ranging from the diminutive Brighton Terrier 0-6-0Ts, built in 1872, to Bulleid's semi-streamlined Southern Railway Pacifics of the 1940s.

The Bluebell is especially proud of its set of restored Pullman coaches of 1920–1930s vintage. An outing on the line to take advantage of the *Golden Arrow* dining service, where lunch or dinner is served in the Pullmans, is a memorable occasion. The evening dinner train leaves Sheffield Park at

The Golden Arrow dining service features faithfully restored Pullman coaches that give the traveler a taste of times past.

FIELD NOTES

DISTANCE 9 miles (14.5 km)
BEST TIME TO TRAVEL Spring and summer to see the bluebells for which the line is named
GETTING THERE Frequent trains from London's Victoria Station to Haywards Heath or Uckfield for Sheffield Park, or to East Grinstead for Kingscote

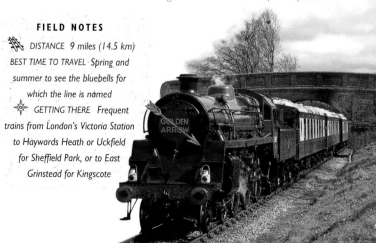

Prince, a vintage 0-4-0STT, on a spiral section on the Ffestiniog line

The Ffestiniog Railway

North Wales, Great Britain

When the Industrial Revolution created enormous demand for urban housing, endless lines of gray slate roofs became an intrinsic part of the landscape. The mountains of North Wales contained vast quantities of slate, and a labyrinth of railways was built to connect the mines with seaports or the mainline railway. Opened in 1836, the Ffestiniog Railway carried slate from the mines in Blaenau Ffestiniog to the harbor at Porthmadog, 13½ miles (22 km) away on the north Welsh coast.

Built to a gauge of 1 foot 11½ inches, the Ffestiniog also carried passengers. It was the first narrow-gauge railway in the world to do so, and it exerted a great influence on future railway development.

The line was horsedrawn until 1863, when steam locomotives took over, despite the doubts of Robert Stephenson as to their suitability for so small a gauge. But the railway prospered and in 1872 became the first user of bogie passenger coaches in Britain.

The Ffestiniog's choice of motive power also broke new ground by successfully pioneering the Fairlie type locomotive in 1869. This was, in effect, two engines placed back to back and mounted on separate power bogies. These powerful machines were ideal for hauling heavy trains around the sinuous curves and steep grades that were a feature of the mountainous line.

By the mid-20th century the demand for slate had declined, tiles having become a much cheaper roofing alternative, and by 1946 the line lay moribund. Following the successful reopening of the Talyllyn further south (the first line ever to be restored), a preservation society was founded to reopen Ffestiniog.

The preservation bid created enormous public interest and, over the latter half of the 20th century, the line was transformed into a superb operating railway—a glowing credit to the entire preservation movement. The full restoration included building a 2½-mile (4 km)

MILES
0   2   4

KM
0   5

Blaenau Ffestiniog
Tanygrisiau
Tan-y-bwlch
Penrhyn
Porthmadog

engineering plate from No. 589

HUNSLET ENGINE Co
LEEDS
No 589, 1893

stretch of new railway to replace a section of the original track bed that had been flooded some years earlier to make way for a hydroelectric power station.

The Ffestiniog Railway is marketed as one of the "Great Little Trains of Wales" and it is a major tourist attraction in its own right. It operates over the full distance between Porthmadog and Blaenau Ffestiniog, where it shares a station with Railtrack's Conway Valley branchline from Llandudno Junction, which is on the North Wales mainline. Traversing Snowdonia National Park, the Ffestiniog provides spectacular views of the region's lakes, waterfalls, valleys, pastures, mountain scenery, and dense forests. At Dduallt, the line spirals to gain height, the

FIELD NOTES

DISTANCE 13¹/₂ miles (22 km)

BEST TIME TO TRAVEL June to October

GETTING THERE Connects with the national railway network at Blaenau Ffestiniog, accessed from Llandudno Junction. Porthmadog Harbor Station is located on the A487 Welsh coast road

only example of this kind of operation in Britain.

The Llechwedd slate caverns, a major visitor attraction in its own right, can also be reached by the railway. These caverns provide an experience of life in a slate mine 150 years ago.

Some of the line's original 0-4-0 Tender Saddle Tanks, dating from 1863, can still be seen, along with the now unique Fairlies with their two-way engines. One of these, the *Earl of Merioneth,* was built at the railway's Boston Lodge engineering works in 1979.

The Merddin Emrys, a 0-4-4-0 Fairlie tank engine at the Dduallt spiral.

The Steam Railway

Isle of Man, Great Britain

For lovers of vintage transport, a visit to the Isle of Man off the northwest coast of England is a must. The island has five separate heritage rail systems, all of Victorian origin. Pride of place goes to the 3-foot-gauge steam railway that runs between the capital, Douglas, and Port Erin, a seaside resort, a distance of 15½ miles (25 km).

At Douglas, the trains connect with horse-drawn trams that have been in service since 1876. These run along the promenade to Derby Castle, where the electric Manx railway begins the 17½-mile (28 km) trip along the east coast to Laxey and Ramsey. This route also links with the charming 2-foot-gauge Groundle Glen Railway and the ever-popular Snaefell Mountain Railway. The island's tranquillity is a perfect setting in which to enjoy the Steam Railway; the countryside is a profusion of broad meadows and rolling hills, with quiet villages and very little traffic.

The colorful trains are hauled by engines with copper-capped chimneys and brass domes, and serve stations steeped in the atmosphere of a bygone age. At one road crossing, the lady keeper hoists a white flag high above the surrounding hedges to inform the train driver that the crossing gates are closed to road traffic. After the train has passed, she resets the gates and returns to her knitting.

The island's engines were delivered from the legendary Beyer Peacock works at Gorton, in Manchester, a company with a flair for design. They are all 2-4-0Ts, the first of which, *Loch,* arrived on the island in 1874 to coincide with the opening of the first line. The most recent engine on the roster is *Kissak* built in 1910. They represent a smaller version of Beyer Peacock's celebrated 4-4-0Ts, built for the London Metropolitan Railway's Inner Circle line from 1864.

The colorful and evocative insignia for the Isle of Man Railways signals a bygone era.

A 2-4-0T leaving the Douglas terminal station bound for Port Erin

The line from Douglas to Port Erin is all that remains of a once-thriving system of railways that embraced the entire island. The system was designed to cope with the enormous holiday traffic of the Victorian period. However, widespread closure of many rural railways in Britain over the years following World War II also affected the Isle of Man and by 1965 the entire system was closed. The Marquis of Ailsa launched a vigorous action to get the railway reopened but, in fact, only the small section from Douglas to Port Erin could be saved.

FIELD NOTES

DISTANCE 15½ miles (25 km)

BEST TIME TO TRAVEL June to October

GETTING THERE Located in the Irish Sea, midway between England and Ireland, with frequent air and ferry services to and from Douglas, the island's capital

The red brick station at Douglas is a typically imposing Victorian edifice, and one can easily imagine how busy it was in its heyday. The departing trains face a 2½-mile (4 km) climb to the clifftops above Port Soderick, famous in Victorian times for its smugglers' caves.

As the trains coast downward to Ballasalla, a magnificent ocean vista opens up, including the island of St. Michael's. After Castletown, the former capital of the Isle of Man, the railway heads across the plains and passes through lush meadows between the foothills and the sea. Port St. Mary is famous for its sandy beaches, and the cliffs between here and Port Erin are truly spectacular.

Meeting the crew of the Isle of Man's steam trains is a part of the whole experience of traveling on the island's historic railways.

183

Handsome 64-ton (65 t) 2-10-2Ts haul most HSB trains

Harz Narrow-Gauge Railways

Germany

Deep in the Harz Mountains of former East Germany, concealed from the West for decades by the Iron Curtain, a scenic and countrified meter-gauge railroad charges up mountains and rambles across meadows.

The Harz Narrow-Gauge Railways, or Harzer Schmalspur Bahnen (HSB) was privately built in the late 19th century primarily to serve the mining and timber industries. In 1949 the East German nationalized railways, Deutsche Reichsbahn, now part of Deutsche Bahn (DB), took over the system. Under communism, the 82-mile (132 km) system was highly subsidized, but with reunification this became unacceptable. By then, however, the narrow-gauge line's recreational potential had been recognized, and it was split off from DB, Germany's then newly unified

Alexisbad Station

national rail system, and taken over by local governments. The HSB is in three parts, but operates as a single railroad. The Harzquerbahn (or Trans-Harz Railway) runs north–south from Wernigerode, the railroad's headquarters and an enchantingly beautiful medieval city, to Nordhausen Nord. At Drei Annen Hohne, the Brockenbahn (Brocken Mountain Railway) veers off to ascend the mountain to Brocken. Further on, at Eisfelder Talmühle, the Selketalbahn (Selke Valley Railway) branches eastward to Alexisbad and Gernrode, with lines continuing on to Hasselfelde and Harzgerode. At Wernigerode, Nordhausen Nord, and Gernrode, the HSB connects with the standard-gauge DB.

The most scenic line is the Brockenbahn. While the other routes—less traveled by tourists —often operate with diesel locomotives or miniature 1950s passenger railcars known as railbuses, the trains to Brocken generally draw steam, in the form of burly, low-drivered 2-10-2Ts. Being "tank" engines, they have no tender,

Map labels

Brocken

Wernigerode

Drei Annen Hohne

Gernrode

Hasselfelde

Harzgerode

Eisfelder Talmühle

MILES
0   8   16

0   20
KM

Nordhausen

An HSB locomotive makes its way to Brocken

A HSB locomotive takes on water at Drei Annen Hohne, the junction for the scenic line to Brocken.

FIELD NOTES

DISTANCE 82 miles (132 km)
BEST TIME TO TRAVEL Runs daily
but with reduced
frequency in winter
GETTING THERE The HSB
connects with the
Deutsche Bahn, Germany's
national rail system,
at Wernigerode,
Nordhausen, and Gernrode

effectively making these locomotives bidirectional and therefore ideal for HSB's network, which lacks turning facilities at the ends of the lines. The HSB schedules 18 of these locomotives (which burn oil instead of coal), all but one of which was built in the 1950s, plus eight older steamers of various classes that are used on special occasions.

From Wernigerode, the 21-mile (34 km) ride to Brocken takes one hour and 40 minutes. It is a steep, looping ascent into Hochharz National Park that ends with the line wrapping around the mountain in a tight spiral. Given that the highest summit in the Harz Mountains is at 3,691 feet (1,126 m), and Brocken is in a part of former East Germany that bulged into the West, the mountain made a perfect top-secret Soviet listening post and radar location. This accounts for the Sputnik-like tower, bristling with antennae, that remains. It also explains why Brocken was off-limits and the line closed to passengers from 1961 to 1992. Now hikers are back, many using the train for the upgrade leg of their trip. From the top, views to Wernigerode, 2,900 feet (884 m) below, are outstanding.

With views, hiking, and steep grades, the Brockenbahn is by far the most popular line, but the others—low key and bucolic—have their own charms.

185

Outeniqua Choo-Tjoe

George to Knysna, South Africa

With the Indian Ocean roiling in the background, a curved bridge soars over the broad estuary of the Kaaimans River. Across this much-photographed viaduct run the rails of the 38-mile (61 km) George–Knysna Branch, a railway preservation currently operated by South Africa's Transnet Heritage Foundation. Once or twice daily (depending on the season), Sundays excepted, the *Outeniqua Choo-Tjoe* plies the scenic route, generally powered by steam, a Class 24 branchline 2-8-4. This excursion train—its name onomatopoetic and bilingual (English and the Dutch-based Afrikaans) and noting a mountain range along the route—takes two and a half hours each way for a run that offers fine views of crashing surf, broad beaches, and interesting seaside villages.

Transnet, South Africa's public transport company, encompasses rail (Spoornet), marine (Portnet), and air (South African Airways). The Heritage Foundation, a separate arm under the Transnet umbrella, operates historic aircraft, railway museums at George and Kimberley, and multi-day excursions on the *Union Limited,* as well as the *Choo-Tjoe.* South African

Railways (Spoornet's predecessor) ran substantial regular-service steam into the 1980s, and many of these locomotives—some 75 of them operable—are preserved in the Heritage Foundation collection and used on both the *Union Limited* and the *Outeniqua Choo-Tjoe* journeys.

At George, a completely authentic, fully functional steam locomotive terminal is tucked within the wye where the branch to Knysna swings away from the "Garden Route" mainline, which connects Cape Town with Port Elizabeth. Enginehouse, sandhouse, and a "cocopan" coaling system (where dump cars are loaded by hand) remain in everyday use; switching and the line's limited freight service are still largely operated by steam supplemented by historic diesel locomotives,

nameplate

The Outeniqua Choo-Tjoe crosses the Kaaiman's River Bridge

A 4-8-2 and a Garratt make a photo run-by during an excursion on the Union Limited *on the branch line from George to Knysna.*

also in the Transnet Heritage Foundation collection. While the *Choo-Tjoe* offers an outstanding excursion, the branch, and particularly the complex at George, preserves an authentic slice of steam railroading in its totality.

Another arrow in the Transnet Heritage Foundation quiver is the *Union Limited,* a train of historic coaches that makes regularly scheduled multi-day excursions, pulled largely by steam locomotives.

Named for the predecessor of the famous *Blue Train,* the *Union Limited* spends much of the year in five-night "Golden Thread" tours from Cape Town. (Longer trips with a greater variety of locomotives are run a few times each year.) The Golden Thread itinerary leads first into the wine country of the Western Cape, then along the Garden Route to George. From there the train ventures

north over Montagu Pass to the town of Oudtshoorn, and then over the preserved railway to Knysna.

Steam locomotives are in charge most of the way. Typically, a mainline 4-8-4 might handle the train in and out of Cape Town, before giving way to double-headed 19Ds, branchline 4-8-2s. On the Garden Route and the line to Knysna, a 19D might double-head with a GMAM 4-8-2+2-8-4. (Like the 19Ds, this eccentric locomotive, an articulated Beyer Garratt, was built to operate on the light rail of secondary lines.)

Though many of the passengers are excursionists rather than train enthusiasts, each day sees at least one "photo run-by," with the train unloading photographers and spectators before backing up, then charging past with a great show of smoke and whistling. **187**

FIELD NOTES

DISTANCE 38 miles (61 km)

BEST TIME TO TRAVEL Year-round

GETTING THERE George is near the Indian Ocean coast, between Cape Town and Port Elizabeth, with access by road or on the weekly Southern Cross train from Cape Town

The Zig Zag Railway

New South Wales, Australia

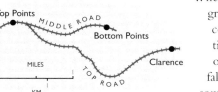

Australia's Zig Zag Railway is the restoration of a spectacular piece of line in the Blue Mountains, about 81 miles (130 km) west of Sydney. Located near Lithgow, the Zig Zag was a remarkable feat of engineering when constructed between 1866 and 1869 by the Great Western Railway. Narrow ledges were blasted from sheer cliffs, while the repeating arches of three sandstone viaducts provided an extraordinary aesthetic highlight. But it is its zig-zag for which this line is renowned.

Zig-zags (generally called "switchbacks" in North America) are a railway builder's last resort.

When confronted with topography too steep to be conquered by conventional methods, engineers occasionally are forced to fall back on this cumbersome expedient. A zig-zag requires a train to reverse direction and back through the middle leg of the switchback, then reverse direction again to complete the transit.

The famous Great Lithgow Zig Zag was on the original mainline west from Sydney. (It was actually one of two; not far away, at Lapstone Hill, the "Little Zig Zag" was a feature of the railroad up the escarpment that the Lithgow Zig Zag later allowed it to descend.)

But the line's single track, steep grades, and the switchbacks in particular soon created a bottleneck. In 1910 it was replaced by an alignment that uses 10 tunnels to go through the mountains, not up them. The original line to Lithgow was abandoned in 1910 but came to life again in 1975, when volunteers relaid about a mile of track on the Middle Road (or middle leg) of that zig-zag. In 1986 to 1988 more track

No. 1072, a former Queensland steam locomotive, prepares for its departure from Lithgow Station.

In 1901 this goods train ran out of control on the descent from Clarence Tunnel. It climbed the buffers and mounted the parapet.

was relaid on the Top Road as far as Clarence, currently the upper terminus. (Today's intercity mainline uses the Bottom Road.)

Though the Zig Zag Railway was originally standard gauge, the restoration is 3-foot-6-inch gauge. This allows historic steam equipment from the state of Queensland (where the railways are all 3-foot-6-inch gauge) to be used. Weekday services for much of the year are aboard sleek, vintage diesel rail motors, while on weekends, and public and school holidays steam locomotives do the honors. These historic locomotives include a 4-8-0, a 2-8-2, a 4-6-2, and a trio of 4-6-4Ts from among a dozen that were built between 1948 and 1952 for commuter service in the city of Brisbane, Queensland. (These "tank" engines were bidirectional, making them ideal for commuter work because they did not need to be turned at the end of short but frequent trips.)

Excursionists who arrive at the Zig Zag Railway by train (a two-and-a-half-hour ride on City-Rail from Sydney) start

their journey at Bottom Points, the lower of the two switches on the original arrangement. Those who come by car begin at the upper terminus, at Clarence.

Leaving there the train drops down through a long tunnel and, on the Top Road, travels across No. 1 Viaduct. At Top Points, the engine moves to the other end of the train and the journey continues down the Middle Road. The train traverses No. 2 and No. 3 Viaducts before it arrives at Bottom Points. The engine switches ends one more time and undertakes the strenuous climb back up a grade of 1 in 42 (or 2.4 percent) to Top Points and Clarence.

FIELD NOTES

DISTANCE 4 miles (6.4 km)

BEST TIME TO TRAVEL

Runs every day except Christmas Day

GETTING THERE Located near Lithgow in the Blue Mountains, around 81 miles (130 km) west of Sydney; linking with mainline rail from Sydney's Central Station

Soon after leaving Belgrave, 2-6-2T No. 7A crosses the Trestle Bridge

Puffing Billy

Victoria, Australia

The oldest preserved railway in Australia is the 2-foot-6-inch-gauge Puffing Billy, located in the Dandenong Ranges 26 miles (42 km) east of Melbourne, Victoria. The 14-mile (23 km) line hosts three to six daily trains (depending on the season and day of the week). All are steam hauled, as the name suggests, except on "total fire ban" days in the heat of summer, when a diesel takes over. The diminutive locomotives and coaches offer a nostalgic ride through rural country, traversing lush, fern-filled valleys and providing fine mountain views.

Belgrave
Menzies Creek
Lakeside
Emerald
Cockatoo
Gembrook

MILES
0   5
0   5
KM

The Puffing Billy was one of four narrow-gauge "developmental railways" (branch lines in American parlance) built by Victorian Railways (VR) around the turn of the 20th century. The line began in Upper Ferntree Gully, about 3 miles (5 km) south of Belgrave, the current terminus, which interchanges with the broad-gauge line to the Victorian capital, Melbourne. It then ran southeast to Gembrook, 18 miles (29 km) away, to collect timber from Gembrook's mills, as well as potatoes from local farms, shrubs from a nursery at Nobelius, and—right from the beginning—excursionists wanting to visit the scenic area.

The majority of the line was closed in 1953 after a landslide, but the railway still hosted excursions on the short stretch from Ferntree Gully to Belgrave until that was broad-gauged in 1958. By this time the Puffing Billy Preservation Society had been formed, and in 1962 a portion of the line was reopened for excursions

An army of volunteers supplements the 30 paid staff on the Puffing Billy preserved line.

Puffing Billy's 2-6-2T arrives back at Belgrave in the afternoon

Maintenance is all in a day's work for volunteers helping to preserve Puffing Billy in Victoria's Dandenong Ranges.

from the new terminus at Belgrave, where a station, yard, and locomotive depot were constructed by volunteers. By 1975 operations had reached Lakeside, about 8 miles (13 km) from Belgrave, which remained the terminus until 1998, when the line was reopened all the way to Gembrook.

The railroad's workhorse locomotives are five NA–class (N for narrow gauge) 2-6-2Ts, from among an original fleet of 17 used throughout VR's 2-foot-6-inch system. The first two were built in 1898 by the Baldwin Locomotive Company in Philadelphia as "pattern engines." The rest were constructed on the same plans at VR's Newport Workshops in Melbourne between 1900 and 1915. Other locomotives on the roster include a VR 1926 Beyer-Garratt (a unique articulated design built in Manchester, England, by Beyer Peacock and widely used on secondary lines in many parts of the British Empire) and a Climax geared locomotive from the state's Forests Commission.

In spite of its whimsical name (the moniker "Puffing Billy" is reminiscent of one of Britain's earliest locomotives, itself preserved and the oldest original locomotive in existence), the railroad is highly professional, with 30 paid staff in addition to the 500 volunteers who help make the operation work. As multiple trains run on the line at the same time, there is a system of "tokens," which the train drivers carry, giving them authority to travel on each particular stretch of line.

Trains run every day of the year except Christmas Day, with day-long round trips the entire length of the line to Gembrook (a run of a little under two hours each way, with a substantial layover in Gembrook to enjoy its shops and museums). There is also a short one-hour round trip to Menzies Creek. Most trains turn at the long-time terminus of Lakeside at Emerald Lake Park, a journey of about one hour each way.

FIELD NOTES

DISTANCE 14 miles (23 km)

BEST TIME TO TRAVEL Runs every day except Christmas

GETTING THERE About one hour from Melbourne, with frequent electric trains from Flinders Street Station

191

Wingatui Viaduct with its soaring iron trestles, is a highlight of the journey

Taieri Gorge Limited

Dunedin, South Island, New Zealand

Dunedin, in New Zealand's South Island, is rich in Scottish tradition, but its finest building, the railway station, is a two-storied stone building of Flemish Renaissance architecture, completed in 1907. From the station the diesel-hauled passenger train, the *Taieri Gorge Limited*, departs on its daily trip through the Taieri Gorge, a journey dubbed "the Denver and Rio Grande of New Zealand."

The Flemish-styled railway station is one of Dunedin's finest buildings.

The *Taieri Gorge Limited* runs to the town of Pukerangi, a distance of 35 miles (56 km), but every Sunday from October to March the train travels to Middlemarch, the end of the line, 12 miles (19 km) farther. The Pukerangi return journey takes four hours, with an extra hour for the Middlemarch return trip.

The train runs on what was formerly the Otago Central Branch of New Zealand Railways (NZR); it is now known as Taieri Gorge Railway. Construction began in 1879, and it took 42 years for the line to reach Cromwell, 147 miles (237 km) from Dunedin. NZR operated both passenger and freight services on the line, which also served the construction of the nearby Clyde Dam. Then in 1976 it announced that it would cease operating the passenger trains.

So the Otago Branch of the New Zealand Railway and Locomotive Society decided to run its own passenger trains and purchased some old carriages. The Society's operating organization, the Otago Excursion Train Trust, ran the first excursion to Central Otago in October 1979. Following the completion of the dam and

The Taieri Gorge Railway offers spectacular scenery

a decline in other freight traffic, NZR announced that it would close the line completely on April 30, 1990. However, the scenic beauty of the Otago Central had made the excursions so popular that enthusiasts were not willing to let the line go. The Society launched a successful public appeal to purchase it as far as Middlemarch. This was also vested with the Otago Excursion Train Trust.

After leaving Dunedin, the train travels southwest across the fertile Taieri Plains for 7 miles (11 km) to Wingatui on the South Island Main Trunk Railway and then turns northwest onto the Taieri Gorge Railway. A gradual climb up to Salisbury follows, and then there is the descent into the rocky Taieri Gorge.

On the descent the train crosses the slender wrought-iron 113-year-old Wingatui Viaduct. At 646 feet (197 m) long and 154 feet (47 m) high, it is the longest and highest viaduct on the line. The train clings to the rocky schist outcrops of the Taieri

FIELD NOTES

✳ DISTANCE 47 miles (76 km)

BEST TIME TO TRAVEL Autumn colors, from March to May, are spectacular

✳ GETTING THERE Dunedin is 225 miles (362 km) south of Christchurch, with daily train, coach, and air services

Gorge, which are interspersed with tussocks and small trees, through to Pukerangi. It crosses 22 more viaducts and bridges, and passes through 10 tunnels. After Pukerangi, the barren gorge opens onto the South Taieri Plain as the train descends into Middlemarch, the largest town in the area, with a population of 250. The train stops occasionally in the course of the journey to allow passengers to disembark to take photographs or to enjoy the ruggedness of this wilderness region. Those who are adventurous and fit can leave the train at Middlemarch and cycle 93 miles (150 km) on the old rail line as far as Clyde, on New Zealand's first Rail Trail.

The area is home to native lizards and birds such as hawks, bellbirds, and tui. It is especially beautiful in autumn, from March to May, when the trees turn golden and the landscape is a riot of color.

The tiled floor of Dunedin railway station features quaint representations of the trains.

193

On a train, all things are possible.

PAUL THEROUX (b. 1941), American travel writer and novelist

CHAPTER SEVEN
GREAT RAIL JOURNEYS

WHAT MAKES *a* GREAT RAILWAY JOURNEY?

Luxury or adventure, history or modernity, scenery or mechanics, great rail journeys are made of these.

Dependent as we are on automobiles, the magic of rail travel is powerful. Our fascination with the passenger train, itself surprisingly resilient against long odds, has survived jet planes, interstate highways, and autobahns. In the United States, it's helped an often struggling Amtrak to survive. In Europe, it's been the icing on the cake of practicality that has led most countries to make huge investments in passenger railroading.

What makes some rail journeys special, while others remain merely routine? Since trains offer an ideal window to the world, scenery—the more spectacular the better—is a big part of the magic. Some trains, such as Amtrak's *California Zephyr*, VIA Rail's *Canadian*, and Swiss Federal Railway's *Glacier Express*, are famous for it. Often the spectacle involves mountain ranges and rivers, but for the savvy traveler it could just as well be a cityscape lit at night.

A journey's purpose is another factor. The 5:11 local carrying commuters home won't qualify as a great train journey, but Australia's *Indian Pacific,* spanning the continent from ocean to ocean, certainly will. So will the *Rossia* on its epic Trans-Siberian route from Moscow to Vladivostok.

And though the last years of the 20th century saw a growth in the popularity of trains that act like cruise ships (the *American Orient Express* is a fine example), great rail journeys—even when taken primarily for their own sake—almost always retain a sense of destination. The Cunard Line's famous slogan, "Getting there is half the fun," was about line voyages by steamship, not about cruises.

Food and service might also elevate a rail journey to greatness. Dinner in the diner is an article of faith among train devotees, and the lure of fine, fresh food stylishly served on crisp linen decked out with fresh flowers and brightly polished silver is a powerful draw. This is an evocative part of the legacy of many now-vanished trains— the *20th Century Limited,* or the *Super Chief*—but also a current reality on such trains

STUNNING LANDSCAPES *are part of the story—the California Zephyr nears Thompson, Utah, hauled by a modern Amtrak GE AMD-103 engine.*

as the *Venice Simplon-Orient-Express* (*VSOE*), where the dining-car cuisine has been taken to new heights and the service is white glove.

The lavishness of the accommodation obviously plays a role too. On Rovos Rail's *Pride of Africa*, a suite may fill half a coach, offering a double bed and a bathtub. The competing *Blue Train*'s newly refurbished rooms have the finely crafted stylishness of the most elegant yacht. And the *VSOE* is literally a rolling museum, in which elegance combines with historical authenticity.

Not all great train trips are luxurious, however. In fact the adventurous can be as wonderful as the plush. Rattling down Patagonia's Esquel Branch behind steam; hanging on as India's "Toy Train" climbs to Darjeeling; bartering with vendors selling food and crafts on a platform overlooking Mexico's Copper Canyon—these experiences can be memorable, too, whatever physical hardships they might impose on the traveler.

Though many of the world's great rail journeys have not survived, they still

Yet there isn't a train I wouldn't take, / No matter where it's going.

From *"Travel,"*
EDNA ST. VINCENT MILLAY
(1892–1950), American poet

hold magic for those lucky enough to have experienced them, such as a ride on one of Java's once-rich collection of historic working steam engines, now replaced by the ubiquitous diesel.

There are yet others that have been destroyed, through war or commercial neglect, that may once again be revived. Here the resourcefulness of the tiny nation of Eritrea is to be marveled at in their commitment to rebuild

the once-enthralling railway above the Red Sea coast.

With any great rail journey it's safe to say that the whole equals more than the sum of the parts. There's the rush of anticipation as, walking beside a train that stretches far down the platform, you read car numbers in a quest for yours; the cozy security of a berth at night, from which you peek at the lonely lights of farmhouses as the train hurtles into the darkness. There's that special enjoyment of dining in motion, when a freshly cooked meal and the endlessly unfolding vistas outside the window vie for attention, and the conviviality of the lounge car, where strangers become instant friends and confidantes through some alchemy unique to train travel. And always there's the rumble underfoot of wheel on rail, at once soothing but also exhilarating, which tells you that you're going somewhere.

No doubt some would agree with the sentiment of Edna St. Vincent Millay's poem (above). Others are much fussier, opting only for the best.

THE WOOD-PANELED LOUNGE *of*
Southeast Asia's Eastern and Oriental
Express *is lavishly furnished.*

A GREAT JOURNEY
that ONCE WAS

Some of the world's most memorable train journeys no longer exist.

One in Indonesia was neither luxurious nor even comfortable,

yet the memory of it still evokes the magic of steam.

During the 1970s the Indonesian State Railway possessed historic locomotives of an incredible diversity. Most were of European origin from the early 20th century, when the country was still part of the Dutch East Indies. Java was especially rich in vintage locomotives, and they were characterized by an amazing decrepitude. They ranged from enormous four-cylinder compound Mallets to the world's last 2-4-0 passenger engines and steam trams.

With diesel's ascension, all these locomotives were out of service by the mid-1980s; many branch lines had been closed even before then. At least 60 engines have been preserved, however. Most are in the Transportation Museum in Jakarta or the museum in Ambarawa, central Java. In the latter there is a 5½-mile (9 km) preserved line. Visitors are able to hire a century-old locomotive and carriages.

A MAGICAL JOURNEY

But the experience of riding an original steam engine before the closure of the lines in part sums up steam's magic. One such branch line ran from Tanahaban to Labuan on Java's west coast via the town of Rangkasbitung. Among the veteran engines still in service

A B51 CLASS 4-4-0 *reveals its solid Prussian ancestry as it takes on water at Rangkasbitung. More than 40 of these locomotives were built for the Dutch East Indies in the early 1900s by both Dutch and German builders, and survived until the 1980s.*

in the 1970s was a B51 Class two-cylinder compound 4-4-0 built in 1909 by Werkspoor, Amsterdam, its lineage from 19th-century Prussia.

The train consisted of six ancient coaches that heaved with humanity one warm evening in 1974. There was no lighting, seats were missing, and the windows were either jammed open or jammed shut. Many passengers chose to ride on the roof. The engine had no steam brake, a shortage of suitable brake shoes having caused it to be disconnected, so a dubious-looking tender handbrake was the train's sole means of stopping.

Yet engine B5138 stormed out of Rangkasbitung, doing its Prussian ancestry proud.

The fuel was a mix of coal, wood, and oil, and black smoke pumped into the darkening sky. The grand locomotive heaved violently over the track. A roar of escaping steam from a leak in the front end contrasted with the throbbing rasps of the exhaust. Suddenly, the engine picked up speed dramatically, its machinery churning and pulsating with the effort.

The whistle screamed as the train sped past vast sugar-cane plantations, tiny villages, and small open crossings at which ox carts were briefly lit by the engine's incandescence. The white-hot fire threw vivid reflections in the thick exhaust trail, causing the smoke to flutter with crimson

AMONG THE LAST *express passenger steam trains to remain in world service were these B51 Class 4-4-0s, pictured at Rangkasbitung (left). A B5138 arrives at the village of Pandeglang between Labuan and Rangkasbitung (below).*

flashes. Stops were made at several small stations sullenly lit by oil lamps, and shadowy figures carrying sacks and boxes emerged from the train to vanish into the gloom.

Under a star-sown sky, the train ran though miles of rice paddies over which galaxies of fireflies were visible, so dense that many merged into blazing clusters of light. Just at that moment the engine's coal supply ran out and logs alone became the source of fuel. The B51 responded with a flurry of wood sparks from the chimney which cascaded amid the fireflies. The darkness burst into a bright tapestry as darting spirals and pinpoints of silver and orange formed constantly changing patterns.

On that beautiful island was found the all-consuming magic of the steam train.

A GREAT JOURNEY
that MIGHT BE AGAIN

The impoverished African nation of Eritrea is battling all odds

to rebuild one of the world's most spectacular mountain railways.

One nation has rediscovered the steam age. Eritrea is one of Africa's youngest countries, having gained its independence from Ethiopia in 1993 after a bitter civil war that lasted 30 years. Despite being one of the poorest nations on Earth, Eritrea is committed to restoring its Italian-built railway between the port of Massawa, on the Red Sea coast, and the capital of Asmara, 74 miles (119 km) inland, in the hope of attracting tourists and supporting freight traffic from the port.

The line has been relaid to about half of the total distance, from Massawa to Ghinda, and, despite still-volatile relations with Ethiopia, some optimistic tour companies are planning for the full journey.

THE LEGACY OF WAR
Once completed, trains on this unique 950-millimeter-gauge railway will again struggle up the fog-shrouded Arborobu escarpment. The climb is to an incredible 7,143 feet (2,179 m) above sea level, with 30 tunnels and 65 bridges, making this one of the world's most spectacular mountain railways.

The railway was wrecked during the civil war, with track ripped up for use in

A 0-4-4-0 MALLET
No. 442.59, built by Ansaldo of Milan in 1938, is back on track, hauling an engineer's train on the restored main-line outside Massawa.

military bunkers and passenger coaches transported away to be used as military sleeping quarters. The line's restoration is one of the world's most exciting railway stories since, with little outside involvement, this poor and fragile nation is achieving the work

Our railway system will

serve as a historical

monument.

ATO AMANUEL GHEBRESILASIE,
Head of Eritrean Railway
Transport, October 1997

almost with bare hands. The whole country has been mobilized for the task, even school-children on holidays and youth in military service. Volunteers have gone to the old battlefields to recover rails and sleepers from the trenches, with each rail having to be reshaped manually. Septuagenarian engineers, engine drivers, and other experts have also been recalled, the younger generations having no experience of the railways.

Asmara's old engine shed has been reopened and its machine tools coaxed back to life to overhaul the steam locomotives—0-4-0WTs built in Italy by Breda in the 1920s and 1930s, and the superb 0-4-4-0T four-cylinder compound Mallets built by Ansaldo in 1938.

No less exciting are the system's two historic art deco Littorina diesel railcars built by Fiat in 1936. Several Well Tanks and two Mallets have been steamed and are ready to return to service.

THE LOCOMOTIVE SHED *in Asmara came back to life in 1998 when Italian-built Breda 0-4-0WTs of the 1920s and 1930s were overhauled after lying derelict for 25 years (above). Rail workers use the workshop's turntable to steam-test Well Tank 202-004 (left). This 1936 Fiat-built art deco diesel rail-car (below) will also return to service.*

The two Mallets have been used to haul engineers' trains, along with a pair of former Russian lorries, known as Orals. The lorries have been modified to run on railway tracks through considerable improvization. A further example of the Eritreans' amazing resourcefulness is the track inspection trolley built out of a classic Motoguzzi motorcycle of the 1930s, complete with a gear change on the side of the petrol tank.

The ultimate hope is to restore the line even beyond Asmara over a further 117-mile (188 km) section to transport both freight and passengers to Keren and Agordat, close to the Eritrean border with Sudan.

Passengers aboard the Canadian get a close look at wildlife

The Canadian

Toronto to Vancouver, Canada

Though rerouted from its original Canadian Pacific (CP) rails, the *Canadian* from Toronto to Vancouver remains one of the world's greatest train rides.

Both a time machine and a magic carpet, it whisks its passengers across the vast variety of Canadian topography. This is a leisurely journey, however, taking some 74 hours to travel 2,760 miles (4,444 km) over the Canadian National (CN) line. VIA Rail Canada, the national rail passenger corporation, which operates the *Canadian,* essentially owns no track but runs on the CP and CN rails.

The *Canadian*'s journey embraces the wild terrain of the Canadian Shield, a rugged expanse of Precambrian rock, muskeg swamps, countless lakes, rushing rivers, and endless forests; the fertile wheatfields of Saskatchewan; and the mountains of Western Canada—the Rockies, the

Selkirks, later the Coastal Range—some crowned in snow year-round. This country, among the most beautiful in North America, includes such highlights as Pyramid Falls, the Albreda Glacier, Moose Lake, and Mount Robson.

And the *Canadian* itself is beautiful to look at—a sinuous silver train of perfectly matched stainless steel cars that occasionally number as many as 35 in peak summer season. (In winter and the shoulder seasons, the train is often a third that size or smaller, providing a travel experience in many ways preferable.) These cars comprise day coaches, a mid-train dome lounge, a smartly appointed diner, dome-observation car with rounded "bullet lounge" at the train's end, and sleeping cars.

The sleeping cars offer roomettes, bedrooms, and drawing rooms (now called

The Canadian *winds through deep forests on the Canadian National route via Yellowhead Pass.*

202

observation dome

single, double, and triple bedrooms), all with showers. There are also "open sections," upper and lower berths that are made down at night and hung with heavy curtains, a sight more familiar in old movies than contemporary train travel.

Canadian Pacific Railway placed this equipment into service in 1955 as the *Canadian*, running between Vancouver and both Montreal and Toronto. In the early 1990s it was thoroughly rebuilt mechanically (changing to a "head-end-powered" electrical system for heating, air-conditioning, and lighting) and refurbished cosmetically. Modern art now adorns the walls, and the color scheme throughout runs to blues and grays, with rose accents in the dining car.

With this upgrading VIA introduced the Silver & Blue (or Bleu d'Argent) class: riding in sleepers, with meals included in the ticket price. Ironically, the upgrading followed massive cuts in VIA service. This included cancelling the original *Canadian* service on the CP line. This route hugged the shore of Lake Superior in Ontario, served

Banff and Lake Louise in Alberta, then cork-screwed through the famous Spiral Tunnels. But VIA moved the "Canadian" name and equipment to the CN route to the north.

While the loss of service on the historic CP route in the west is lamentable (though the *Rocky Mountaineer,* a privately owned tour train, does serve it in summer), the *Canadian*'s current run via Jasper and Yellowhead Pass has plenty of scenic charm, especially when seen from the dome windows of a classic 1950s streamliner.

FIELD NOTES

DISTANCE 2,760 miles (4,444 km)

BEST TIME TO TRAVEL *Shoulder seasons to avoid crowds (the train triples in size in summer); winter landscapes can be beautiful*

SPECIAL FEATURES *Spectacular scenery; dome lounge and observation car; well-appointed sleeping and dining cars*

203

Passing through the beautiful Bow Valley in Banff National Park

The Rocky Mountaineer

Calgary, Banff, and Jasper to Vancouver, Canada

Dome cars have been a staple amid the snowcapped peaks of the Canadian Rockies since 1955, when Canadian Pacific (CP) introduced them onto its new streamliner, the *Canadian*. But with its full-length Gold Leaf domes, built by Denver's Rader Railcar and introduced in 1995, the privately operated *Rocky Mountaineer* has improved on a good thing.

The *Rocky Mountaineer*'s principal route is from Calgary to Vancouver (with a stop at Banff, where most passengers board or disembark for sightseeing). It's a trip of 667 miles (1,074 km) that takes two full days, including an overnight hotel stop midway at Kamloops, British Columbia.

In 1990, the *Canadian* was rerouted from the CP line north to the Canadian National (CN) tracks through Jasper. Since then the *Rocky Mountaineer* has been the only train to make the scenic run beneath the turreted Castle Mountain, by the spectacular Mount Victoria Glacier, over Kicking Horse Pass, through the famous and fascinating Spiral Tunnels, across Stoney Creek Bridge, and along houseboat-strewn Shuswap Lake.

For five years, until 1995, the *Rocky Mountaineer* operated strictly with ordinary coaches, a class of service now called "Red Leaf." With limited visibility and airline-style meals, the experience of riding these former CN cars is a far cry from the amenities of "Gold Leaf," where passengers are accommodated in the upper-level dome of the double-decker cars.

There's not a bad seat in the house. And on the lower level scrumptious breakfasts and lunches are served on linen-covered tables. The cars' open observation platforms are another bonus, an ideal place to watch mountains, rivers, and lakes slide by, hour after scenic hour.

The *Rocky Mountaineer*'s secondary route is Jasper–Vancouver (550 miles, or 886 km), where VIA's *Canadian* also operates. Canadian Northern opened the Jasper–Kamloops line in 1915. (The railway company almost immediately fell into bankruptcy and became part of Canadian National, until recently a ward of the Canadian government.) The route from Jasper to Vancouver is generally considered to be less scenic than the CP line to the south, and it is certainly less acclaimed.

Map labels: Jasper — Banff — Calgary — Kamloops — Vancouver — MILES 0 160 — KM 0 200

The Canadian Pacific route through Banff was the nation's first transcontinental railroad. Completed in 1885, when the last spike (of utilitarian iron rather than ceremonial gold) was driven at Craigellachie, British Columbia, the line bound that state to the rest of Canada and arguably preserved the shape of the nation as it exists today. Without question the building of the CP is one of the great Canadian epics, and travel over this endlessly scenic route is further enriched by its history.

East of Kamloops, the CP line is no stranger to rivers: the Bow, the Kicking Horse, the Columbia, the Beaver, the Illecillewaet, the Eagle, the South Thompson, each joined and abandoned as the tracks jump from watershed to

Passengers are treated to in-seat service in the upper level of the train's Gold Leaf dome cars as the scenery slips by. Breakfast and lunch are served downstairs.

watershed, crossing the Continental Divide and winding their way westward.

Beyond Kamloops, the running is exclusively at waterside—a gathering flow that funnels to the Pacific via Kamloops Lake, the Thompson River, and finally the powerful Fraser. (Here the *Rocky Mountaineer* uses CN tracks, generally right across one river or another from the CP.) It's a great potpourri of scenery, from the alpine heights of the Rockies to the classic cowboy, sagebrush West around Kamloops, and the lushness of the Coastal Range into Vancouver.

The Adirondack runs along Lake Champlain's Willsboro Bay

The Adirondack

New York City, United States of America, to Montreal, Canada

Say Amtrak and scenery and most people think West, but there is one train in the Northeast whose journey can rival any through the Rockies. In its 381-mile (613 km) daylight run, taking nine and a half hours, the *Adirondack* follows the Hudson River north to Albany, then shadows Lake Champlain for its substantial length of over 100 miles (161 km). There's rarely a dull moment from departure to arrival.

Leaving New York's Pennsylvania Station, the *Adirondack* follows the Empire Connection out of Manhattan, passing under George Washington Bridge. For the next 140 miles (225 km), the Hudson River is rarely far away. Across the broad waters the impressive cliffs of New Jersey's Palisades loom. Soon comes the long, curving Tappan Zee Bridge, then Bear Mountain Bridge, nestled in the picturesque Highlands of the Hudson. There are the daunting fortresses of West

Point, the castle-like arsenal on Bannerman's Island, various lighthouses, and both commercial and recreational river traffic.

About an hour and a half beyond Albany, the train reaches the pinched southern tip of Lake Champlain, swerving to echo every bend in the shoreline. From there all the way to Plattsburgh the track flirts with the lake, running high above it in the Red Rocks at Willsboro Bay.

Though somewhat offset by the inevitable, annoying delay for customs at the border, the international flavor of the train is attractive, the French atmosphere of Montreal making this all the more piquant.

The *Adirondack*'s immediate ancestor was the *Laurentian,* run on essentially the same route by

Amtrack's Adirondack in its period as a Turboliner.

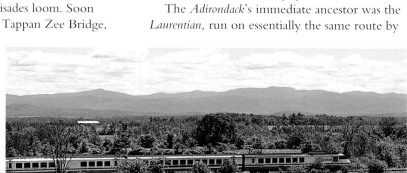

Laurentian, Adirondack's predecessor, skirts a frozen Lake Champlain

the Delaware & Hudson (D&H) north of Albany and south of there by the New York Central (later Penn Central). It lasted until the formation of Amtrak in 1971, at which time the train was dropped. But it had gained attention from railfans beginning in 1968, when it was re-equipped with glamorous sleek Alco PA diesels from the Santa Fe, and stylish streamlined coaches and diners from the Denver & Rio Grande Western.

FIELD NOTES

DISTANCE 381 miles (613 km)

BEST TIME TO TRAVEL Autumn colors are especially beautiful

SPECIAL FEATURES A run along the Hudson River and Lake Champlain with Heritage Fleet equipment

In 1974 the *Laurentian* was reborn in the Amtrak era as the *Adirondack,* thanks to financial support from New York State. Bruce Sterzing, the D&H's iconoclastic young president, took a unique position. He wanted the train to bear the D&H imprint, rather than the homogenous Amtrak style and colors. As a result, the PAs (rebuilt by Morrison-Knudsen) were returned to service and the surviving coaches and diner-lounges refurbished.

For a few years, the *Adirondack* wore eye-catching D&H gray, blue, and yellow livery, sometimes sported dome cars, and set diner tables with crockery bearing the D&H logo and New York State seal. But Sterzing and Amtrak knocked heads, and before long Amtrak's Turboliners and later Amfleet equipment (with slim windows unfortunate for such a scenic run) took over. Then, in the 1990s, Amtrak decided to refurbish some of its older Heritage Fleet equipment with large windows expressly for service on the *Adirondack,* bringing back better viewing of this wonderful scenic line.

The northbound Adirondack *has just traversed Breakneck Tunnel in its run alongside the Hudson River.*

The California Zephyr

Chicago to Oakland, United States of America

With a 2,436-mile (3,929 km) route that traverses Colorado's Rocky Mountains and California's Sierras as it links Chicago with the San Francisco Bay, Amtrak's *California Zephyr* (*CZ*) offers a 52-hour rail journey unsurpassed for scenery.

Westbound from Chicago, the *CZ* runs through Illinois farm country before crossing the Mississippi River at Burlington, Iowa, in mid-evening. The next morning, at Denver, the main event begins as the train makes a sweeping, looping ascent of the Front Range of the Rockies, with views back toward the city and the Great Plains beyond. After cresting the Continental Divide in 6-mile (10 km) Moffat Tunnel, the tracks join the Colorado River; before leaving it 238 miles (383 km) later they will have traversed no fewer than five canyons—Byers, Gore, Red, Glenwood, and Ruby—each quite different, and all beautiful.

The next day the train reaches California's Sierra Nevada Mountains, which are hardly less spectacular. After cresting Donner Pass, where

in winter the railroad battles some of the fiercest snow conditions in North America, it winds its way through the American River Canyon, where the North Fork of the river roars along far below the rails.

The first *CZ* was inaugurated in 1949 with sleek "moderne" cars of fluted stainless steel, which were delivered by North America's preeminent builder of streamliners, the Budd Company of Philadelphia. This all-new train—owned and run jointly by a consortium of the Chicago, Burlington & Quincy (CB&Q), Denver & Rio Grande Western (D&RGW),

Silver Crescent, the dome observation car of the original streamlined California Zephyr, was built by the Budd Company.

Winter running offers spectacular snowscapes

Vista-Dome observation car

and Western Pacific (WP)—sported five of the then-novel Vista-Dome cars, with glass bubbles projecting above the roofline for unobstructed viewing.

The *CZ* quickly grew famous as a train scheduled for scenery, traveling the Rockies and Sierras in daylight and the Great Plains and the Nevada desert at night, as it still does for today's passengers. But stylish equipment, fine food in the diner, and special onboard services were also important as the train established a reputation for excellence.

This self-proclaimed "most talked about train in America" became a cause célèbre in the late 1960s when WP and then D&RGW filed with the Interstate Commerce Commission (ICC) for permission to discontinue it because of operating losses. The ICC at first declined, describing the train as "a unique national asset," but then finally agreed. The original train made its final departure on March 20, 1970. More than the loss of any other train, the demise of the *CZ*, much chronicled in the press, alerted politicians and the public to the real peril that the United States could become a country without long-distance passenger trains. Then, in 1971, Amtrak was created to save some of what little remained of America's once-proud fleet.

Happily, Amtrak's *CZ* (which reclaimed the name in 1983 when it returned to its original route through the Rockies) is a more than reasonable facsimile of the original. With its double-decker Superliner cars (in use since 1980) offering comfortable sleeping berths (standard, deluxe, family, and disabled-accessible), tasty meals served in the diner, and the Sightseer lounge car with its broad, tall windows, today's *CZ* is worthy of its illustrious heritage.

FIELD NOTES

DISTANCE 2,436 miles (3,929 km)

BEST TIME TO TRAVEL Shoulder seasons to avoid summer crowds; aspens can be beautiful in autumn

SPECIAL FEATURES Scheduled for scenery; double-decker sleeping cars; dining and lounge cars

209

The Coast Starlight on Cuesta Grade in the San Lucia Mountains

The Coast Starlight

Los Angeles to Seattle, United States of America

For all their strengths—and these include fine scenery, broad-windowed lounges and dining cars, and comfortable sleeping cars—Amtrak's Western trains of bilevel Superliner equipment typically suffer from sameness. Other than route and small touches here and there, the *Empire Builder*, *Southwest Chief*, *Sunset Limited*, and *Texas Chief* are much like the *California Zephyr*.

One train does stand out from the others, however, and that's the *Coast Starlight*, which takes two full days and a night to traverse the 1,389 miles (2,236 km) between Los Angeles and Seattle, via Oakland, Sacramento, and Portland. In the mid-1990s Amtrak wanted to make this train something special, and it succeeded. A number of features and amenities were added, many centering around the Pacific Parlour Car, which provides lounge space exclusively for sleeping-car passengers. On no other train does Amtrak offer this service.

The Pacific Parlour Cars—spacious, airy, and handsomely appointed—are actually clever retreads. They were built in 1956 as lounge cars for the Santa Fe's all-coach Chicago–Los

Angeles *El Capitan*. (Though it had no sleepers, the double-decker *El Capitan* would be the model for Amtrak's Superliner fleet.) Dolled up at Amtrak's Beech Grove Shops, the Pacific Parlours now host champagne receptions and wine tastings, and provide entertainment. They also hold a library and, perhaps most important of all, provide a perfect spot for gazing out the window or chatting with fellow passengers.

While elsewhere on Amtrak wine generally means a screw-top split, good local vintages are poured from corked bottles in the Pacific Parlour and in the *Coast Starlight*'s diner. Quality micro-brew beers from producers along the route are also available. Menus are specific to the train and feature local specialties. Fresh flowers adorn not only the public rooms but also the sleeping compartments.

Coach travel on the *Coast Starlight* has its attractions as well. The Sightseer Lounge is open to all passengers. A children's playroom offers games and activities—and visits from an entertainer, often a magician, who also performs in the Pacific Parlour Car.

There's plenty to see from the lounge and elsewhere, as the train passes some of the finest

Seattle
Portland
Sacramento
Oakland
Los Angeles

MILES
0   300   600
0   750
KM

FIELD NOTES

DISTANCE 1,389 miles
(2,236 km)
BEST TIME TO TRAVEL Year-round
(in autumn and winter
north from Los Angeles
is best direction for scenery)
SPECIAL FEATURES Dramatic
and varied scenery; Pacific Parlour Cars
offer lounge space for sleeping-car
passengers, including entertainment;
Sightseer Lounge is open to all and
has a children's playroom

The Coast Starlight moves through signals in the Salinas Valley in Harlem, California.

and most varied scenery in the West. Particularly in seasons short on daylight, and considering the possibility of en-route delays, north from Los Angeles is the preferred direction of travel to take advantage of the scenery.

After winding through the Santa Susanna Mountains, the tracks—the Coast Line of the Southern Pacific, now part of the Union Pacific—run along the Pacific Ocean for some 110 miles (177 km), through Santa Barbara and on to Pismo Beach. Then, almost immediately,

at San Luis Obispo, they begin to climb toward Cuesta Pass, looping through two graceful horseshoe curves in the process.

The following morning brings another of the scenic highlights, the passage through the Cascade Mountains, with features including Upper Klamath Lake, the Williamson River, and the climb to Cascade Summit. The line then drops a dramatic 2,700 feet (823 m) to travel through Willamette Pass and Salt Creek Canyon. In early evening it's back to tidewater, as the train runs along Commencement Bay of Puget Sound and into Tacoma before logging the final miles into Seattle.

The Sierra Madre Express nears the Copper Canyon

The Copper Canyon

Chihuahua to Los Mochis, Mexico

If Mexico's Copper Canyon is an astonishing spectacle—and it is deeper and wider than the Grand Canyon—then the railroad that serves it is hardly less remarkable. Completed in 1961 and named El Ferrocarril Chihuahua al Pacifico, the line needs 86 tunnels, 36 major bridges, and assorted spirals and horseshoes to wend its 405 miles (652 km) from Chihuahua City to Los Mochis near the Sea of Cortez, an arm of the Pacific Ocean.

The railroad has an intriguing history. Though it has even older roots, it was effectively begun in 1900 by North American

A Los Mochis-bound train at Temoris, where the completion of the railroad to the Copper Canyon was celebrated in 1961.

businessman Arthur E. Stillwell as the Kansas City, Mexico & Orient—the Orient Line—in hope of linking the Midwest with the Pacific. When, six decades later, the last rails finally were laid through the Sierra Madre Occidental by the government of Mexico to finish the line, earlier completed sections of it had already been abandoned, so it never did function as the intended through route.

Though the railroad doesn't actually enter the Copper Canyon, it passes just a stone's throw from the rim at Divisadero and does traverse other canyons. Amid miles of beautiful scenery, with towering crags and cascading rivers punctuated by tunnels and other virtuoso performances of railroad engineering, one

MILES
0   120
0   160
KM

Chihuahua
Cuauntemo
Creel
Divisadero
El Fuerte
Los Mochis

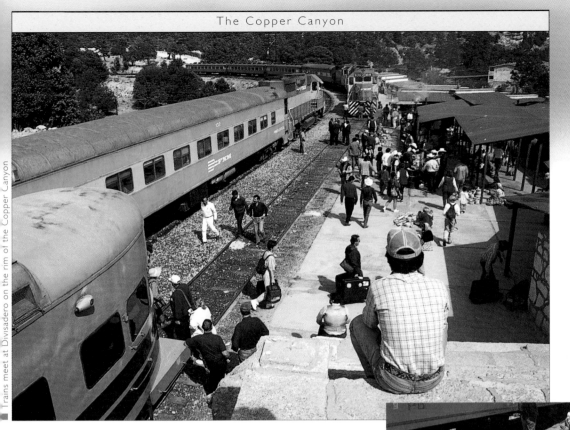

Trains meet at Divisadero on the rim of the Copper Canyon

location stands out: Estation Temoris. Here the line drops into the Santa Barbara Canyon using three levels of track, turning at one end in a tunnel (aptly named La Pera, "the pear," with its 180-degree turn) and at the other end on a graceful curved bridge across the Rio Septentrion.

FIELD NOTES

DISTANCE 405 miles (652 km)

BEST TIME TO TRAVEL Winter and early spring, to avoid summer heat

SPECIAL FEATURES Miles of beautiful scenery, with towering crags and cascading rivers punctuated by tunnels, bridges, spirals, and horseshoes, with overnight stopovers

At Divisadero local people sell their produce and crafts to travelers.

There are distinctly different ways to go by train to the Copper Canyon. The most economical is to take the regular daily train between Chihuahua and Los Mochis, stopping for hotel overnights along the way. In July 1999, as part of a countrywide initiative to privatize the railroads, the Copper Canyon line was sold to Ferrocarril Mexicano (or FerroMex), a wholly owned subsidiary of Grupo Mexico (which also owns mines served by the railroad) and the Union Pacific railway. The new owner has upgraded passenger service, now offering Express Class with refurbished cars and light meals on board. At midday the eastbound and westbound trains meet at Divisadero, where canyon views are superb and the platform teems with vendors hawking crafts and food.

More luxurious is a pair of U.S.-based private trains, the *Sierra Madre Express* (*SME*) and the *South Orient Express* (*SOE*). With an eclectic group of cars that includes an ex-Union Pacific dome diner and an ex-Northern Pacific round-end observation car (a *North Coast Limited* veteran), the *SME* offers six-day round trips from Nogales to Creel, with two nights on the train and three nights off the train to explore the Copper Canyon and surrounding areas.

The *SOE* has no sleeping cars, so all four nights on tour are spent in hotels. Passengers travel in Budd-built stainless steel cars that include domes of *California Zephyr* heritage and an ex-New York Central round-end observation car. The *SOE* runs one-way and round trips in either direction between Chihuahua and Los Mochis. But whatever the conveyance, the goal is the same: Barranca del Cobre, the Copper Canyon.

213

Mary Queen of Scots at Loch Dubh on the West Highland Railway

Fort William to Mallaig

Scotland, Great Britain

Completed in 1901, the 42-mile (68 km) Mallaig Extension of Scotland's West Highland Railway was among Great Britain's last major rail-building projects. It is also among the most spectacular. Anyone who thinks that all British countryside is tame, cozy, cultivated, and contained by hedgerows should ride this line as it plunges into wild, remote, and brilliantly scenic country on Scotland's rugged western shoreline.

Four trains—modern Super Sprinter diesel-electric railcars—operate in each direction between Fort William and Mallaig every Monday through Saturday, with one on Sunday. The ride takes one hour and 20 minutes. These services are run by ScotRail Railways Ltd., one of 25 train-operating companies created when British Rail was privatized in 1994. The Jacobite Steam Train also runs in summer, from Sunday to Friday, under the aegis of the West Coast Railway Company.

Whether behind steam or aboard a Super Sprinter, passengers leaving Fort William

see Ben Nevis, Britain's highest mountain, towering in the distance. After running along narrow Loch Eil, the train crosses Glenfinnan Viaduct—a beautiful, curved, 1,248-foot-long (380 m) structure that was revolutionary for its time because it was built of concrete. In fact, the use of this material in railway construction was pioneered on the Mallaig Extension. The line uses 21 arches to cross the valley near where Bonnie Prince Charlie (Charles Stuart) gathered the clans for the Stuart claim to the British throne against King George II in 1745.

A kaleidoscope of water and mountain views follows as the line touches Lochs Ailort, Dubh, and Nam Uamh. Then comes Borrodale Bridge, a single span 128 feet (39 m) long that was a pioneering landmark for Robert MacAlpine, the line's civil engineer.

Ben Nevis, here looming behind the train from Fort William to Mallaig, is Scotland's highest mountain.

Loch Eil is just one of the many lakes the West Highland line passes en route to Mallaig.

He came to be known as "Concrete Bob" for his work with that material. (Ironically, the concrete bridge was given decorative stonework and battlements to satisfy the landowner, who apparently had little appreciation for the aesthetics of Concrete Bob's important innovation.)

Water vistas change from fresh to salt as the train skirts the Sound of Sleat before coming to a stop at the terminal at Mallaig; this little fishing village is also the port for the ferry to Ardrasar on the Isle of Skye. Initially Mallaig's herring harvest was the main reason for the extension, along with the sheep and cattle

raised along the route. And right from the beginning the summer tourist trade was significant.

Many passengers on the Mallaig Extension will have made the rail trip from Glasgow over the original section of the West Highland line, completed to Fort William in 1894. Taking close to four hours, this 122-mile (196 km) route is no slouch for scenery either. Rannoch Moor is an extraordinary expanse of peat bog and rock, brightened in season by the yellow flowers of Scotch broom and the purple flowers of heather. Corrour Summit is 1,347 feet (411 m) above sea level, making it the highest point on any of Britain's railways. Passengers coming from London can take the overnight Caledonian Sleeper through Glasgow right to Fort William. Making this journey in a comfortable sleeping compartment brings the mountainous and remote region of western Scotland into surprisingly easy reach.

FIELD NOTES

DISTANCE 42 miles (68 km)

BEST TIME TO TRAVEL Spring and summer (the Jacobite Steam Train operates in summer only)

SPECIAL FEATURES A run of almost one and a half hours through wild Scottish terrain

215

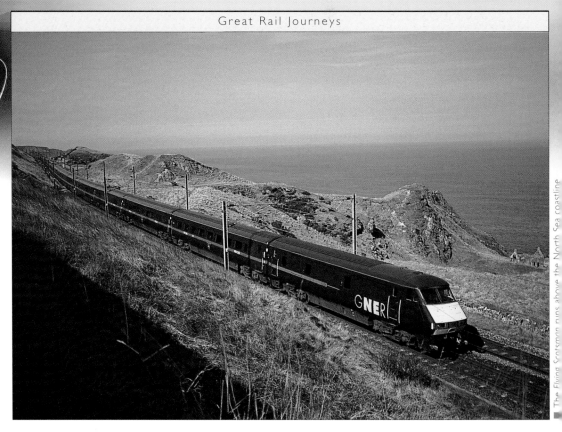

The Flying Scotsman runs above the North Sea coastline

The Flying Scotsman

London to Edinburgh and Glasgow, Great Britain

Every day at 10 o'clock in the morning, a storied train called the *Flying Scotsman* slips away from the platform at London's King's Cross Station, bound north up the East Coast mainline to Edinburgh, its traditional destination, 394 miles (634 km) away. It then travels on to Glasgow 47 miles (76 km) west.

This ritual began in June of 1862, when the train was called the *Special Scotch Express* and was operated by a trio of companies: Great Northern Railway, North Eastern Railway, and North British Railway. About a quarter-century later, in response to the performance of a competing train on the West Coast mainline, the *Express* increased its speed, earning it the nickname the "Flying Scotsman." This soon became its official title.

However, a ride on the *Flying Scotsman* has more than speed to recommend

it. Arrival in the city of York is under an elegant curved train shed, its ironwork intricately painted. Later the train passes through Darlington—a terminus of the Stockton & Darlington, the world's first railway. It then speeds on to Durham, where a high-level entry to the city offers virtually an aerial view of Durham Cathedral. Over the border into Scotland, the train skirts the North Sea.

Today's *Flying Scotsman* is operated by the Great North Eastern Railway (GNER). In truth, the train is just one of GNER's substantial fleet of Britain's fastest— *InterCity 225* speedsters capable of 140 miles per hour (225 km/h). The high-speed services run from King's Cross to Edinburgh's Waverley Station and beyond, to Glasgow, Inverness, or Aberdeen. The coaches generically carry the notation "Route of the Flying Scotsman" above GNER's crest.

Smart red-banded, dark blue coaches of the Flying Scotsman *carry the crest of the Great North Eastern Railway.*

ROUTE OF THE FLYING SCOTSMAN

Electric locomotives (left) stand ready for the England to Scotland journey.

GNER's *Flying Scotsman* makes the run from London to Edinburgh on this high-speed line in just over four hours. But in the 1880s Parliament urged both the East and West Coast operators to take double that time, in the wake of concerns about rough and dangerous journeys, to which the railways agreed. Like all of GNER's best trains, the *Flying Scotsman* offers dining-car service—an amenity it acquired in 1900—and carries first- and second-class cars.

Part of the cachet of the *Flying Scotsman* no doubt stems from the famous steam locomotive of the same name that once hauled it and continues to operate in preservation. Pacific No. 4472, built in 1923, stands elegant in the apple-green livery it introduced for the London & North Eastern Railway (LNER), and was part of its first class of locomotive. LNER was one of four railways formed that year by grouping more than 100 previously independent lines. In 1928, when its namesake train began to run London–Edinburgh non-stop, a corridor was installed in the tender so that a relief crew could reach the locomotive cab at the journey's midpoint. In 1963 the 4472 was rescued from the scrapyard by enthusiast Alan Pegler. It has survived since in a succession of private ownerships, has toured the United States and Australia, and was restored once again in 1999 to run in excursion service.

So both the locomotive and the train survive. The latter speeds its way along the electrified East Coast mainline, a scenic and comfortable journey behind streamlined electric power units and aboard Mark 4 coaches. And it's still a fine ride. **217**

FIELD NOTES

DISTANCE 441 miles (710 km)

BEST TIME TO TRAVEL Year-round

SPECIAL FEATURES A modern high-speed journey over a historic route, traditionally known for speed

A Leeds–Carlisle diesel railcar service crossing Ribblehead Viaduct

Settle & Carlisle Line

Yorkshire to Cumbria, Great Britain

When the 24-arch Ribblehead Viaduct was declared unsafe in 1981, it seemed that the Settle & Carlisle Line (S&C), crossing some of England's most rugged and spectacular landscapes, would be consigned to the history books. To the British, the S&C is known as the line that refused to die. Miraculously, the government's threat of closure was lifted after economical ways were found to repair Ribblehead's crumbling stonework. Since then a huge national upturn in rail traffic has returned the S&C to its former role as a key passenger and freight artery linking England and Scotland.

This is a route of contrasts. Along the line's 73-mile (118 km) length the landscape changes from rolling Yorkshire countryside at its southern end to windswept moors and mountains, all of which tested the skills of its Victorian builders to the limit. Mile after mile of embankments, magnificent viaducts, and tunnels are testament to their determination and engineering prowess.

One of the country's last mainlines to be built, it reflected the Midland Railway's drive to have its own route to the north in competition with the neighboring London & North Western (LNWR), which was becoming less and less willing to allow competitors to run over its own route from Birmingham to Carlisle via the main industrial centers of Crewe, Wigan, and Preston. The Midland board voted in 1865 to have an independent line, and its application to Parliament, plus talk of amalgamation with two southern Scottish companies (Glasgow & South Western and Caledonian Railways) caused such a stir that LNWR offered reconciliation. Midland considered abandoning its S&C proposals, but it was compelled by its partners, Lancashire & Yorkshire and North British Railways, to press on.

Construction took six and a half years, two more than expected, and cost almost twice the original budget. Scores of the 7,000 navvies (laborers) died in the process, many buried in churchyards alongside the line. The S&C starts from its southern end at Settle Junction with a punishing climb of 15 miles (24 km) at an almost continuous 1 in 100 gradient. A total of 13 tunnels and 21 viaducts are needed to reach Carlisle, almost at sea level.

The line was never profitable, and operations were made more difficult because of the harsh

Map labels:
Carlisle
Appleby
Crosby Garrett
MILES
0   15   30
0   40
KM
Ribblehead
Settle

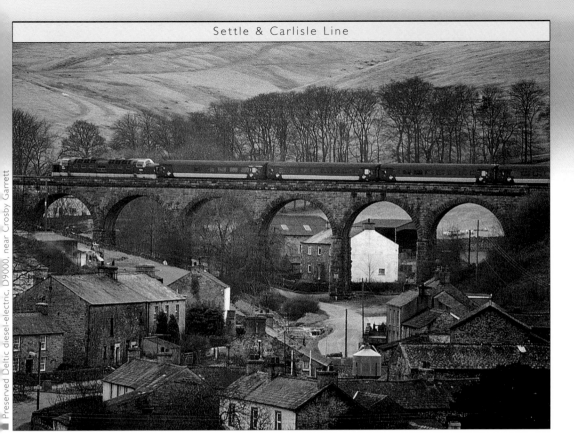

Preserved Deltic diesel-electric, D9000, near Crosby Garrett

The Flying Scotsman *hauls the southbound* Cumbrian Mountain Express *up to the summit of the Settle & Carlisle Line.*

year-round weather conditions, with the line commonly blocked by snow in winter. As the railways drifted into decline after World War II, the viability of duplicate routes was inevitably questioned. The lack of home-generated traffic also led to major cutbacks being wreaked on the S&C. Wayside stops were closed, and intercity passenger and freight trains were transferred to other lines. The publication by British Rail of formal closure notices in 1983 could have been the end of the story but for a vigorous national campaign by local authorities.

The Friends of the Settle & Carlisle Line, and others, succeeded in delaying a decision by some six years. British Rail's figures for its losses and maintenance costs were openly challenged. Also during this time the tourist potential of the line was being exploited to the full, including the running of almost weekly *Cumbrian Mountain Express* excursions hauled by privately owned steam locomotives.

To the joy of over 30,000 petitioners, the government announced the line's reprieve in April 1989. A program of investment was instituted, including repairs to Ribblehead Viaduct and renovation of the eight intermediate stations, which now record high levels of business from locals and tourists. Turning the wheel full circle, extensive track repairs at the end of the 1990s allowed the return of the heavy freight and passenger trains for which the line was built.

219

The Venice Simplon–Orient-Express

London, Great Britain, to Venice, Italy

In the lexicon of railroading, no name has more cachet than *Orient-Express*. Ever since Georges Nagelmackers rolled out the *Express d'Orient* in 1883, the words have held magic.

Nagelmackers, a Belgian, was founder of the grandly and evocatively named Compagnie Internationale des Wagons-Lits et des Grands Express Européens, the sleeping-car company often known simply as Wagons-Lits. His most famous train, which in time would be chronicled by Graham Greene and Agatha Christie among many other authors, linked Paris with Constantinople (now Istanbul), the gateway to Asia—hence the name *Orient-Express*. In its long career it came to embody a delicious combination of luxury, intrigue, and adventure.

Genteel service is part of the experience of this classic journey.

But in 1977, not quite a century after its birth, it died an unceremonious death. By then it was just a single sleeper and some coaches. There was no dining car, no elegance, and no glamor—but there was a wonderful, evocative name, one which has proven too good to die. Now there are a handful of *Orient-Express* trains scattered across three continents (including the "ordinary," prosaic *Orient-Express* trains D262/263, which run daily between Paris, Vienna, and Budapest and twice a week to and from Bucharest).

But when people say "*Orient-Express*," they generally mean the *Venice Simplon-Orient-Express,* the *VSOE,* which runs from March through November between London and Venice via Paris (a journey of about 31 hours), and on alternate routes as well.

Dating from 1982, this train is the brainchild of James P. Sherwood, president of the Sea Containers Group. He was impressed by the publicity surrounding the original train's demise and bought a pair of Wagons-Lits sleepers at a

A cabin on a *VSOE* passenger car is made up for the night

Sotheby's auction—then went on to hunt up more sleepers and some British Pullmans. In total, he purchased 35 cars and these carriages were then impeccably restored at great expense.

The *VSOE*'s bread-and-butter journey starts in London, with a rake of stylish Pullmans, gleaming in traditional cream and brown livery, pulling out of Victoria Station. (In Britain and on the Continent, Pullmans are luxury cars for daytime travel, not sleepers.)

Passengers in plush wing-backed chairs lunch at tables elegantly laid with crisp white linen, brightly polished silver, crystal, and fine china, on a short leisurely journey to Folkestone. With classical names like *Minerva, Phoenix,* and *Ione,* the historic Pullmans, most dating from the 1920s and 1930s, are veterans of such trains as the *Golden Arrow* and the *Brighton Belle.* Each car's interior features unique marquetry, which has been lovingly restored. At Folkestone passengers board a high-speed ferry to cross the English Channel to Boulogne.

The Continental rake of Wagons-Lits cars is every bit as elegant. The sleepers, wearing the company's traditional dark blue livery adorned

FIELD NOTES

DISTANCE 1,044 miles (1,681 km)

BEST TIME TO TRAVEL Runs from March through November

SPECIAL FEATURES A delicious combination of luxury, intrigue, and adventure; fine food and service; lovingly restored dining and sleeping cars, and British Pullmans

The cabin facilities on the Venice Simplon-Orient-Express are stylish even though they don't stretch to showers.

with raised brass lettering and crest, are all museum pieces, except that you're invited (for an undeniably costly fare) to live in them.

Though some mechanical upgrades have been made to accommodate safety requirements, most of the cars remain without air-conditioning. Toilets are at the end of the corridors, and there are no showers. Roughly the same age as the British Pullmans, the carriages are paneled in lustrous inlaid wood. A gracefully rounded door in the corner of each compartment conceals a washbasin. By day, there's a plush sofa. At night, the cabin makes down into an upper and a lower berth.

221

The dining cars are, if anything, more beautiful. One, a Pullman decorated by René Lalique, has "Bacchanalian maidens," triple-relief panels of opaque glass. Food and service are exquisite, and the atmosphere is formal, with black-tie common.

The *VSOE*'s most direct predecessor started in 1919 as the *Simplon-Orient-Express,* which traveled to Istanbul from Paris via Lausanne, the Simplon Tunnel, Milan, and Venice. This was the route to Venice initially selected by the *VSOE,* though the train now makes a more northerly trek, through scenic Arlberg Pass and Innsbrück. This keeps its non-air-conditioned cars in the Alps longer and out of the Mediterranean heat.

Though London–Venice is the staple run, there are other itineraries as well. Some trips from London and Paris extend overnight to Rome, adding a second night. Rome–Venice (with a stop of more than three hours for a walking tour of Florence) is offered as a stand-alone one-night excursion. More like rail cruises are Venice–Prague–Paris–London (four nights,

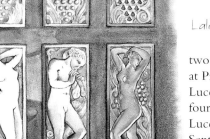

Lalique glass panels

two of them off the train at Prague) and Venice–Lucerne–Paris–London (also four nights, two of them in Lucerne). Once a year, in September, the train returns to its roots with a four-night Paris–Istanbul tour (also run in reverse), with off-train overnight stops at Budapest and Bucharest.

THE OTHER ORIENT-EXPRESSES
The United States, Mexico, and Southeast Asia all feature trains using variations on the name *Orient-Express* to catch some reflected glory. The *VSOE* operators also offer other luxury trains in Great Britain, as well as the *Great South Pacific Express* in Australia.

The *Eastern & Oriental Express* (*E&O*) runs from Bangkok, Thailand, to Singapore via Kuala Lumpur, Malaysia (two nights, with stops for touring) and Bangkok to Chiang Mai, Thailand (one night). It was inaugurated in 1993 and is operated by the company that runs the *VSOE.*

With thoroughly rebuilt cars that were once part of Australia's Sydney–Melbourne *Southern*

A journey on the Eastern & Oriental Express *offers the delights of fresh local produce.*

Aurora, the *E&O* achieves a level of elegance and service comparable to the *VSOE.* Beautiful wood veneers and inlays are featured throughout, and all compartments offer private bathrooms with showers. At the rear of the train is an observation car with an open platform, an ideal spot to savor the tropical climate and scenery.

In North America, the *American Orient Express* (*AOE*) emulates its namesake, but with cars that are a faithful evocation, rather than an accurate restoration, of the great days of luxury rail travel. The *AOE*'s roots are in the *American European Express* (*AEE*), which began service in 1989. It ran between Washington and Chicago, attached to an Amtrak train.

The *AEE* cars, which began life as workaday streamliners built mostly in the 1940s and 1950s, were transformed into lavish wood-paneled carriages. Especially handsome were pairs of diners and club cars, the latter equipped with baby grand pianos. Within two years the *AEE* failed, but the equipment was resurrected in 1994 as the *AOE.* The *AOE* concept evolved through various operators to become what it is today, a true cruise train offering seven different itineraries, over 7 to 10 nights, across North America. The *AOE* features exquisite cuisine and many bus tours at stops along the way.

And, finally, the *South Orient Express* (*SOE*) is one of two private trains that travel to Mexico's Copper Canyon—on a route that was originally called the Orient Line, which gives the train's name some credibility. Using stainless steel streamlined cars that include domes and a round-end observation car, the *SOE* operates round trips from Los Mochis, near the Pacific coast, to Divisadero, right on the rim of the Canyon, as well as one-way trips between Los Mochis and Chihuahua City.

223

The Glacier Express

Zermatt to Chur and St. Moritz, Switzerland

The mountains of Switzerland are spider-webbed with dozens of meter-gauge railways, a network over which trains shuttle with the precision of a Swiss watch. Though all but one of these narrow-gauge lines is independent, they are seamlessly integrated with each other and with the Swiss Federal Railways. To run the famous *Glacier Express,* an all-day journey that connects the chic resorts of Zermatt and St. Moritz, it takes three private railways: the Brig-Visp-Zermatt (BVZ), the Furka-Oberalp (FO), and the Rhaetian Railway (or Rhätische

The Solis Viaduct is one of many highlights on the Glacier Express *route.*

Bahn, RhB). From Zermatt, an automobile-free community at the foot of the Matterhorn (among the most famous and most photographed mountains in the world), cars of the *Glacier Express* roll over the BVZ, down into the Rhône Valley and on to Brig. This major railway junction links the standard-gauge Bern–Lötschberg–Simplon and Swiss Federal with the meter-gauge BVZ and FO. Then the train heads east, running under the Furka Pass in a tunnel 9 miles (15 km) long. (Before the Furka base tunnel's completion in 1982, the line was closed each winter and one of the bridges disassembled to prevent its destruction by avalanche.)

At Andermatt, a spur drops down to connect with the Swiss Federal north–south artery at Göschenen, right at the northern portal of the Gotthard Tunnel. Meanwhile, the *Glacier Express* climbs a steep mountain, with breath-taking views at the townsite. Here and else-where on the FO, and on the BVZ as well, trains use rack and pinion to hoist themselves up grades as steep as 11 percent (1 in 9). On the RhB, where grades top out at 7 percent (1 in 14), traction is entirely by adhesion. Further east is the 6,666-foot (2,033 m) Oberalp Pass.

At Disentis/Muster, the FO hands the *Glacier Express* over to the RhB to complete the journey to St. Moritz (or Chur, where some trains terminate). The line to St. Moritz on the RhB is the most spectacular, crossing the elegant stone Landwasser Viaduct and negotiating a series of spirals above Bergün.

In summer up to four services carry the name *Glacier Express.* Typically, these trains carry Panorama cars, with broad windows and skylights above, and dining cars for at least part of the trip. These are perhaps the only diners anywhere to operate over rack-and-pinion trackage. They offer wine glasses with skewed stems as souvenirs, testimony to the pronounced tilt of the cars on the steep grades.

RhB runs another train, the *Bernina Express,* that for scenery rivals or even outstrips the *Glacier Express.* From Chur to Samedan the trains share the same spectacular route across the Landwasser Viaduct and through Bergün's five ingeniously engineered loop tunnels. When the *Bernina Express* strikes out on its own, it crests Bernina Pass (said to be the only Alpine crossing made above ground) and passes through an otherworldly landscape along the shores of Lago Bianca ("White Lake"), named for the milky green color of the water, the result of "glacier milk," melting glacial waters. From there the rails seesaw down a series of switchbacks into a lush, Mediterranean valley en route to Tirano, which is across the Italian border and 89 miles (144 km) from Chur.

FIELD NOTES

DISTANCE 180 miles (290 km)

BEST TIME TO TRAVEL Fewer crowds and superb colors in spring and summer

SPECIAL FEATURES A beautiful all-day journey from the foot of the Matterhorn to the resort of St. Moritz or to Chur

The Bernina Express *runs alongside the road through the picturesque town of Tirano, Italy, where it terminates.*

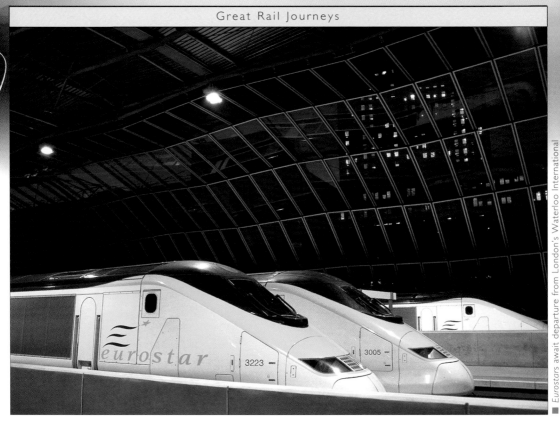

Eurostar and TGV

London, Great Britain, to Bern, Switzerland, via Paris, France

Enter the airy, space-age *Eurostar* terminal at London's Waterloo International and you'll know right away that an uncommon journey lies ahead. From here the sleek *Eurostar*s, introduced in 1994, race through the Channel Tunnel, making 18 daily round trips between London and Paris and 10 from London to Brussels. Stylishly painted in white, with blue roofs and window bands and yellow stripes, the *Eurostar*s flaunt their futuristic credentials. Built by GEC-Alstom (like the French *TGV*s to which they are closely akin), these articulated, permanently coupled train sets are 18 coaches long, with a locomotive at each end.

Aboard *Eurostar,* first-class passengers enjoy comfortable two-and-one seating and complimentary food and beverage service, while those traveling in standard class may patronize the bar car or trolley cart for snacks and refreshments. Rolling through the British countryside, speeds are moderate (although a dedicated high-speed line is to open in 2007) and views remain in

focus: tiled-roof brick cottages, grazing sheep, the vivid yellow of mustard seed plants. Near the Channel Tunnel entrance, the sharp-eyed traveler can glimpse freight trains and the cars and locomotives of *Le Shuttle,* which ferries automobiles through the Tunnel. The ride through the 31-mile (50 km) "Chunnel" itself takes only about 20 minutes, but the quirky experience of popping out into daylight on the far side of the English Channel is something to be savored. Then the high-speed running begins—at up to 186 miles per hour (300 km/h)—for the trip into the Gare du Nord in Paris, the whole journey from London taking just three hours.

Map labels: London · Calais · Paris · Dijon · Neuchâtel · Bern · MILES 0 100 200 · KM 0 250

Le Shuttle ferries automobiles through the 31-mile (50 km) Channel Tunnel, which opened in 1994.

French TGVs now hold the world speed record

In Paris passengers from the *Eurostar* can link with any of France's *TGV* services to make possible a high-speed journey from London to international as well as French destinations. Bern is reached from the Gare de Lyon, the heart of France's growing *TGV* network and a few minutes ride across town from the Gare du Nord by Métro or RER (local train). The French National Railroads, or SNCF (Société Nationale des Chemins de Fer Français), operates the *TGV*s, which began commercial service in 1981. The aerodynamic *TGV* holds the world speed record of 319 miles per hour (514 km/h), which was achieved in trials. It records service speeds of up to 186 miles per hour, as for the *Eurostar*.

The original *TGV* route, the Sud Est, is plied by sleek gray and blue train sets of eight or 16 cars, with slant-nosed power cars at the ends of each eight-car unit. The trains travel south and east from Paris, serving such cities as Lyon, Dijon, Avignon, and Grenoble. They also reach into Switzerland, to Lausanne, Geneva, Bern, and Zürich. To meet demand, some trains have *TGV* Duplex equipment—spacious double-decker coaches that substantially increase their

FIELD NOTES

DISTANCE 645 miles (1,038 km)

BEST TIME TO TRAVEL Year-round

SPECIAL FEATURES The experience of the "Chunnel" and dedicated high-speed train travel; the TGV run to Bern includes classic mountain railroading—at speed

capacity. A second *TGV* route, the Atlantique, runs west from Paris with 10-car silver and blue train sets that feature enhanced technology and amenities. In 2001 the *TGV* Méditerranean line was completed to Marseille and Montpellier, and construction started on *TGV* Est from Paris to Strasbourg.

To complete the three-capital route that began in London, board the *TGV* bound for Bern, a 338-mile (544 km) journey of just four and a half hours. South from Paris the train rolls at top speed down the *TGV* Sud Est line, then shows off the *TGV*'s extraordinary versatility by running equally smoothly on the classic route into Switzerland, twisting and turning through the Jura Mountains. On *TGV*s operating at mealtimes, passengers in first class can order meals served at their seats; those in second class can repair to the bar car for lighter fare.

Speed is the calling card of all members of the *TGV* family. When they roll free from their city terminals and enter the dedicated high-speed lines, first-time passengers will hear a different pitch to the traction motors' whine and sense an exhilaration of speed they've never felt anywhere before but on an airport runway.

227

A train approaches the Kleven Bridge between Finse and Myrdal

Oslo to Bergen

Norway

Stretching for 300 miles (483 km) from Oslo to Bergen, Norway's Bergensbanen is among the most spectacularly engineered railways in the world. Completed in 1909 and electrified in 1964, this remarkable line requires no fewer than 184 tunnels and 300 bridges, as well as 18 miles (29 km) of snowsheds, to traverse some extraordinarily somber, breath-taking, and otherworldly landscapes in making the twisting climb across the roof of Norway.

NSB (the Norwegian State Railways, or Norges Statsbanen) operates four trains daily between Oslo and Bergen, the country's two largest cities, and the ride takes roughly seven hours. Along the way passengers encounter deep forests, lakes, waterfalls, and snowy mountains.

The most spectacular part of the run is the stretch above the timberline, where undulating plateaus, windswept and barren, extend in all directions. Elevation tops out at 4,267 feet (1,301 m) at Taugevatn, near the tiny settlement of Finse, which provides a base for snow clearing in the winter and line maintenance at other times of the year.

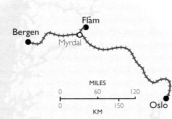

Bergen — Flåm — Myrdal — Oslo

MILES
0   60   120
0   150
KM

This is a world of gray-greens: scrub vegetation struggling against the prevalence of rock, old snow in pockets, faded snow fences angular against the bolder-strewn landscape. For sightseeing, the many tunnels—at about 5 miles (8 km), Ulriken is the longest—and snowsheds, which in winter offer some shelter from blizzards and avalanches, can be frustrating. Shutterbugs often have photos lined up through the windows, only to be plunged suddenly and unexpectedly into darkness. But, when you can see, the views are extraordinary. Water is everywhere: frozen in glaciers and snow banks, tumbling in waterfalls, torrential in rivers, luminous in lakes.

One of the Oslo–Bergen services runs over-night, with sleeping cars. The other three are express day trains with a number of special features, including bistro cars that serve a traditional Scandinavian breakfast smorgasbord and hot and cold meals later in the day.

First-class cars offer a lounge section, where meals are served. One of the second-class cars includes a children's playroom. And high-speed *Signatur* tilting trains will soon be on the route.

The line runs through rugged country between Bergen and Voss

Electric trains take 50 minutes to travel from Flåm station (left) to Myrdal. The route takes in spectacular and, from an engineer's perspective, extremely challenging terrain.

largest and deepest fjord in the world), the line plunges down grades of 1 in 18, Norway's steepest, and slips through 20 tunnels totaling almost 4 miles (6 km). This descent is so extreme that the coaches are equipped for safety with five separate braking circuits, any one of which could independently stop the train.

The ride takes 50 minutes at a leisurely pace, with the train slowing for scenic highlights, even stopping at the best spots, including Nali. Here the Flåm River breaks into a spectacular water-

THE FLÅM LINE

Connecting with the line from Oslo to Bergen at Myrdal, at an elevation of 2,840 feet (866 m), is the 13-mile-long (20 km) Flåmsbana, or Flåm railway. This awe-inspiring branch line drops precipitously from Myrdal's heights to sea level, running down the narrow and beautifully scenic Flåm Valley.

To reach the terminus at Flåm, which is situated at the head of the Aurlandsfjord (an arm of the Sognefjord, the

FIELD NOTES

DISTANCE 300 miles (483 km)

BEST TIME TO TRAVEL Spring and summer

SPECIAL FEATURES The engineering highlights include 184 tunnels, 300 bridges, and 18 miles (29 km) of snowsheds through remarkable terrain; offers one overnight and three express day services with bistro cars, children's playroom, and first-class lounge

fall. From one point you can see three levels of track as the railway scales the mountainside.

The Flåmsbana (and the Bergensbanen) are part of an attractive one-day circle tour, aptly named "Norway in a Nutshell," which also includes a boat trip on the Sognefjord and return by motor coach to either Oslo or Bergen. Another pleasant return option is to take the express ferry that runs from Flåm to Bergen.

229

The journey takes in spectacular coastal views

Rome to Palermo

Sicily and mainland Italy

To ride along Italy's western coastline from Rome to the Sicilian capital of Palermo is to view some of the Mediterranean's most spectacular coastlines. There are glimpses of 2,000 years of civilization, dating back to Roman times, and vistas of the rugged terrain around Europe's most active volcanoes. The 569-mile (916 km) journey can take a marathon 11½ hours. However a 40-minute time saving is possible by taking a *Pendolino* tilt train over the brand new 140-mile (225 km) high-speed line between Rome and Naples, which follows a more direct inland alignment.

Electrified throughout with 3,000v DC overhead current collection, the "traditional" Rome–Palermo mainline has been part of Italian State Railways (Ferrovie dello Stato, or FS) since nationalization in 1905–1907, although its management changed in 1985 from a government department to a state corporation. The route's principal engineering features include three of the world's longest tunnels. Two of them are between Rome and Naples: the Monte Orso, at 4 miles, 1,230 yards (7,562 m)

long, and the Vivola, at 4 miles, 1,004 yards (7,355 m). Both opened on October 28, 1927. However, both are significantly outdistanced by the 6-mile-662-yard (10,262 m) Santa Lucia tunnel, which opened between Naples and Salerno in 1977. The Rome–Naples section of the line is famous for a spectacular speed run on July 27, 1938, when a three-car electric train covered the 132.9 miles (213.9 km) at an average speed of 96.1 miles per hour (154.7 km/h) with a top speed of 125 miles per hour (201 km/h).

The departure from Rome, through its drab, sprawling suburbs, gives little hint that the city is a world cultural center, but history is soon apparent as the countryside opens up into the flat, fertile plain that is the Campagna. The train runs parallel to the Via Appia Antica road once used by Spartacus and his followers; it still has its original cobbles. Other notable sights are the hundreds of arches of the ancient Colli Albani aqueduct, and the Pontine Marshes, which were drained by the ancient Romans and again in the 20th century by Mussolini.

The train reaches the chaotic metropolitan city of Naples, with its extensive suburban rail system that includes a metro, tramways, and

Trains cross the St. Severino Viaduct

funiculars, in two hours. This railroad played a vital role in the mass migration of impoverished agricultural workers from the south in the early 20th century to feed the country's rapid industrial expansion.

The landscape is dominated by the volcano Vesuvio (Mount Vesuvius), which normally erupts every 30–50 years. It had its own funicular railway from 1880 until an eruption in March 1944. This was the first and only line to be built on top of a volcano. Today, frequent services on the SFSM Circumvesuviana narrow-gauge railway serve the area around the volcano, but the top is now reached by a bus service from Pugliano and a chairlift.

The view of Vesuvio is soon replaced by the Bay of Naples and Sorrento peninsula and the islands of Capri, Ischia, and Procidia. The train hugs the coastline for the rest of the journey. After the modest intermediate towns of Battipaglia, Sapri, and Paola, the end of the Italian mainland is reached at Villa San Giovanni, just north of Italy's southernmost major town, Reggio di Calabrio. Here the train is split into sections and shunted aboard one of Europe's last

> **FIELD NOTES**
>
> DISTANCE 569 miles (916 km)
>
> BEST TIME TO TRAVEL Year-round
>
> SPECIAL FEATURES A spectacular coastline journey, with a ride on one of Europe's last train ferries; historical, geographical, and engineering highlights; ride the Pendolino for the Rome–Naples leg to experience high-speed tilt train technology

A rail ramp allows the train to roll on and off the ferry for the crossing to Sicily from Villa San Giovanni.

train ferries for the short crossing of the Strait of Messina to Sicily. The final 113-mile (182 km) section of the journey is along the northern coast of this picturesque island to Palermo, infamous home of the Sicilian Mafia. It takes a marathon three hours because the railway is single track.

But the views of the Tyrrhenian Sea are compensation. To the south there is the spectacular sight of a second great volcano, which at 10,902 feet (3,323 m) is one of the world's largest and the highest point in Italy south of the Alps—Mount Etna.

The Blue Train's club car offers all the trimmings of a luxury hotel

The Blue Train and the Pride of Africa

South Africa

In South Africa, two trains vie for the title of most luxurious. One, Spoornet's *Blue Train,* has a reputation of long standing. The other, Rovos Rail's *Pride of Africa,* is a relative newcomer. Though both are opulent and offer some similar itineraries, they are quite different from one another in many respects.

Today's *Blue Train* features décor of unequaled elegance—and butlers. The rooms are all Deluxe Suites or Luxury Suites, the latter equipped with VCRs and CD players, and all are finished in finely crafted honey-colored paneling. A remote control raises, lowers, and adjusts the angle of the venetian blinds and also adjusts the television, which shows an engineer's-eye view from a camera mounted on the front of the train. There's a cell phone to call the butler.

Featuring Italian marble, the bathrooms have either a shower or a tub. Built-in seats piled high with cushions make down at night into either twin lowers or a double bed, all with puffy duvets embroidered with the train's

sweeping "B" logo. For daytime use there's also a fold-down table and movable chair. This luxury is all the more impressive when you consider that South African trains run on 3-foot-6-inch-gauge rails, much narrower than standard. No less stylish are the public rooms: lounge car, club car (smoking allowed), finely appointed dining car with an equally fine menu, and, in one of the two trains, an observation car with a rear-facing glass wall.

The *Blue Train*'s direct ancestor was the *Union Limited,* which began service in 1923 as a biweekly luxury train running from Pretoria and Johannesburg to Cape Town, connecting with the Union Castle Line mailships to and from England. (In the other direction the train was called the *Union Express.*) The train's cars initially had unpainted exteriors, but a blue-and-cream color scheme was introduced in 1933 with Protea, a luxurious new dining car. These colors, eventually adopted throughout, led to the nickname "Blue Train." When this luxury service was resumed in 1946 after a four-year

MILES
0   325   650
0   750
KM

Victoria Falls
Bulawayo
Beit Bridge
Kruger National Park
Pretoria
Hoedspruit
Maputo
Kimberley
De Aar
Cape Town
Port Elizabeth

The new Blue Train, hauled by three Class 5 E-1 electric locomotives

The Blue Train's ornate logo (above) is featured on everything from chairs to duvets. The train's lounge car (left) affords sweeping views of the surrounding countryside on the Pretoria-to-Cape Town route.

hiatus during World War II, the name became official. In 1972 the *Blue Train* received new equipment—cars that were rebuilt in 1997 and 1998 to become today's super-luxury trains.

The classic journey is the 27-hour, 994-mile (1,600 km) trip from Pretoria (Johannesburg is no longer a stop) to Cape Town. This now includes a layover of a few hours for touring. Southbound it's at Kimberley, to visit the town's Mine Museum and the "Big Hole," where De Beers once dug diamonds. Northbound the stop is at Matjiesfontein, a preserved Victorian town on the vast, arid Karoo. Scenic highlights come at the southern end of the route, where the train passes through the mountainous Hex River Valley and the lush wine country of Western Cape.

As the *Blue Train* has moved from being primarily transportation to being an event, itineraries have been added. It is now also possible to travel from Pretoria to Victoria Falls, from Pretoria east to Hoedspruit in the Valley of the Olifants, and from Cape Town to Port Elizabeth along the Garden Route.

While the *Blue Train* has always been run by the national system—South African Railways, which became Spoornet—Rovos Rail's *Pride of Africa* is the vision of one man, Rohan Vos (hence Rovos). Vos, a train enthusiast who

FIELD NOTES

DISTANCE 994 miles (1,600 km) Pretoria–Cape Town (other itineraries available)

BEST TIME TO TRAVEL Spring and autumn

SPECIAL FEATURES Deluxe or Luxury Suites that feature décor of unequaled elegance, bathrooms with either tub or shower, butler service, opulent lounge, observation, club, and dining cars

233

■ The diner on the *Pride of Africa* features fine wood paneling

made his fortune in the auto-parts business, bought a few railway cars to use for vacation travel with his family. Chagrined at the cost of operating them, he took a suggestion from the railway and decided to invite paying guests, which led to the inauguration of the *Pride of Africa* in 1989. The first train, now called the *Edwardian* and used for charters, was made up of older, wooden cars. The two trains that are now in regular operation, *Classic 1* and *Classic 2,* contain newer steel-sided sleepers, thoroughly rebuilt with wood-paneled interiors that give them an appearance that belies their relatively young age.

Rovos Rail's sleeping accommodations are extravagantly large, with either twin or double beds that remain in place day and night. There's even plenty of room (in a Deluxe Suite) for a credenza with minibar, two comfortable chairs, ample closet space, and a bathroom with a stall shower. Royal Suites have all this plus a claw-footed bathtub, in which a sybaritic passenger can soak while gazing at the passing scenery.

But the *Pride of Africa*'s crown jewels are its diners. The first acquired, Shangani, is a wood-paneled beauty, with carved pillars and arches, a style characteristic of South African trains. Other feature cars are the observation cars, which provide fine rearward views.

Steam engines were originally a major part of the Rovos Rail program, but steam mileage has dwindled dramatically as the infrastructure needed to support the locomotives has declined. Now Spoornet diesel and electric locomotives do most of the hauling. Rovos still schedules five operable, beautifully restored steam loco-

The Royal Suites on the Pride of Africa *offer the combination of the opulence of pre-war travel with subtle modern innovations.*

A Rovos Rail steam train at Capital Park, the company's headquarters

FIELD NOTES

DISTANCE Varies depending on chosen itinerary

BEST TIME TO TRAVEL Spring and autumn

SPECIAL FEATURES Extravagantly large sleeping accommodations with permanent twin or double beds, bathroom with stall shower (Royal Suites have a claw-footed bathtub); ornate dining cars; and rear-facing observation car

The bridge at Victoria Falls was part of Cecil Rhodes' dream for a Cape-to-Cairo railway.

motives, which glitter with the polished ornamentation typical of the most lovingly tended South African power. Three are Class 19D light 4-8-2s with long, graceful "torpedo" tenders that ride on six-wheel "Buckeye" trucks, designed to negotiate the branchline trackage for which these engines were built. The latest restoration, including conversion from coal to oil, was a mainline 4-8-4 locomotive. The antique of the roster is a diminutive 4-6-0 built in 1893.

Rovos Rail's operations are now based at the immaculately groomed Capital Park complex, just north of Pretoria. Here Vos has transformed a fairly pedestrian building, where apprentice engineers once trained, into a plush and elegant station with extensive shops where the locomotives and cars are rebuilt. Now Rovos steam engines range no more than about an hour from there. But even this whiff of steam nicely complements the spacious sleepers and historic diners aboard the *Pride of Africa*.

Rovos Rail itineraries include Pretoria to Cape Town, Pretoria to Victoria Falls (flying on a historic aircraft to the falls from Pietersburg), Pretoria to Kruger Park, Cape Town to George, and Pretoria to Durban. The longest is an exclusive 12-night trek from Cape Town to Dar es Salaam on the Tanzania coast. Offered only once a year, it features the spectacular bridge crossing at Victoria Falls.

235

One of five zig-zags, or switchbacks, where the train gains height

Darjeeling Himalayan Railway

Siliguri to Darjeeling, India

Everyone should visit the Darjeeling Himalayan Railway at least once in a lifetime. An ingenious and awe-inspiring example of Victorian engineering, it is the world's most outstanding example of a hill passenger railway. The mountainous terrain through which it passes is of great beauty, and on a clear day the distant views of the snow-capped peaks of Everest and Kanchenjunga, the first and third highest mountains on Earth, constitute one of the world's most memorable sights.

The railway's original purpose was to serve the celebrated summer hill station of Darjeeling and enable the British to escape from the torrid heat of the plains in the summer. Under the Raj, Darjeeling was of immense social significance and housed some of India's finest schools. The trains also transported tea from the famous Darjeeling plantations.

The 2-foot-gauge railway climbs through the foothills of the Himalayas from the plain at Siliguri and reaches Darjeeling, 51 miles (82 km) away. Darjeeling is 6,810 feet (2,077 m) above sea level and the line abounds in short radius loops, spirals, and reversing stations. At one loop, it is possible to jump from the toiling train, gently stroll to the opposite track, take a photograph, and rejoin the train as it passes. Although the gradients are as steep as 1 in 25, remarkably there are no rack-and-pinion sections. The journey takes an enjoyable eight hours uphill and only a little less coming down.

The principal motive power has always been the celebrated B Class steam locomotive, a 0-4-0ST, the first of which arrived from Sharp Stewart of Glasgow in 1889; by 1927 there was

Map labels: Darjeeling, Ghum, Kurseong, Tindharia, Agony Point, Sukna, Siliguri Junction, To Calcutta, New Jalpaiguri, To Assam, MILES, KM, 0, 11, 17

Locomotive No. 805 attacks one of the steepest sections of the Darjeeling Himalayan Railway as it climbs through Tindharia.

With a backdrop of the Himalayas, the train tackles the Batasia loop

a total of 30 B Class locomotives. They were infinitely successful and are still active on the line.

Though the railway paid good dividends over much of its existence, its future has been questioned in recent years. The road that parallels it has become an ever greater threat, while the wash-outs during the monsoon period, along with escalating maintenance costs, have caused Indian Railways to threaten closure. But this "toy railway of the Himalayas" enjoys world fame and has long been a major tourist attraction in its own right.

Any worries about the railway's long-term future were resolved in 2000, when it was guaranteed permanent protection by UNESCO as a world heritage site. In the same year, two new 250-horsepower diesel locomotives arrived. Many felt this to be an abuse of the UNESCO declaration, but Indian Railways deemed that the B Class would remain for tourist trains. The Bs are also still in charge of shorter workings at the upper end of the line between Darjeeling and Kurseong.

During the 1970s, not all of Darjeeling's B Class 0-4-0STs were required for the line.

FIELD NOTES

DISTANCE 51 miles (82 km)

BEST TIME TO TRAVEL November to March

SPECIAL FEATURES The world's most outstanding example of a hill passenger railway, climbing grades as steep as 1 in 25 by way of short radius loops, spirals, and reversing stations

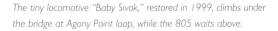

The tiny locomotive "Baby Sivok," restored in 1999, climbs under the bridge at Agony Point loop, while the 805 waits above.

Indian Railways gave some of the engines major overhauls and transferred them to the coalfields of Upper Assam, close to the Burmese and Chinese border, where a network of 2-foot-gauge lines operated. Here the Bs worked in turn with Assam's Bagnall 0-4-0STs, which were first delivered to the Assam Railway and Trading Company during the 1890s from the Castle Engine Works at Stafford, England.

In late 2000 India's Ministry of Railways called for tenders to supply three new oil-fired steam locomotives for the line, along with others for the Nilgiri Mountain Railway. It is unclear, however, whether orders will be placed.

The Trans-Siberian's final station at Vladivostok

The Trans-Siberian Railway

Moscow to Vladivostok, Russia

There is nothing else remotely like the Trans-Siberian Railway—5,777 miles (9,297 km) of unbroken railway stretching from Moscow, across Europe and Asia to the Pacific at Vladivostok. Traveling the entire distance is the equivalent of two trips across the Atlantic, and when it is midday in Moscow, it is already 7 p.m. in Vladivostok. The Trans-Siberian is still the only fixed link between eastern and western Russia—the vital means of communication in the world's largest country.

The Trans-Siberian has always attracted romantics wanting to experience the world's greatest railway journey. In the time of the Czars, well-heeled passengers could enjoy *Orient-Express*-style luxury, but under Communism Siberia became a severely restricted area. Now, visitors can again travel freely.

The adventure begins at Moscow's Yaroslavl Station, a substantial gray and white building based on a traditional Russian fort. Contrary to popular belief, the train itself has never been called the "Trans-Siberian." It is Train 1, *Rossia*, Russia's premier train, that awaits at platform

MILES
0   1150   2300
0   3000
KM

St.Petersburg
Moscow   Yekaterinburg
Novosibirsk   Kharbarovsk
Irkutsk   Vladivostok

two. Train 2 is for the return service. The 15 coaches, the majority of them sleeping cars, are hauled by a powerful electric locomotive.

They have to withstand winter temperatures of -40°F (-40°C) or below, as does all the railway's equipment. For "soft class" travelers, home for the next eight days is a two-berth compartment in one of these coaches. The cheaper "hard class" option has four berths.

At 3.05 p.m. Moscow time (the railway uses Moscow time throughout to avoid confusion), the *Rossia* departs. As the days pass, the train will dictate the passengers' way of life. Berths will be festooned with possessions, and washing strung across the compartments. Toilets are at the end of the corridor and hot water must be obtained from the carriage attendants, or *provodnitsi*, who keep the samovar stoves on the boil throughout the journey.

Soon, Moscow's factories and apartments give way to open country and the broad, 5-foot-gauge track snakes lazily along, allowing a clear view of the line ahead. The amount of traffic shows how important the railway is, with a train running in each direction every 20 minutes.

The train passes through an autumn landscape in a Siberian forest

In Soviet times trains ran every four minutes. Not all go to Vladivostok; many clatter their way over shorter distances, hauled by streamlined 1960s-style electric locomotives. Other trains use the Trans-Siberian before traveling on to Mongolia and Beijing. But the majority of trains are long-distance freights, crashing and clanging their way across the emptiness.

Over the next few days a variety of sights will pass the windows, brought, as it were, to the traveler's seat. When the train is 180 miles (289 km) out of Moscow, it rumbles over the River Volga on one of the railway's distinctive, long cantilever bridges. These are considered so important that the army permanently guards them. Of all the great rivers that the train will cross, the Volga is the one indelibly linked with Russia's culture and history. Europe's longest river, it stretches for 2,000 miles (3,200 km) across Russia to the Caspian Sea.

The first stop is at Danilov, 43 miles (70 km) further on, where the *Rossia*

FIELD NOTES

DISTANCE 5,777 miles (9,297 km)

BEST TIME TO TRAVEL Spring or autumn

SPECIAL FEATURES World's longest continuous train journey, from Europe to Asia, across the Russian steppe, through primeval rainforest, over the Ural mountains and through Siberia

changes engines. Here the passengers have a chance to stretch their legs and indulge in a little free-market trading. As soon as the train stops it is surrounded by women selling fruit and vegetables, bread, pickles, meat, and, of course, vodka. Some stations, particularly those near the borders of Mongolia or Manchuria, become open-air markets, but everywhere the stations are the center of local life. Often the only building in sight or, at most, seeming to serve a few huts, the neat little stations are always bustling with humanity.

Between the stations the landscape mostly takes two forms: the great open plains of the steppe; or the dense primeval forest called the taiga, which

Two of the electric locomotives that work the vast length of the Trans-Siberian route.

■ The precarious stretch of line around Lake Baikal

hugs the line for mile after mile. Things don't start to change until after Perm. This is the 890 milepost (1,433 km) and the scenery becomes more rugged as the train climbs high into the Ural mountains. Soon an important point in the trip is reached at the mist-shrouded 1,104 milepost (1,777 km). To the right of the train a nondescript stone obelisk marks the boundary between Europe and Asia.

Though the weather is forbidding at times, travelers make the journey in comfort.

The train soon rolls into Yekaterinburg for another engine change. Here, in the cellar of a house, the last Czar and his family were killed by the Bolsheviks in 1918. The house was recently demolished, and now only a small cross marks the spot for the many pilgrims.

Siberia is arrived at on day two, at the 1,291-mile (2,078 km) mark. The next places of any notable size are Tyumen (the oldest Siberian town, founded in 1586) and Omsk, before the train runs over the 2,100-foot-long (640 m) River Ob bridge and into Novosibirsk. This is the largest city in Siberia and capital of the region. Novosibirsk owes its existence to the railway, the first settlers being railway builders. Nowadays, with a population of 1,250,000, the city is a large industrial center, and railway

enthusiasts will see plenty that will interest them, from the vast marshaling yards to the locomotive depot and the constant shunting. There may be some steam engines, part of the "Strategic Reserve" maintained in working order in case of crisis. At the time of the Soviet Union's collapse there were still thousands of engines parked up, though the figure has much declined since then. They are kept in guarded dumps beside the mainline, ready to roll at short notice. The most numerous type in the reserve is the L Class 2-10-0 freight engine, of which over 4,000 were built from 1945 to 1955.

From Novosibirsk the line runs through more taiga, stopping at Taiga Station itself at 2,215 miles (3,565 km) on day three, before reaching perhaps the most beautiful sight on the whole trip—Lake Baikal. Leaving Irkutsk, the city known somewhat optimistically as the "Pearl of Siberia" on day four, the train climbs the notoriously steep "Devil's Mountain," then winds sharply down the other side toward the lake. Baikal is the world's deepest freshwater lake. Almost a mile (1.6 km) deep, 400 miles

A Trans-Siberian coach displays the railway's insignia

(650 km) long, and up to 40 miles (65 km) wide, it contains an amazing 20 percent of the world's fresh water. Many animals and plants unique to the area live here, including the Baikal seal.

On a railway full of engineering headaches, driving the line round Baikal was the biggest, and for the first few years passengers had to cross the lake on a ship (which was brought in pieces from England and assembled on the lakeside), joining another train on the far side. In winter rails were once laid across the ice, but this resulted in a disaster when a heavily laden troop train crashed through in 1904. Later that year the Circumbaikal Loop opened. It clings to the edge of the lakeside cliffs, affording travelers a spectacular ride as the train snakes along the edge of the water and bursts in and out of tunnels.

After Baikal the countryside changes and becomes more hilly and varied. The train arrives at Ulan Ude, 280 miles (450 km) from Irkutsk. The majority of people who live here are descended from the Mongols. From here the Trans-Mongolian line branches away, heading south via Ulan Bator to Beijing in China.

Some 3,506 miles (5,642 km) and five days from Moscow, there are still another 2,268 miles (3,650 km) and three days to go. The train now travels through the wild far-eastern regions of Siberia. Here, some of the world's most extreme

The chefs are important members of the Trans-Siberian's crew on its eight-day journey.

temperature ranges have been recorded—a savage, numbing -76°F (-60°C) in winter, and a scorching 113°F (45°C) in summer. Fortunately Russian carriages are well insulated.

The train makes its way through Chita and Belogorsk, arriving at Khabarovsk on day seven. In Soviet times foreigners had to end their journey at Nakhodka on the Sea of Japan—the important naval port of Vladivostok was a closed city. Travelers can still disembark here to catch a ferry to Japan, or remain on board for the final 470-mile (750 km) run due south parallel to the Chinese border to Vladivostok. *Rossia* arrives at 1.30 p.m. Moscow time (8.30 p.m. in Vladivostok), eight days after leaving Moscow. In that time Train 1 has completed the longest continuous train journey in the world, bringing its passengers from the borders of China, Japan, and Korea. The greatest railway adventure is over.

241

The Indian Pacific nears Spencer Gulf on its run to Port Augusta

The Indian Pacific

Sydney to Perth, Australia

The name *Indian Pacific* is among the most evocative in train travel. It is also one of the most descriptive, defining a journey by streamliner across the full breadth of Australia, from the Pacific to the Indian Ocean—an epic trek of 2,703 miles (4,352 km) that takes three and a half days. In large measure it's a traverse of the Outback, including the vast, empty Nullarbor Plain ("Nullarbor" is Latin for "treeless"). There the *Indian Pacific* encounters the Long Straight—at 297 miles (478 km), the world's longest railway tangent,

true as an arrow. There is conventionally attractive scenery as well, including the Blue Mountains northwest of Sydney at the eastern end of the train's journey, and the serpentine Avon River at the western. North of Adelaide, South Australia's capital, are the Flinders Ranges.

Inaugurated in 1970, when Australia's east and west coasts were finally linked by a standard-gauge route across the continent, the Sydney–Perth (via Adelaide) *Indian Pacific* today runs with its original equipment. These stainless steel cars were built under license from the Budd Company of Philadelphia and they have a distinctively North American look, reminiscent of such famous trains as the *California Zephyr* (1949) and the *Canadian* (1955). In the 1990s they were buffed up in a major renovation.

The *Indian Pacific* offers three levels of service, beginning with a basic, no frills "sitting car" called Economy Class. A big step up is Holiday Class, with small sleeping rooms for two called "twinettes" (showers and toilets are down the corridor), a comfortable lounge car, and Matilda's,

Indian Pacific's sister train, the Ghan, relives the historic journey from Alice Springs to Adelaide.

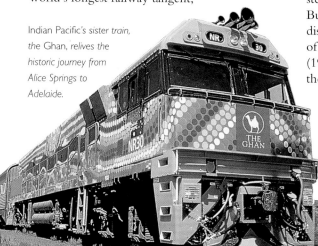

Map labels: Alice Springs, Kalgoorlie, Cook, Tarcoola, Broken Hill, Perth, Port Augusta, Adelaide, Sydney, Melbourne

MILES
0   525   1050
0   1000
KM

The transcontinental Indian Pacific streamliner sports the wedge-tailed eagle, Australia's largest eagle, as its emblem.

FIELD NOTES

DISTANCE 2,703 miles (4,352 km)

BEST TIME TO TRAVEL Year-round, but Australian spring (September to November) can offer unique desert wildflowers, especially in Western Australia

SPECIAL FEATURES A journey that traverses the breadth of the country, including the world's longest straight stretch of rail, with three classes of travel

The *Indian Pacific*, currently operated by the Great Southern Railway, has become something of a "cruise train" by offering off-train tours of one to two hours at Adelaide, the silver-mining town of Broken Hill, and Kalgoorlie, the heart of the goldfields region of Western Australia. But it really is the continent-spanning journey itself that most passengers will find memorable.

Australia also offers a second substantial rail journey into the Outback, and that's the *Ghan,* named for the Afghan cameliers who once transported supplies (for railroad building, among other purposes) into the remote central regions. The *Ghan* operates weekly from Melbourne via Adelaide to Alice Springs (1,481 miles, or 2,384 km) and from Sydney via Adelaide to Alice Springs (2,015 miles or 3,243 km), both trips taking 45 hours. Its equipment and services are almost identical to the *Indian Pacific,* using cars built for that train. Though the original *Ghan,* which first saw service in 1929, was a narrow-gauge train famous for decrepitude and poor timekeeping, the modern version is very much up to snuff.

a restaurant offering buffet-style meal service. In First Class, the single and twin cabins are wood-paneled and commodious, with private toilets and showers. Meals are graciously served in the Queen Adelaide Restaurant, which is decorated in Victorian style.

The smart plush club cars (four are needed to meet the twice-weekly *Indian Pacific* schedule) have been refurbished with a theme for each car. Hannan's Lounge, for instance, is decked out with photos and artifacts paying tribute to Paddy Hannan, whose discovery of gold in 1893 set off Western Australia's gold rush, establishing the city of Kalgoorlie.

In summer flowering wild lupins blanket the lineside near Arthur's Pass

The TranzAlpine Express

Christchurch to Greymouth, South Island, New Zealand

Joining the east and west coasts of New Zealand's South Island are two ribbons of steel known as the Midland Line. Over this railway line, New Zealand's most famous passenger train, the *TranzAlpine Express,* makes its daily return journey.

Departing the very English city of Christchurch (complete with city square, cathedral, and red buses), the train travels southwest and then northwest over the Canterbury Plains, passing through the small towns of Darfield, Sheffield, and Springfield. The English-based New Zealand Midland Railway Company began building the railway in 1888. They soon ran out of funds, and the New Zealand Government was forced to complete the line and take over its operation.

After leaving Springfield, 43 miles (69 km) from Christchurch, the line clings to the rugged Waimakariri Gorge, and travelers can enjoy spectacular views of the snow-fed Waimakariri River from the comfort of the heated carriages. For the next 42 miles (67 km) till the *TranzAlpine Express* reaches

Arthur's Pass, the train is in the "Giant's Backyard," an area where the Waimakariri River and its tributaries have carved into the landscape for centuries. Traveling through this area is only possible by passing through 16 tunnels and crossing nine viaducts and bridges with names such as Broken River, Staircase, and Pattersons Creek. Pattersons Creek viaduct, though not the highest on the line, is the longest, spanning 610 feet (186 m) across a 118-foot-deep (36 m) ravine. The area is surrounded by snowcapped mountains of the Torlesse Range and the Southern Alps. Near Cass the railway skirts around the pretty Lake Sarah, where the grandeur of the surrounding mountains is reflected in the still waters, fringed by poplar trees.

Arthur's Pass, with its chalet-style railway station, is the center of Arthur's Pass National Park, a great spot for mountaineers, trampers, and daytrippers. On leaving the station the *TranzAlpine* plunges into the 5¼-mile (8.5 km) Otira Tunnel, which pierces the Southern Alps and extends down a 1-in-33 grade to reach Otira in the Westland region. The next 50-mile (81 km) stretch to Greymouth, journey's end,

The kea is one of many bird species
in Arthur's Pass National Park.

The *TranzAlpine* rounds Lake Brunner

provides an utter contrast as the Midland Line passes through lush rainforest and at one point is virtually in the bed of the Taramakau River.

Another town that the *Tranz-Alpine* passes through is Moana, a holiday resort with a rural atmosphere, on the shores of Lake Brunner. Westland was a center for coal mining and sawmilling activities, and relics of these industries remain, such as the old sawmills at Stillwater and the remains of the Brunner coal mine, where, in 1896, an explosion caused the deaths of 65 men and boys.

Greymouth, at the mouth of the Grey River, has a population of 8,000, and during the one-hour stopover passengers can enjoy walking and shopping in the town or take a tour of the area, reboarding the train for the four-hour return journey to

FIELD NOTES

DISTANCE 144 miles (232 km)

BEST TIME TO TRAVEL Winter (July to September) offers spectacular snowscapes around Arthur's Pass

SPECIAL FEATURES A journey of contrast between the rugged and barren landscape from Springfield to Arthur's Pass and the indigenous forests and fast-flowing rivers of Westland

Christchurch. Tours of the region, from one to three days, are also available.

As with most travel in New Zealand, the *TranzAlpine Express* can be enjoyed in all seasons, although during July to September much of the area from Springfield to Arthur's Pass is covered in snow, a bonus that makes the trip an absolute delight.

At the line's terminus at Greymouth dolphin-watching trips can be organized.

I travel not to go anywhere, but to go. I travel for travel's sake. The great affair is to move.

Songs of Travel,
ROBERT LOUIS STEVENSON (1850–1894), Scottish writer

INDEX and GLOSSARY

INDEX and GLOSSARY

In this combined index and glossary, **bold** page numbers indicate the main reference and *italic* page numbers indicate illustrations and photographs.

The Whyte System of wheel notation for steam locomotives

The first figure refers to the leading wheels, the second to the coupled wheels, and the third to the supporting wheels.

Notation	Front ... rear	Known as
0-4-0*		
4-4-0		American
0-6-0		
4-6-0		Ten-Wheeler
4-6-2		Pacific
2-8-0		Consolidation
4-8-4		Northern
4-8-8-4		Big Boy
4-8-4+4-8-4		Beyer-Garratt

* The addition of a suffix "T" denotes a tank engine, "ST" a saddle tank.

European practice for steam locomotives is to count axles, not wheels—thus 0-6-0 becomes 0-3-0, 4-6-2 becomes 2-3-1, and so on

Notation for diesel and electric locomotives

(also used in Europe for steam locomotives)

Letters denote numbers of axles (A=1 and so on), with suffix "o" if axles are individually powered. Numbers denote unpowered or "idler" axles.

Notation	Arrangement	Type
B		rigid frame
C		rigid frame
D		rigid frame
1C-C1		rigid frames
B-B		bogies
Bo-Bo		bogies
Co-Co		bogies
1Co-Co1		bogies
A1A-A1A		bogies

CONTRIBUTORS

Graeme Carter lives in Wanganui, New Zealand, and sells out-of-print and new transport books, including railway titles. He is also the editor of *New Zealand Railway Observer* and *Tramway Topics*.

David Jackson has been a railway enthusiast since his childhood years in England. He now resides in Sydney, Australia. David worked in the advertising industry for many years. He subsequently took up an appointment with The Australian Railway Historical Society and developed a particular interest in the publishing arm of the society.

Colin Garratt is both an authority on the history of rail and a professional railway photographer, with over 40 books to his credit. His company, Milepost 92½, specializes in writing and photographic assignments for the railway industry. Colin has devoted himself to documenting the last steam locomotives of the world, making expeditions to some 50 countries. He resides in England.

Howard Johnston is a former newspaper editor who has written extensively about transport, modern and historical, for over 20 years. Director of his own publishing firm in England, he also advises railway companies in the United Kingdom that are undergoing the upheaval of privatization.

William D. Middleton is a frequent contributor to *Trains* magazine in the United States. He is the author of numerous books, including *The Interurban Era*, *The Time of the Trolley*, and *When the Steam Railroads Electrified*.

Karl Zimmermann is the author of 13 books about railroading, including *CZ: The Story of the California*. His stories on trains and travel have appeared in newspapers across North America, including the *New York Times* and the *Los Angeles Times*. A frequent contributor to *Trains* magazine, he has written for *Travel & Leisure*, *Railfan & Railroad*, and other magazines, and currently is contributing editor to *The International Railway Traveler*.

CAPTIONS

Page 1: Northern Pacific #328—detail 4-6-0
Page 2: Switzerland's *Glacier Express* crosses a bridge over a river
Page 3: Locomotive moving through steel bridge, surrounded by steam
Pages 4–5: Bullet trains in station, Tokyo, Japan
Pages 6–7: Steam trains waiting at Shenyang station in winter, Liaoning, China
Pages 8–9: Interior view of metro station at Komsomoloskaya, Moscow, Russia
Pages 10–11: Eastern Mojave Railroad and desert, California

Pages 12–13: Railway construction workers dismantling the old gantry at Waterloo Station, London, to make way for a new electric signal box
Pages 60–61: A *TGV* (*Train á Grande Vitesse*) station in France
Pages 74–75: Signals and tracks in fog
Pages 96–97: Oriente station, Lisbon, Portugal
Pages 116–117: President Lincoln's funeral train, 1865
Pages 142–143: Old Noojee Trestle Bridge at Noojee
Pages 194–195: Railway tracks and sunset
Pages 246–247: Steam train crossing Horseshoe Curve Viaduct, Perthshire, Scotland

ACKNOWLEDGMENTS

John Bull (cover design and bandings); Sarah Anderson, Kate Brady, Peta Gorman (editorial assistance); Angela Handley (proofreading); Nancy Sibtain (indexing); Mel Holley, Tony Streeter, Philip Haigh, Sue Graves, Colin Nash, and the staff of Milepost 92½.

PHOTOGRAPH AND ILLUSTRATION CREDITS

Photograph credits

1c MPT/Brian Solomon 2c APL/Corbis/Tim Thompson 3c TPL/TSI/Richard A. Cooke 5c GI/TSI 6–7c TPL/TSI/Yann Layma 8–9c TPL/TSI 10–11c APL/Corbis/C. Aurness 12–13c TPL/HG 13t Cor 14r GI/TSI; tl PE 15t PD; b AAP Image/AAP 16c AAP 17t Adtranz; b TPL 18t APL/Archive Photos; c APL/Corbis; b APL/Corbis 19t APL/Corbis; b Victoria and Albert Museum, London, UK/TPL 20t APL/Corbis 21t GI/HG; cr APL/Corbis; br KZ 22t MEPL/Institution of Civil Engineers; b AP via AAP/Danielle Smith 23t REU; b Adtranz 24tr AT; b BP 25tl BP; tr BP 26cl APL; b Adtranz 27tl MPT; tr MPT; b MPT 28tl APL/Bettmann; tr SS; br SS 29t SS 30t SS; bl SS 31b APL/Corbis/Hulton-Deutsch Collection; t SS 32tl SS; cr SS; br SS 33t SS 34t SS; b SS 35cr MEPL; b SS 36tr MEPL; c AKG 37b APL/Corbis 38t APL/Corbis 39t APL/Corbis; b HG/GI 40c SS; b TPL/BAL 41t AKG/Eric Lessing; b GI/HG 42t APL/Corbis; b APL/Corbis 43t APL/Corbis 44t SS/NRM; b APL/Corbis 45t SS/NRM; c SS/NRM; b APL/Corbis 46t MPT; b SS 47t MPT 48tl APL/Corbis; b AKG/Jean-Louis Nou 49t APL/Corbis; b APL/Corbis 50t PD 51t APL/Corbis; b APL/Corbis 52bl AKG/History Archive; br SS 53t APL/Corbis/Bettmann 53b GI/HG 54tl MEPL; c MEPL; b GI/Hulton Archive 55t APL/Corbis; c APL/Corbis 56t APL/Corbis/Hulton-Deutsch Collection 57t MPT/W. A. Sharman; cl APL/Corbis; b SS/NRM 58t PD 59b AAP Images 60–61c APL/Corbis/Grant Smith 61t PD 62t MEPL/Illustrated London News b NRM/SS 63t London Transport Museum/Gavin Dunn; b APL/Corbis 64t MEPL; b Chicago Transport Authority 65tr AKG; cr TPL; b AKG 66t MEPL; b MEPL 67t APL/Corbis; b MEPL 68t MPT; b Adtranz 69c Inigo Bujedo Aguirre/Arcaid; b AT 70t Dover Royalty-Free Illustration; b MEPL 71t MPT; c MPT; b PD 72t APL/Corbis; b TPL 73t AAP; b MPT 74–75c APL/Zefa 75t Cor 76tl RP/MH; tr SS 77t SS 78t Adtranz; c Adtranz; b MPT 79t MPT; b GI/IB 80t Adtranz; b Adtranz 81t Adtranz; bl Adtranz; br Adtranz 82c MPT 83tl MPT; tr MPT; b RP/MH 84c KZ; b APL/Corbis 85t BP; b MPT 86t MPT; b BP 87t MPT/Alan Pike; c Pilatus Railway; b RP/MH 88tr AT; c The Art Archive; b APL/Corbis 89t BP; b RP/MH 90tl APL/Corbis; b APL/Corbis 91t APL/Corbis; b APL/Corbis 92tl TPL; c APL/Corbis; b QA Photos 93t Adtranz 94c Digital Stock 95t RP; b Pilatus Railway 96–97 Arcaid/John Edward Linden 97t PE 98b KZ 99t MPT; b MPT 100t Peter Newark's American Pictures; b APL/Corbis/Minnesota Historical Society 101t APL/Corbis/Bettmann; b APL/Corbis/Oscar White 102t MEPL; b APL/Corbis 103c MPT; b MPT 104t MPT; c MPT 105t MPT; b MPT 106t APL/Corbis; b APL/Corbis 107t APL/Corbis; b APL/Corbis 108tl MEPL; b GI/HG 109t MPT; bl APL/Corbis; br GI/Hulton Archive 110t MPT; bl MPT 111t APL/Corbis; b MPT 112t The Art Archive/NRM, York/Eileen Tweedy; b APL/Corbis 113t TPL; c MPT; b APL/Corbis 114t APL/Corbis; b APL/Corbis 115t APL/Corbis; c APL/Corbis 116–117c APL/Corbis 117t Digital Stock 118t APL/Corbis 119c APL/Corbis; b APL/Corbis 120t APL/Corbis; b APL/Corbis 121t APL/Corbis; b MPT 122t HG/GI 123tr APL/Corbis; c GI/Hulton Archive; b APL/Corbis 124l APL/Corbis 125t AP via AAP; b GI/HG 126t SS; b TPL 127t APL/Corbis; cl APL/Corbis cr APL/Corbis 128tr MPT/CG; b RP/MH 129t MPT; b MPT 130–131t APL/Corbis 130bl MPT/CG 131cl APL/Corbis; cr APL/Corbis 132t MPT/CG; b AKG 133t APL/Corbis 134b Wildlight/Carolyn Johns 135tl ARHS Railway Resource

Centre/B. Blair; tr Queensland Rail; b Photobank New Zealand 136b MPT/CG 137t MPT/CG; cr MPT/CG; bl MPT/CG 138t BP; b MPT 139t MPT; c MPT; b MPT 140t MPT; c MPT 141t PD; bl Adtranz; br MPT/CG 142–143c APL/John Carnemolla 143t PD 144t MPT; b MPT 145t APL/Corbis 146c APL/Corbis 147tl MPT; tr MPT; bl AAP 148t APL/Corbis/Wolfgang Kaehler; b MPT/Brian Solomon 149t SS/NRM; cr MPT 150t APL/Corbis; tl SS/Science Museum; b APL/Corbis 151t MPT 152t MPT; b MPT 153tl MPT; tr MPT 154t MPT/Brian Solomon; b MPT/CG 155tl MPT/Brian Solomon; tr MPT/Brian Solomon 156t MPT/Brian Solomon 157t APL/Corbis/Lowell Georgia; c APL/Corbis/Lowell Georgia 158t MPT/Brian Solomon; c MPT/Brian Solomon 159t KZ; b KZ 160t KZ; b Grand Canyon Railway 161t Grand Canyon Railway; c Grand Canyon Railway 162t APL/Corbis/Lee Snider; b APL/Corbis/Underwood & Underwood 163t AT; r APL/Corbis/Lee Snider 164t KZ 165t KZ; c KZ 166t BP/Donnelle Oxley; b Cass Scenic Railway 167t BP/Gary J. Benson; b BP/Donelle Oxley 168t APL/Corbis; b APL/Corbis 169t APL/Corbis; b APL/Corbis 170t KZ; b KZ 171t KZ; b KZ 172t The Great Central Railway 173tc The Great Central Railway; c The Great Central Railway 174t MPT 175t MPT; c Paul Lewis; 176t APL/Corbis; b MPT/W. A. Sharman 177t MPT/W. A. Sharman; b MPT/W. A. Sharman 178c MPT/Mike Esau 179t MPT/Mike Esau; c MPT/Mike Esau 180c MPT/John R Jones 181t MPT/John R. Jones; b MPT/John R. Jones 182t MPT; b Michele Burgess 183t MPT; b Michele Burgess 184t KZ 185t KZ; c KZ 186t MPT 187t APL/Corbis; c KZ 188t AT; b AT 189t TPL; c Australian Railway Historical Society 190t TPL; b APL/Corbis/Douglas Peebles 191t KZ; cr KZ 192b Lindsay McLeod; t Photobank 193t Taieri Gorge Railway, NZ; b Lindsay McLeod 194–195c APL/Sharp Shooters 195t PD 196b Gary Benson 197t DHRS/PJ; b TPL 198t MPT 199t MPT; b HB 200c MPT 201t MPT; c MPT 201b MPT 202t VIA Rail Inc.; b VIA Rail Inc. 203t VIA Rail Inc. 204t APL/José Fuste Raga 205t APL/Corbis; b KZ 206t AMTRAK; b BP/Gary J. Benson 207t Laurel Zimmerman; b MPT/Brian Solomon 208t MPT/BrianSolomon; b KZ 209t AMTRAK 210t AMTRAK 211t AMTRAK; c MPT/Brian Solomon 212t KZ; b KZ 213t KZ; c KZ 214t MPT/W. A. Sharman; b MPT/W. A. Sharman 215t MPT/W. A. Sharman; c APL/Corbis 216t MPT; b MPT 217t Peter J. Robinson; c MPT 218t HB 219t HB; b HB 220t KZ; b KZ 221t APL/Corbis; cr TPL 222t KZ 223t TPL b APL/R. Ian Lloyd 224t Herbert Aurenz; b Stefan Drigenburg 225t Stefan Drigenburg; b Stefan Drigenburg 226t MPT; b QA Photos 227t APL/Guy Marche Studios 228t NSB/Rolf M. Sorenson; t NSB/Rolf M. Sorenson 229c KZ 230t AA Photo Library 231t AA Photo Library; c AA Photo Library 232t KZ 233t MPT/Garry Buchanan; cl KZ; cr KZ 234t KZ; b KZ 235t KZ; b Rovos Rail DHRS/PJ; b DHRS/PJ 237t DHRS/PJ; b DHRS/PJ 238t APL/Corbis 239t APL/Corbis; b Howard Johnston/Tony Streeter 240t APL/Corbis; c Tatjana Pozar-Burgar 241t APL/Corbis; c APL/Corbis 242t Southlight Photo Library/Milton Wordley; b Great Southern Railway 243t Great Southern Railway; c Great Southern Railway 244t Tranz Rail; b G. R. Dick Roberts Photo Library 245t Tranz Rail; b D.L.A Turner 246–247c GI/TSI

Illustration credits

Inklink Firenze 76. **Lorenzo Lucia/Stuart McVicar** 156, 158, 160, 162, 164, 168, 170, 182, 186, 190, 204, 206, 208, 210, 214, 218, 224, 230, 232, 234, 236, 245. **Edwina Riddell** 157, 164, 186, 209, 222.

Cover credits

BCtl VIA Rail Inc., tr Adtranz, bl MPT, br HB; **FC**tl PL, tr APL/Corbis, tcl APL, tc APL, tcr Karl Zimmerman, cl APL, c PL, bl PD, br PL; **Spine** Lindsay McLeod.